YALE ROMANIC STUDIES: *Second Series*

IV

STUDIES IN THE BAROQUE FROM

MONTAIGNE TO ROTROU

Studies in the Baroque

from Montaigne to Rotrou

BY IMBRIE BUFFUM

NEW HAVEN AND LONDON: YALE UNIVERSITY PRESS

Paris: Presses Universitaires de France

INTRODUCTION

THE AIM OF THIS BOOK is to arrive at a definition of the baroque style in French literature between 1570 and 1650. Critics have long been aware of the fact that literary works of this period are significantly different in form and spirit from those of the Renaissance or of classicism. However, until comparatively recent times, the tendency has been, at least among French scholars such as Lanson, to dismiss them as irregular, extravagant, or mediocre. It is the revival of interest in baroque art and architecture, initiated in large measure by the Swiss scholar Wölfflin, which has led to a reappraisal of the literature of the period. And so, within the last generation, we have witnessed the rehabilitation or rediscovery of such writers as Donne or Crashaw in England, or Sponde, d'Aubigné, La Ceppède, and the early Corneille in France. Noteworthy in this respect have been the scholarly works of Wellek, Austin Warren, Boase, Rousset, Lebègue, and de Mourgues. In my own book on d'Aubigné I sought to present *Les Tragiques* as an outstanding example of the baroque style in poetry. In doing so, I was influenced by the fact that, in the history of criticism, the existence of the baroque as an important and independent style was first recognized in the field of the fine arts. I therefore attempted to establish stylistic parallels between the poetry of d'Aubigné and contemporary painting, sculpture, and architecture. My method was a posteriori rather than a priori; by examining in detail the text of a specific work by a specific author, I endeavored to make an analysis of the baroque which would correlate stylistic and ideological criteria.

A broader exploration of the period as a whole now seems desirable. If we examine a variety of writers of the baroque age, it is likely that we shall find stylistic and ideological characteristics common to the majority of them; and this in turn will be most helpful for the solution of the problem of the baroque.

The question arises: Why choose these particular dates, 1570 and 1650, as limits? Any such choice is, of course, somewhat arbitrary. In my opinion, however, a chronological delimitation is necessary. Otherwise we are forced into the conclusion that the baroque is a universal human phenomenon recurring at various periods of history. Certain scholars, such as Focillon and d'Ors, have in fact adopted this position; but the result is to make the baroque a concept so vast as to be almost meaningless: we are finally led

v

to define as baroque any work of art or literature not governed by the strictest principles of balance, order, and reason.

A number of factors have influenced my choice of 1570 as an opening date. By this year the greatest works of the Pléiade, with the exception of Ronsard's *Sonets pour Hélène,* had been written. In 1571 Montaigne retired from public affairs to the seclusion of his tower library; and almost immediately thereafter he began the composition of one of the major works of the baroque age: the *Essais.* The year 1572 is of course the date of the Massacre of St. Bartholomew; and this tragic event, representing as it does the destruction of the high hopes of such early Renaissance writers as Rabelais, exercised a decisive influence on the spirit of the time. This spirit animates Agrippa d'Aubigné; and a large part of *Les Tragiques* was composed in 1578, six years after the massacre.

In explaining my selection of 1650 as the closing date, I should perhaps pause to emphasize the fact that I do not regard the great masterpieces of the 1660's and 1670's as baroque. I have no desire to destroy the concept of classicism in order to replace it by that of baroque. Such works as La Fontaine's *Fables, Le Misanthrope, Bérénice* (which Fergusson takes as an example of the baroque theatre), or *Phèdre* (even though certain scholars have professed to discern baroque elements in the "Discours de Théramène") do not come within the scope of this study. In my view the history of the French literature of the sixteenth and seventeenth centuries presents us with a succession of three—perhaps four—styles: Renaissance, then mannerism (though this question still remains to be explored), then baroque, and finally classicism. In effect, two further considerations have led me to select 1650. There is the problem of Corneille's revisions of his youthful works. Two of the comedies examined here, *Clitandre* and *Mélite,* in their original versions exhibit many of the characteristics which appear to me baroque; beginning in 1644, but more especially in 1660, Corneille makes many alterations in order to bring them into closer conformity with classical principles. We may be permitted to conclude that some intermediate date—in other words, approximately 1650—represents the dividing line between baroque and classical taste in France. Finally, in the genre of tragedy, perhaps the most unmistakably baroque work is Rotrou's *Saint Genest,* which was first performed in 1646; allowing a little leeway, we again arrive at the year 1650 as a convenient *terminus ad quem.*

The point of departure of this study is Montaigne. As early as 1929, Professor Croll, in an article on the baroque style in prose, drew attention to the manner in which the sentences of the *Essais* are composed: the reader actually gains the impression that he is watching Montaigne think. In this dynamic style, the ideas are born and grow before our very eyes. Now since *movement* has by all critics been considered one of the essential elements of the baroque, it seemed to me likely that a thorough stylistic analysis of the *Essais* would be valuable. This conviction was strengthened by the feeling, arising from twenty years' admiration of Montaigne, that French prose style, though it gained priceless qualities of clarity, precision, and order under the influence of the principles of classicism, also lost certain elements of color, picturesqueness, and vitality from the seventeenth century onward. An examination of the *Essais* might help reveal the exact nature of these characteristics which appear to have been lost; and at the same time it would probably be invaluable as an aid to the definition of the baroque. It should be noted also that the majority of Montaigne scholars, such as Strowski, Villey, and Plattard, have confined their attention to the ideas rather than to the art of this writer. Yet, though Montaigne may be classified as a moralist, it is perhaps as a literary artist that, for the last three hundred and fifty years, he has been able to claim so many enthusiastic friends. Although form and content are actually inseparable, it seems decidedly worth while, at the present stage of scholarship, to concentrate upon Montaigne's distinctively literary qualities.

It so happens that Montaigne has much to say about his own style. This is natural in a writer so concerned with self-examination. It has not escaped previous critics that this self-examination is the key to Montaigne's moral life and to that whole experimental method so much in evidence in the third book of the *Essais;* but his self-awareness as a writer, which, as Villey points out, grows with the years, deserves further study. So let us begin by gathering together all Montaigne's most important remarks on his literary traits. This is what I have done in the first section of my first chapter.

If we approach the *Essais* from the point of view which I have just suggested—that is, literary rather than ideological—we eventually come to the conclusion that Montaigne's basic characteristics can be grouped under certain main headings. In the system which I have adopted, there are eight of them. First of all, we notice (and this may seem a partial repudiation of my earlier arguments) that Montaigne is, throughout his book, animated by moral considerations. Not only does he react with strong disapproval to the cruel excesses of the Spaniards in the New World and to the barbarous slaughter of the French civil wars, but also, in his ideas on education and in his self-portraiture, he is forever seeking goodness and wisdom. This is not to diminish his role as an artist, it is simply to say that he is not a believer in art for art's sake; he is what we in the twentieth century would call *un écrivain engagé:* the felicities of his style gain in power because of the underlying moral purpose.

As we look further, another important trait seems to be a tendency to exaggerate, to delight in overemphasis, to express ideas in the most striking manner possible. Hyperbole, the heaping up of evidence to prove his points, the fondness for forceful verbs—these are basic attributes. Perhaps we may in part explain them away by recalling Montaigne's Gascon temperament; nevertheless, they are there and must be reckoned with. Exaggeration is but one step away from violence; and a careful examination of the *Essais* shows that Montaigne, for all his urbanity and gentlemanliness, has a certain inclination to linger over scenes of horror. To be sure, the religious wars gave him ample occasion for this; but not content with describing the brutalities of his own country and age, he often dwells at considerable length upon tales of Spanish or ancient cruelty.

A very striking stylistic trait in his marked taste, in expressing abstract ideas, for concrete expression. It is perhaps here—especially when we compare his prose with that of seventeenth- or eighteenth-century masters such as Descartes or Voltaire, that we most realize how disembodied and intellectual later French literature became—at least until the advent of romanticism. In Montaigne, even when he is discussing subjects as philosophical as epistemology, there is always a direct and vivid appeal to our senses.

We further discern in the author of the *Essais* a marked flair for the dramatic. Many of the stories which he quotes to us from antiquity, and many of the accounts of his personal experiences, are presented with great theatrical effect. Here again it is not merely a question of the Gascon spirit; in numerous cases it is clearly conscious artistry. A deliberate attempt to achieve the dramatic argues a mind which delights in illusion for its own sake; and this also we find to be true. Such essays as the *Apologie de Raymond Sebond* deal extensively with the problem of the contrast between illusion and reality. This may seem to be primarily a philosophical problem rather than one of form; yet we soon see that Montaigne, as a literary artist, delights in creating illusions, and that much of his skill is directed to this end. I have mentioned the word "contrast"; the previous considerations lead us to observe that Montaigne derives a keen pleasure from antithesis and the diversity of phenomena. This is true not only of the philosopher who looks at the world but also of the literary stylist who is seeking to captivate the attention of his readers. Unlike the classicist who glories in an attitude of *nil admirari,* Montaigne enjoys being surprised, and enjoys surprising us.

Returning to Professor Croll's theory that Montaigne's prose is such as to give the reader the sensation of being actually present while thoughts are being formed, we come to another basic category for the consideration of this style: movement and metamorphosis. And this idea seems to receive additional confirmation when we remember the writer's constant interest in evolution: "Ie ne peints pas l'estre, je peints le passage." What, after all, are the *Essais* considered as a whole but the record of the evolution of a mind over twenty years?

Finally, we are struck by two aspects of Montaigne which are especially noticeable in the Book III. Superficially, they appear to be mutually independent, for one is concerned with the way in which these last essays are composed, while the other is nothing less than his fundamental attitude toward life. But here as elsewhere, the two things cannot be separate: Montaigne himself has asserted that his book is consubstantial with its author. Specifically, I mean this: upon a first reading, our impression is that essays like *Des coches* and *De la vanité* are made up of such diverse elements as to have no orderly plan whatever; the writer seems merely to be following his stream of consciousness, delighting in the complexity of the world, but mindful of no principles of artistic composition. Careful study, however, will reveal that, despite all apparent disorder, each essay does possess an organic unity. The delight in complexity just mentioned points to another aspect of the problem. The variety and mutability of phenomena cause Montaigne neither bewilderment nor distress; just as the essays, viewed as literary compositions, are really not disorganized, so is Montaigne's own life not in a state of chaos. His study of himself has taught him that, underlying all contradictions and inconsistencies, there exists in his personality a basic pattern; this pattern he cannot change, and does not want to change: he accepts it in the same way that he accepts the whole physical world. Similarly, no matter how different each man is from every other, there exists a fundamental reality which we can know and love: human nature. The mature Montaigne insists that, despite all pain and complexities, life has meaning and value. This brings back to mind the writer's love of sensuous expression, and suggests once more that his view of the world is essentially incarnational. Of the religious implications of this attitude we shall have much to say in another place.

To recapitulate the main headings under which I have chosen to consider the style of Montaigne: it will be found that I postulate eight categories, which though distinct are in many ways interrelated. I term them as follows: moral purpose; emphasis and exaggeration; horror; incarnation; theatricality and illusion; contrast and surprise; movement and metamorphosis; organic unity and the acceptance of life. These eight categories are discussed, respectively, in sections two through nine of my chapter on Montaigne, by means of a close examination of applicable texts. And, in order to show that these particular characteristics should indeed be regarded as baroque, I endeavor, wherever possible, to point out parallels with the fine arts of the period.

In view of the importance which I attach to the last of these categories (the problem of the *forme maistresse,* the underlying pattern which Montaigne discerns and accepts in himself, in mankind, and in his own Book III), it has seemed desirable to devote a tenth section of the Montaigne chapter to the stylistic analysis of a single essay. For this purpose, especially since many readers have considered it confused, disorganized, and misleading in its title, I have chosen *De la vanité.* We shall thus be able to review the principal characteristics found in Montaigne, and to observe how they work together to form an artistic unit.

However, so far we have been discussing the baroque aspects of a single author; and while the *Essais* are a good place to begin our inquiry, the purpose of the present study, as I have already indicated, is to reach an understanding of the basic characteristics of the whole baroque period in France. It remains to be seen whether some or all of these eight categories discovered in Montaigne are applicable to a wide variety of writers active between 1570 and 1650. Which writers, and which works, shall we examine? My book is not an encyclopaedia, and since my method involves detailed textual analysis, a choice must be made. It seems evident that this study will be most valuable and meaningful if we select diversified genres, and writers who, at the outset, appear very different from each other. Then, if we continue to recognize the eight categories, our conclusions will begin to take on much greater significance, and we shall come closer to perceiving, as regards both form and spirit, the nature of the baroque style.

Let us look, for example, at the *Introduction à la vie dévote,* by St. François de Sales. Here is a book which surely is very different from the *Essais:* it is a manual to teach the reader how to lead a devout life. There are indications, however, that it may include features which are useful to our inquiry. For example, the imagery is suggestive. These frequent and exuberant references to flowers, to bees and honey, to birds and animals both domestic and exotic possess that ornate quality which we associate with the baroque. Then the basic idea underlying the book is interesting: it is possible for man to lead simultaneously a worldly and a religious life. Calvin, who in so many ways is a characteristic product of Renaissance humanism, would never have tolerated such a concept; and neither, in the following century, would a typical Jansenist like Pascal. Can it be that St. François de Sales, living in an intermediate period, attempting to reconcile the demands of God and of the world, is representative of the baroque spirit? And we are further tempted to examine St. François' book when we remember that he was instrumental in the construction of one of the few really baroque churches in France, the Chapel of the Visitation at Nevers. Chapter 2, then, is an analysis of the style of the *Introduction à la vie dévote.*

It is time that we turn to poetry. Can we find, in the France of this period, a religious poet possessing some of the qualities to be seen in the *Holy Sonnets* of Donne? A number of years ago, it might have been difficult to answer this question affirmatively; but now, thanks in large measure to the efforts of two recent French scholars, Jean Rousset and François Ruchon, readers are beginning to be familiar with a truly great figure, unjustly neglected for three centuries: Jean de La Ceppède. Not wholly neglected, however: at the time of the First World War, the Abbé Brémond pointed out the spectacular, colorful qualities of this poet, and compared him to Rubens. My third chapter is devoted to certain typical sonnets chosen from the *Théorèmes* of La Ceppède.

And now, in virtue of our principle of variety of examples, let us choose a poet of a very different kind, one who differs also fundamentally from the conventional conception of the seventeenth century, one noteworthy for his feeling for nature, his melancholy, his love of the fantastic, his picturesqueness, realism, and epicureanism: Saint-Amant (1594–1661). In the fourth chapter we shall direct our attention to the detailed analysis of three of his most curious and characteristic poems: "La Solitude," "Le Contemplateur," and "Le Melon."

Obviously one of the major figures of the first half of the seventeenth century, but one who at first sight does not appear to come within the scope of this book, is Pierre Corneille. It has always been the custom to pigeonhole him among the classicists. Yet, if we examine some of his early comedies, we find that they are very far removed from the rules of Boileau. For example, that strange *Illusion comique,* with its amusingly deceptive play within a play, suggestive of some kind of magic television performance, is worth analyzing. And then, for our purposes, we discover a highly significant fact: in his old age, having lived to see the great classical generation of 1660, Corneille grew ashamed of the style of his youthful comedies. He began to correct them, to tone them down, to bring them more nearly into conformity with the taste of a Boileau. Recently, scholars have come to realize the importance of the earlier versions of these plays: Mario Roques and Marion Lièvre have published an edition of *Mélite* based on the original text; and R.-L. Wagner has done the same thing for *Clitandre.* If we study these two comedies, and analyze the changes made by Corneille, we shall learn much about the baroque style. Chapter 5 contains three sections: the first presents *L'Illusion comique* as an outstanding baroque comedy, while the second and third, respectively, scrutinize the changes which the elderly Corneille made in *Clitandre* and *Mélite.*

So far, then, what are the different kinds of works which we have considered? A book of essays by a humanistic moralist; a manual of religious instruction; a series of sonnets on the Passion of Our Lord; three picturesque and fanciful poems by a somewhat libertine and reputedly drunkard poet; the early comedies of a great dramatist normally regarded as a classicist. In order to round out our selection, we need a tragedy. This tragedy is furnished to us in the form of a masterpiece by the greatest of second-rate dramatists of the seventeenth century: Rotrou. It is, indeed, the only one of his works which deserves to rank beside those of Corneille and Racine: *Saint Genest.* This is the subject of my final chapter. Here again, as in the case of *L'Illusion comique,* we have a play within a play: a situation which, in view of our category of theatricality and illusion, is likely to be significant. But what is more important, in the play within the play the actor who is pretending to be a Christian is converted by his own art and *becomes* a Christian: so here is metamorphosis as well. With this diversified and representative selection of works we can, I think, draw our investigation to a close.

In this attempt to locate the baroque, I should like to compare my method to that of the navigator who has taken a number of star sights. A star, when observed by the sextant and timed by the chronometer, enables him to draw upon his chart a line of position. His ship, he knows, is somewhere along this line. A second star, similarly observed, provides a second line of position, and the ship is presumably at the intersection of these two lines. The first two sights, however, may be in error; and the crucial test is when additional stars provide a third, fourth, or fifth line of position upon the chart. If all go through a single point, or very nearly, the navigator is happy, because he knows that his calculations are accurate. Here in this book I take sights on a number of stars at different points of the 1570–1650 horizon: Montaigne, St. François de Sales, La Ceppède, Saint-Amant, Corneille, and Rotrou; it is my hope that the various kinds of information which each in his way provides will assist us toward a precise location of the baroque.

A few concluding comments are in order. Since the baroque, as a critical term, is by now completely accepted in the history of art but not in the history of literature, it has been my aim, wherever possible, to illustrate my literary examples through pertinent comparisons drawn from painting, sculpture, and architecture. It is hoped that these parallels may prove convincing and lead the reader to accept the literary works discussed here as baroque. If my knowledge had been expert enough, I should have liked to include musical parallels also—Monteverdi for example—but this would have been the impressionism of an amateur, and so I prefer to abstain. It will be observed also that often I fail to draw a decisive line between form and content. It may sometimes appear that, in discussing questions of style, I am in reality talking about ideas. But this problem, inescapable in all literary criticism, is all the more so in connection with the baroque. For the baroque is, as I trust that I shall have persuaded the reader when he has finished these pages, an art where, to borrow Montaigne's expression, spirit and style are *consubstantial;* where the word is made flesh, and dwells among us, full of grace and truth.

ACKNOWLEDGMENTS

A GUGGENHEIM FELLOWSHIP and a Fulbright grant made possible the travel, research, and time for thought which have resulted in this book. To these two foundations I am happy to express my deep gratitude. I should like also to express my thanks to Eugene Davidson, Editor of the Yale University Press, and to Henri Peyre and Jean Boorsch of the Yale French Department, whose advice and encouragement have been invaluable.

CONTENTS

CHAPTER I. The Basic Baroque Categories as Exemplified by Montaigne

1. MONTAIGNE'S COMMENTS ON HIS OWN STYLE

IN STUDYING the style of a writer, it is often illuminating to see what he himself says about it. To be sure, writers, like all artists, are sometimes incompletely aware of their own characteristics—indeed, if it were not so, critics would have no function. But in the case of Montaigne, we have a man who, to an exceptional degree, has devoted his attention to self-analysis. Since the *Essais* are, according to Montaigne's own expression, "consubstantial" with their author, it is natural that they should contain many passages dealing with the stylistic matters. And so, before proceeding to a discussion of the baroque elements in Montaigne, I shall let him speak for himself. His statements will, I think, lead us to an understanding of the baroque style in general.

What sort of language does Montaigne like? He tells us this in a famous passage in the *Institution des enfans,* and his remarks explicitly apply to the spoken and written language alike:

Je tors bien plus volontiers une bonne sentence pour la coudre sur moy, que je ne tors mon fil pour l'aller querir. Au rebours c'est aux paroles à servir et à suyvre, et que le Gascon y arrive, si le François n'y peut aller.

Je veux que les choses surmontent, et qu'elles remplyssent l'imagination de celuy qui escoute, qu'il n'aye aucune souvenance des mots. Le parler que j'ayme, c'est un parler simple et naïf, tel sur le papier qu'à la bouche; un parler succulent et nerveux, court et serré, non tant delicat et peigné comme vehement et brusque:

Haec demum sapiet dictio, quae feriet,

plustost difficile qu'ennuieux, esloigné d'affectation, desreglé, descousu et hardy: chaque lopin y face son corps; non pedantesque, non fratesque, non pleidaresque, mais plustost soldatesque, comme Suetone appelle celuy de Julius Caesar . . .[1]

The passage begins by stating that ideas are more important than words, and content than form. This means, essentially, that Montaigne is not a believer in art for art's sake: the writer's point of departure should be an intellectual and moral purpose. Then, even in a literary work, the style should be conversational, direct, and down to earth. It should be "succulent

1. I, 26, 220. (References are to books, chapters, and pages of the *Essais* respectively.)

et nerveux," that is, full of flavor and muscular. The writer's words should appeal to our senses, should be physical, vigorous, and full of movement. Montaigne does not seek classical polish and perfection: he wants above all to strike the reader. Realizing that perfection is often boring, he chooses rather to be disorderly, disconnected, and bold. On the other hand, he also rejects the style of the scholar, the preacher, and the lawyer. His ideal is the rough speech of the soldier.

We find similar ideas in the essay on presumption:

Tout est grossier chez moy; il y a faute de gentillesse et de beauté. Je ne sçay faire valoir les choses pour le plus que ce qu'elles valent, ma façon n'ayde rien à la matiere. Voilà pourquoy il me la faut forte, qui aye beaucoup de prise et qui luise d'elle-mesme. Quand j'en saisis des populaires et plus gayes, c'est pour me suivre à moy qui n'aime point une sagesse ceremonieuse et triste, comme faict le monde, et pour m'esgayer, non pour esgayer mon stile, qui les veut plustost graves et severes (au moins si je dois nommer stile un parler informe et sans regle, un jargon populaire et un proceder sans definition, sans partition, sans conclusion, trouble . . . Je ne sçay ny plaire, ny rejouyr, ny chatouiller: le meilleur conte du monde se seche entre mes mains et se ternit. Je ne sçay parler qu'en bon escient . . . Au demeurant, mon langage n'a rien de facile et poly: il est aspre et desdaigneux, ayant ses dispositions libres et desreglées; et me plaist ainsi, si non par mon jugement, par mon inclination. Mais je sens bien que par fois je m'y laisse trop aller, et qu'à force de vouloir eviter l'art et l'affectation, j'y retombe d'une autre part . . .[2]

It must be admitted that Montaigne does not do himself justice, especially when he declares that he is unable to please or entertain the reader. As so frequently happens in the *Essais,* we cannot be quite sure whether the self-depreciation is sincere: it may partly be done with the object of arousing our indignant protestations. But here again he recognizes within himself the same characteristics and the same basic principles already mentioned. His style is rough and coarse, lacking in prettiness or formal beauty. In order to write well, he must have something important to say: he is more interested in content than in superficial adornments. He draws upon the amusing language of the common people, not for purposes of stylistic embellishment but because, feeling a temperamental affinity with it, he prefers it to stiff gloomy formality. As a matter of fact, he has doubts as to whether he actually possesses a style: his writing is without form or rules; the essays follow no outline, have no logical divisions, and lead to no conclusions: they are unclear. It is interesting to note that these weaknesses—if indeed they are to be regarded as such—constitute a violation of those basic principles

2. II, 17, 416.

which Descartes was to formulate fifty years later in the *Discours de la méthode*. And this is not surprising, for Descartes is the complete negation of the baroque.

These remarks of Montaigne's on the disorderly arrangement of his essays lead us from questions of language to considerations of composition. Generally speaking, he regards his disorder with indulgence. In this connection, the opening paragraph of the essay on friendship is especially interesting for my purpose. The author compares his art to the art of painting, and feels that perhaps after all the principal merit of his style may lie precisely in its picturesque variety and strangeness:

Considerant la conduite de la besongne d'un peintre que j'ay, il m'a pris envie de l'ensuivre. Il choisit le plus bel endroit et milieu de chaque paroy, pour y loger un tableau élabouré de toute sa suffisance; et, le vuide tout au tour, il le remplit de crotesques, qui sont peintures fantasques, n'ayant grâce qu'en la varieté et estrangeté. Que sont-ce icy aussi, à la verité que crotesques et corps monstrueux, rappiecez de divers membres, sans certaine figure, n'ayants ordre, suite ny proportion que fortuite? [3]

The name of a great French baroque engraver comes to mind at once: Jacques Callot. We may see the technique of filling in empty spaces with grotesques in his series of the deadly sins: in each case, the center of the engraving is occupied by a symbolic woman who represents the sin in question, while around her fly fantastic little winged devils. Many of the great engravings, such as the "Impruneta Fair" or the "Siege of the Ile de Ré," are filled with picturesque extraneous detail: dogs chasing each other or indulging in other doggy activities, prancing horses, sprightly little human figures fighting or cooking dinner or unloading ships. Sometimes the artist adds a fanciful frame for the sheer fun of it: one of the versions of the "Siege of the Ile de Ré" is completely surrounded by a border of convoluted seashells; one scene of a Florentine festival is rimmed by a fan-shaped scroll: the handle of the fan is a grotesque head, while on the folds of the scroll sit groups of elegantly spirited ladies and gentlemen. None of these motifs is essential to the subject; yet the artist obviously delights in them. Or, for monstrous bodies made up of diverse members, consider Callot's amazing "Temptation of St. Anthony": not even Bosch has imagined more fantastic grotesques. Montaigne tells us that, in one respect, his own style resembles that of his Callot-like painter: true, he is not capable of doing the main subject, but he enjoys filling in the empty spaces with fanciful and picturesque detail. He acknowledges that his essays are a heterogeneous collection of odds and ends, and that he works on them only in moments of idleness:

3. I, 28, 235.

Ce fagotage de tant de diverses pieces se faict en cette condition, que je n'y mets la main que lors qu'une trop lasche oisiveté me presse, et non ailleurs que chez moy. Ainsin il s'est basty à diverses poses et intervalles, comme les occasions me detiennent ailleurs par fois plusieurs moys. Au demeurant, je ne corrige point mes premieres imaginations par les secondes; ouy à l'aventure quelque mot, mais pour diversifier, non pour oster. Je veux representer le progrez de mes humeurs, et qu'on voye chaque piece en sa naissance. Je prendrois plaisir d'avoir commencé plustost et à reconnoistre le train de mes mutations.[4]

In other words, he is again insisting that his book has no set plan. He adds picturesque details whenever the fancy strikes him, and whether or not they have any particular connection with what has gone before. Moreover, this passage introduces an idea which is of basic importance in the *Essais:* the evolution of the author's mind is felt to be interesting for its own sake. Not only is variety fascinating but so also is transformation. We have two great baroque themes here: mutability and metamorphosis. Montaigne wrote the above lines in 1579, just before publishing the first edition of the *Essais* and at the moment when he was beginning to be conscious of himself as a literary artist. Nine years later, in the Book III, he returns to the subject again, and gives us perhaps the fullest statement of his attitude toward his writings:

Laisse, lecteur, courir encore ce coup d'essay et ce troisiesme alongeail du reste des pieces de ma peinture.

(The "troisiesme alongeail" is, of course, Book III.)

J'adjouste, mais je ne corrige pas.

This is what he has already told us in *De la ressemblance des enfans aux peres.* Now, however, he gives an additional reason for abstaining from making corrections:

Premierement, par ce que celuy qui a hypothecque au monde son ouvrage, je trouve apparence qu'il n'y aye plus de droict.

In other words, Montaigne has come to feel a responsibility toward his reader. It is partly a matter of commercial honesty: if people have paid their money for the first edition, it is not fair to disavow it. Extensive revision would have the effect of invalidating the earlier text:

Qu'il die, s'il peut, mieux ailleurs, et ne corrompe la besogne qu'il a vendue.

Authors who are forever rewriting their books, Montaigne declares, should allow nothing to be published during their lifetime. I think that he has in mind

4. II, 37, 573.

also another form of honesty. In a book devoted to self-portraiture it would be unfair to alter passages, however questionable they may be, which are a true reflection of the author's thought at a previous period. (This idea, as a matter of fact, is suggested a little further along in this same passage which we are now studying.) In any case, it is easy to see that moral considerations are given precedence over purely literary ones.

It so happens, however, that the early editions very rapidly become out of print. Lest the public be disappointed, Montaigne keeps issuing new editions, and in such cases he feels justified in adding passages here and there. It is to be clearly understood that these additions in no sense constitute a disavowal of the earlier text:

Mon livre est toujours un. Sauf qu'à mesure qu'on se met à le renouveller afin que l'acheteur ne s'en aille les mains du tout vuides, je me donne loy d'y attacher (comme ce n'est qu'une marqueterie mal jointe), quelque embleme supernumeraire. Ce ne sont que surpoids, qui ne condament point la premiere forme, mais donnent quelque pris à chacune des suivantes par une petite subtilité ambitieuse.

Here we have several important points about Montaigne's style. First of all, the essays are composed like ill-fitting marquetry—a piece here, a piece there, with little regard for smoothness or symmetry. And the added bits, even when they do not fit very well, somehow increase the value of what was already there. Disorder and complexity only add to the subtle fascination. Yet we must never forget that Montaigne's book, despite all its diversity, has a fundamental unity ("Mon livre est toujours un"). Those who are unaccustomed to baroque architecture often find themselves distracted by the "emblemes supernumeraires"; in looking at the churches of Rome or of Lecce, they see only a riotous confusion of columns, garlands, seashells, angels blowing trumpets, concavities and convexities: it takes some time to see that the façade constitutes an artistic whole. The unity and diversity give life to each other. So it is with the *Essais*. The uninitiated reader at first finds them confusing; eventually, however, the mass of picturesque but apparently irrelevant and disorderly detail comes to have unified meaning because it gives life to the portrait of an extraordinarily interesting man.

Montaigne then goes on to explain his second reason for not making emendations to his text. He is not at all sure that he becomes wiser as he grows older:

Secondement, que, pour mon regard, je crains de perdre au change: mon entendement ne va pas toujours avant, il va à reculons aussi. Je ne me deffie guiere moins de mes fantasies pour estre secondes ou tierces que premieres, ou presentes que passées. Nous nous corrigeons aussi sottement souvent comme nous corrigeons les autres. Mes premieres publications furent l'an mille cinq cens quatre vingts.

Depuis d'un long traict de temps je suis envieilli, mais assagi je ne le suis certes pas d'un pouce. Moy à cette heure et moy tantost sommes bien deux; mais quand meilleur, je n'en puis rien dire. Il feroit beau estre vieil si nous ne marchions que vers l'amendement. C'est un mouvement d'yvroigne titubant, vertigineux, informe, ou des joncs que l'air manie casuellement selon soy.

In order to give a complete picture of Montaigne, the *Essais* must show what he thought at different periods of his life. The ideas of 1580 are just as important as the ideas of 1588; they may be better or they may be worse, but they are all part of the man. We have just seen that the "emblemes supernumeraires" and ill-fitting bits of marquetry are essential parts of the whole; so also are "me now" and "me some time ago." The art of the *Essais* attempts to depict both the variety and the evolution of the man's experience: diversity and metamorphosis. If Montaigne's life resembles the staggerings of a drunkard or the haphazard swaying of reeds in the wind, his style must take on these characteristics also. Such a style cannot be orderly, logically coherent, and static; it must be confused, contradictory, and dynamic. And, as the images of the drunkard and of the reeds suggest, it must be concrete rather than abstract.

Montaigne concludes this particular discussion of his book by confiding to us that its success has given him self-confidence:

La faveur publique m'a donné un peu plus de hardiesse que je n'esperois, mais ce que je crains le plus, c'est de saouler: j'aimerois mieux poindre que lasser . . .[5]

The final remark is very revealing: he would rather irritate or shock the reader than bore him. Indeed, this trait is often encountered in the *Essais*. Classically minded critics are sometimes offended by Montaigne's lapses from good taste. The explanation he has just given us does not altogether cover the problem. We shall have to admit, I think, that he had a natural inclination toward *polissonnerie*: a casual perusal of *Sur des vers de Virgile,* with its numerous indiscreet references to the author's most intimate habits, should convince anyone of this. And the desire to shock is, after all, merely one aspect of the universal baroque love of surprises. The following example will serve my purpose very well, since in it Montaigne is describing the essays themselves; the startling concreteness of the image, so baroque in spirit, is a specimen of the very thing described:

Se sont icy . . . des excremens d'un vieil esprit, dur tantost, tantost lache, et tousjours indigeste.[6]

There are other passages in the third book where Montaigne discusses his reluctance to correct anything once it is written. And always we see

5. III, 9, 241–2.   6. III, 9, 216.

that his deepest desire is to be true to himself. He prefers honesty of self-portrayal to perfection of style. The purpose of his book, he asserts,

. . . c'est d'estre exactement mien. Je corrigerois bien une erreur accidentale, dequoy je suis plain, ainsi que je cours inadvertemment; mais les imperfections qui sont en moy ordinaires et constantes, ce seroit trahison de les oster.

This is from *Sur des vers de Virgile;* in the same year (1586) Montaigne wrote *Du repentir,* an essay which has always disturbed Christian readers because it fundamentally rejects the idea of repentance. We may disavow our accidental and impulsive sins, the author says, but there is nothing we can do about our deep-rooted vices; in fact, repentance is a "desditte de nostre volonté." We inevitably feel that he disapproves of such a "desditte" because it is really a "trahison." It is interesting to observe that Montaigne's literary theories parallel so closely his moral principles. Revision is the equivalent of repentance, and both are unworthy acts. Montaigne seems to have thought of himself as a moralist primarily, rather than as a literary artist; and such, probably, is the traditional view of him. On the other hand, in this study I am concerned with him as an artist, and indeed I believe that his true greatness lies here, for there have been many moralists whose teachings are greater than his. Yet we must recognize that these two aspects of the writer are as inseparable as form and content. It is perhaps inevitable that this should be so in baroque art, which is so deeply incarnational in nature.

But the chapter goes on to discuss literary matters. Having told us that he has no intention of correcting his work, the author enumerates some of the more frequent criticisms which he hears. The disapproved traits are, for the most part, baroque ones:

Quand on m'a dit ou que moy-mesme me suis dict: Tu es trop espais en figures. Voilà un mot du creu de Gascoigne. Voilà une phrase dangereuse (je n'en refuys aucune de celles qui s'usent emmy les rues françoises; ceux qui veulent combattre l'usage par la grammaire se moquent). Voilà un discours ignorant. Voilà un discours paradoxe. En voilà un trop fol. Tu te joues souvent; on estimera que tu dies à droit, ce que tu dis à feinte.—Oui, fais-je, mais je corrige les fautes d'inadvertence, non celles de coustume.[7]

Again the positive declaration: "I refuse to reform my fundamental nature." But briefly, what are these so-called faults of style? First, an excessive use of imagery. Next, adoption of the language of the streets—in other words, picturesque realism. Ignorance. A love of paradoxes. Crazy ideas. A difficulty, on the part of the reader, in distinguishing between illusion and reality. The excessive use of imagery is common to the majority of baroque writers:

7. III, 5, 121.

Crashaw, Sir Thomas Browne, d'Aubigné, St. François de Sales. For picturesque realism we have only to look at baroque artists: Callot, the Le Nain
brothers, Caravaggio, Rubens. Ignorance I think we can afford to dismiss,
along with craziness: suffice it to say that they are the customary charges
of those who dislike the baroque. Paradox, yes: there is no doubt that
Donne and Sponde delight in it, and seek it deliberately. And of course the
difficulty of distinguishing between illusion and reality is a characteristic of
all baroque art. What is painting, and what is actual architectural space in
Pozzo's ceiling of Sant' Ignazio in Rome? How long is the Scala Regia in
the Vatican? In Corneille's *Illusion comique,* which are the actors and which
are the real people? In Rotrou's *Saint Genest,* is Adrien an illusion, or is
Genest? In *La Vida es Sueño,* how is Sigismondo or the spectator to be
sure which scenes are dreams and which facts?

In considering the twin problems of repentance and literary revision,
Montaigne may claim to distinguish between our fundamental nature and
our accidental, impulsive actions, but it is evident that, feeling a deep fondness for his spontaneous sallies, he is reluctant to repudiate them either. The
best passages in the *Essais,* he suggests, are improvisations; we should not
be misled by the apologetic introduction to the following passage:

> Mais mon ame me desplait de ce qu'elle produict ordinairement ses plus pro-
> fondes resveries, plus folles et qui me plaisent le mieux, à l'improveu et lors que
> je les cerche moins; lesquelles s'esvanouissent soudain, n'ayant sur le champ où
> les attacher: à cheval, à la table, au lit, mais plus à cheval, où sont mes plus
> larges entretiens.[8]

He goes on to explain that, try as he will to commit these flashes of inspiration to memory, many are lost forever; when later, in a perfectly calm frame
of mind, he strives to recover them, it is all in vain. Thus we have another
definition of the style of the *Essais:* a series of unpremeditated improvisations. Spontaneous movement, no matter how surprising and erratic, is the
great thing: Montaigne's book is a record of those sudden, lively, and colorful
fancies which he has been able to preserve.

He is aware of the fact that most of the essays in the first book are derivative
in nature, and, therefore, presumably less good: we know now why he has
not cut them out, but he apologizes for them with a typically startling verb:

> . . . de mes premiers essais, aucuns puent un peu à l'estranger.[9]

A characteristic of these early chapters is that they are extremely short.
In the Villey edition the average of those in Book I is only slightly more
than seven pages, while many are a bare page or two. By Book III the

8. III, 5, 123.   9. III, 5, 122.

average has risen to thirty-five. Montaigne, in explaining to us his reasons for the change, suggests that he wants the reader to follow at some length the movement of the author's mind:

> Par ce que la coupure si frequente des chapitres, de quoy j'usoy au commencement, m'a semble rompre l'attention avant qu'elle soit née, et la dissoudre, desdeignant s'y coucher pour si peu et se recueillir, je me suis mis à les faire plus longs, qui requierent de la proposition et du loisir assigné.[10]

This means that, in spite of the "marqueterie" and all the digressions, there is an underlying current which we are expected to follow. We are not to dip into the essays in order to extract picturesque bits, but to accompany Montaigne's mind in careful sequence as he discovers truth. His voyage of exploration will be our voyage of exploration, so we must participate in all its successive phases; and perhaps the journey will prove to be more interesting than the goal. One thing is certain: the author is not anxious to serve up to us detachable nuggets of moral truth, such as are to be found in Book I.

If now we look back over the different things which Montaigne has said about his writing, I think that we cannot fail to be struck with the recurrence of two ideas: the *Essais* have a practical moral purpose, intimately related to the author's own life, and they record a gradual transformation of the man himself. It is not surprising, therefore, that as time goes on there should be an interaction between the man and the book. Montaigne observes this as early as the essay *Du dementir* (1578–80), and of course continues to be aware of the phenomenon in later years, while writing Book III. Once he has set down, in concrete literary form, a description of himself, there is (despite all mutability and metamorphosis) a tendency to live up to it:

> Moulant sur moy cette figure, il m'a fallu si souvent dresser et composer pour m'extraire, que le patron s'en est fermy et aucunement formé soy-mesmes. Me peignant pour autruy je me suis peint en moy de couleurs plus nettes que n'estoyent les miennes premieres. Je n'ay pas plus faict mon livre que mon livre m'a faict, livre consubstantiel à son autheur, d'une occupation propre, membre de ma vie; non d'une occupation et fin tierce et estrangere comme tous autres livres.[11]

Here, among other things, Montaigne freely admits that he paints in heightened colors: his style is characterized by overemphasis and exaggeration, a well-known baroque trait. It seems to me that this passage contains a warning for the New Critics: if we accept their doctrine of the intentional fallacy, ignoring the life, personality, and opinions of the author, we shall gain a

10. III, 9, 284.   11. II, 18, 432.

very imperfect understanding of the *Essais*. Montaigne's intention of ac-
quiring self-knowledge is the very essence of his literary work; this book
does not exist in a vacuum, independent of its author. I have attempted to
show that it is a mistake to isolate individual pieces of marquetry and to
consider them apart from the whole evolution of Montaigne's being; it is
equally a mistake to consider this literary work for its own sake. The expression "consubstantiel à son autheur" is crucial, and, probably better than any
other, sums up the fundamental nature of the *Essais*. In a sense it is a very
daring phrase, as "consubstantiel" is almost exclusively a theological term.
It seems likely that Montaigne had in mind the definition of Christ in the
Nicene Creed: "Consubstantialem patri." The use of the preposition "à"
constitutes further evidence, for it corresponds to the dative "patri"; we
might have expected "avec" instead. Actually, the analogy of the Trinity
is not so inappropriate as it might seem: the Nicene Creed attempts to
explain the relationship between the Father and the Son—they constitute
one God, but are distinct persons. Montaigne wishes to show that (to paraphrase the Book of Common Prayer) the *Essais* are of the substance
with the author; and yet that they have a life of their own: they develop
and grow and even exert an influence on the author. As he says,

Je n'ay aucunement estudié pour faire un livre; mais j'ay aucunement estudié
pour ce que je l'avoy faict . . .[12]

And still more explicitly, in the essay on vanity:

Je sens ce proffit inesperé de la publication de mes meurs qu'elle me sert aucunement de regle. Il me vient par fois quelque consideration de ne trahir l'histoire
de ma vie.[13]

It is, in a slightly different form, his customary refusal to disavow any part
of his literary work—or his life, but we know now that they are of the same
substance. The interrelationship is further stated in a well-known passage
which explains the meaning of the word "essai";

En fin, toute cette fricassée que je barbouille icy n'est qu'un registre des essais
de ma vie, qui est, pour l'interne santé, exemplaire assez à prendre l'instruction à
contre-poil. Mais quant à la santé corporelle, personne ne peut fournir d'experience plus utile que moy . . .[14]

As Professor Auerbach has pointed out, the title *Essais* may be translated as
Tests upon One's Self or *Self Try-Outs."* [15] The book contains a detailed
record of all the different things, both mental and physical, which Montaigne

---

12. II, 12, 453.   13. III, 9, 263.   14. III, 13, 398.
   15. Erich Auerbach, *Mimesis,* tr. W. R. Trask (Princeton, Princeton Univ. Press, 1953),
chap. 12.

has tried; through these repeated tests he has gained an experience which leads to self-knowledge. Montaigne's book and his life represent a quest for mental and physical health; by studying his *Essais,* he can tell what things are likely to produce well-being. And so the word "essai" has three meanings, referring respectively to Montaigne's mind, to his body, and to his literary work; the three meanings are intimately interrelated and are, in fact, "consubstantial."

We have now reviewed the most important passages where Montaigne discusses his own style as a writer. On the basis of these statements, the characteristics of this style can be classified in certain broad categories. These categories, I think, may serve as criteria for the definition of the baroque style in literature. It is not my contention that every writer of the period 1570–1650 exhibits all of these characteristics; nor do I mean to argue that the presence of one or two of them suffices to classify a writer as baroque; I do believe, however, that the categories are basically significant, and that any literary work of this period which conforms to a majority of these criteria should be regarded as baroque.

2. Moral Purpose

The first category I shall call moral purpose. By this I mean that baroque writers (or painters or sculptors or architects, for that matter) are not, as a rule, exclusively artists. They have an intention which cannot be ignored, and they use their skill for the furtherance of some aim which is outside the realm of pure art. This is not to say that the art is subordinated to that aim: the two things exist side by side, consubstantially, as it were. It would be belittling the baroque to call it an art of propaganda, yet this element is usually present. Agrippa d'Aubigné is a great poet, but at the same time he is a soldier in the Protestant cause. Milton is a still greater poet, but pervading the whole of *Paradise Lost* is the religious aim of justifying the ways of God to man. No one would deny the extraordinary technical virtuosity of Bernini, and some of his works, such as the "Apollo and Daphne" or his lovely Roman fountains, come close to being art for art's sake; however, in many of his masterpieces, the "St. Teresa" or the Cathedra Petri for example, it is impossible to separate art from religion. I say moral purpose, but this of course includes political or religious purposes as well. The aim of Rubens' Medici series is primarily political: the glorification of the French royal family. Caravaggio, on the other hand, in his scenes from the life of St. Matthew in San Luigi dei Francesi, has a religious aim. Sometimes the two purposes exist together: who is to say whether the Piazza San Pietro has been designed for the glory of God or for the temporal prestige of the papacy? Now we have just seen that it is impossible to separate Montaigne the moralist from Montaigne the artist. The author of the *Essais* had no professional literary ambitions (at first at least—later, success made him take a certain pride in his skill as a writer); his contemptuous references to the "fagotage de pieces diverses" and the "excremens d'un vieil esprit" testify to a certain aristocratic disdain of his craft. The moral purpose of Montaigne is self-knowledge—or perhaps rather the pursuit of happiness. As I have pointed out, the word "essai" has simultaneously a moral and a literary meaning. The book is one of substance with the author.

That the *Essais* do have an aim beyond the realm of art has been implicit in Montaigne's remarks about his style; but there are, in addition, a number of direct statements as to his purpose. Furthermore, many passages reveal Montaigne as an *auteur engagé* who has taken a definite position on moral, political, or religious questions. The most explicit declaration of Montaigne's purpose, as he conceived it in 1580, is contained in the celebrated preface *Au lecteur:*

> C'est icy un livre de bonne foy, lecteur. Il t'advertit des l'entrée, que je ne m'y suis proposé aucune fin, que domestique et privée. Je n'y ay eu nulle consideration de ton service, ny de ma gloire. Mes forces ne sont pas capables d'un tel dessein. Je l'ay voué à la commodité particuliere de mes parens et amis: à ce que m'ayant perdu (ce qu'ils ont à faire bien tost) ils y puissent retrouver aucuns traits de mes conditions et humeurs, et que par ce moyen ils nourrissent plus entiere et plus vifve, la connoissance qu'ils ont eu de moy. Si c'eust esté pour rechercher la faveur du monde, je me fusse mieux paré et me presanterois en une marche estudiée. Je veus qu'on m'y voie en ma façon simple, naturelle et ordinaire, sans contention et artifice; car c'est moy que je peins.[1]

A man capable of making such a statement is not consciously creating a work of literature. At the particular moment when Montaigne said this, his words are to be taken at their face value. The *Essais* as he conceived them when the first edition went to press were a private, personal book, destined for his relatives and friends. His object is self-expression for the benefit of a few intimates; at the age of forty-seven he regarded himself as old, and wanted those who liked him to have some means of remembering his personality. He has made no attempt to dress himself up or to give a carefully studied picture of himself. Sincerity and naturalness are the paramount considerations. This means not only that the self-portrait is an honest one, but also that it is devoid of artistic pretensions. Needless to say, the book as it actually turns out is a great work of art; but the point of departure is the desire to communicate with his friends.

We have observed how the favorable reception of the *Essais* by a wide

1. *Au lecteur.*

public gave Montaigne confidence, and led him to think of himself as a writer. This phenomenon belongs to the story of the evolution of Montaigne, and will be further discussed in another place. At the present moment I should simply like to point out that, even when he became aware of himself as a prominent literary figure, he continued to think of his purpose as primarily moral. By 1586 the book may be directed toward all mankind, and its fame may derive in large measure from artistic qualities, but the author still regards himself as a moralist. He continues to strive above all for self-expression; the only difference now is that he believes that the portrait of Michel de Montaigne may be instructive for all men. To be sure, the very term "peinture du moi" suggests art; but in the following passage the artist is claiming for this painting a universal moral usefulness:

> Je propose une vie basse et sans lustre, c'est tout un. On attache aussi bien toute la philosophie morale à une vie populaire et privée que à une vie de plus riche estoffe: chaque homme porte la forme entiere de l'humaine condition.[2]

If we come to know Montaigne well, we shall know ourselves and all men. The author of the *Essais* is therefore morally justified in talking about himself so much. We may feel tempted to compare his self-portraiture to that of a great twentieth-century writer with whom he has much in common; but Proust seeks his justification through art rather than through moral philosophy.

However, Montaigne's self-portraiture is by no means the only aspect of the *Essais* to be permeated by a strong moral purpose. The mere fact of composing a treatise on education is indicative of such an intention. Some of those who have done so are of course great artists—Rabelais and Rousseau for example—but we customarily classify theorists of education, such as John Dewey, as moral philosophers. And Montaigne's ideas on bring up children have, for his century, an exceptionally strong moral orientation. The comparison of his views on the subject with those of Rabelais is a timeworn student exercise; it is evident that, while Rabelais stressed an encyclopaedic absorption of knowledge, Montaigne attached more importance to the development of the judgment. Judgment is an intellectual quality, but it also implies an appreciation of values and therefore a moral sense: the well-made head rather than the full one. Montaigne sums up his attitude in a sentence which he regards as so vital that he awards it an isolated paragraph:

> Le guain de nostre estude, c'est en estre devenu meilleur et plus sage.[3]

This declaration of principle applies not only to education but also to the writing and the reading of the *Essais*. Montaigne has told us that the com-

2. III, 2, 27.   3. I, 26, 195.

position of his book has had a moral influence on his life; he obviously hopes that it will have one on ours also.

Political liberals, from the eighteenth century to the present, have often claimed Montaigne for their own. In doing so, they have provided an illustration of the essayist's theory that we all try to draw an interesting author toward ourselves. It is true, nevertheless, that the ideas on colonialism expressed in the *Essais* are far in advance of their time. In an age when apparently few people found anything to criticize in the activities of the Spaniards in the New World, Montaigne's indignation is noteworthy. He sums up the conquest of South America in terse and bitter words:

> Tant de villes rasées, tant de nations exterminées, tant de millions de peuples passez au fil de l'espée, et la plus riche et belle partie du monde bouleversée pour la negotiation des perles et du poivre: mechaniques victoires.[4]

He is no less violent in his denunciation of that papal bull which arbitrarily awarded the western portions of South America to the Spaniards. He cites with evident and deeply felt approval the reply of the Indians to their invaders:

> La responce fut telle: Que, quand à estre paisibles, ils n'en portoient pas la mine, s'ils l'estoient; Quand à leur Roy, puis qu'il demandoit, il devoit estre indigent et necessiteux; et celuy qui luy avoit faict cette distribution, homme aymant dissention, d'aller donner à un tiers chose qui n'estoit pas sienne, pour le mettre en debat entre les anciens possesseurs . . .[5]

and Montaigne goes on to applaud the desire of the natives to retain their own religion. He speaks with horror of the Spanish treatment of the king of Peru, who, after being robbed of all his treasure, was granted the privilege of being publicly hanged rather than burned alive, upon the condition of submitting to Christian baptism just before his death. The same essay, *Des coches,* describes the roasting of the king of Mexico at the stake, and the execution of four hundred and sixty of his subjects in the name of the Christian religion. When Montaigne writes in this tone, it is obviously not art for art's sake but a burning moral indignation; and in 1586 it required courage and vision to express such views.

A condemnation of colonialism Americans of the twentieth century are prepared to admire; but what are they to say to an ardent plea for the redistribution of wealth? I am referring of course to the famous last page of the essay *Des cannibales.* Montaigne describes the interview which took place at Rouen between King Charles IX and three natives of Brazil. The "cannibales" were shown around the city and then asked for their impres-

---

4. III, 6, 168.   5. III, 6, 169.

sions. They answered three things, of which Montaigne, to his great regret, has forgotten the third. The two he remembers are these. The American savages were astonished that the tall, bearded, armed men of the king's guard should consent to obey a child; it would seem more appropriate to choose one of the soldiers as king.

. . . secondement (ils ont une façon de leur langage telle, qu'ils nomment les hommes moitié les uns des autres) qu'ils aperceu qu'il y avoit parmy nous des hommes pleins et gorgez de toutes sortes de commoditez, et que leur moitiez estoient mendians à leurs portes, decharnez de faim et de pauvreté; et trouvoient estrange comme ces moitiez ici necessiteuses pouvoient souffrir une telle injustice, qu'ils ne prinsent les autres à la gorge, ou missent le feu à leurs maisons.[6]

Montaigne makes no direct comment, but the whole essay reveals his sympathy and interest for the "cannibales," and the final ironic sentence of the chapter ("This may be all very well, but they don't wear trousers") indicates that he considers it worth while to listen to these savages. The tone of the passage I have just quoted is unusually passionate for him. It seems clear that he feels genuine moral indignation at the inequalities of wealth in France. We can almost hear his voice rising to a scream, as if he were summoning us to revolutionary action. Inasmuch as this particular effect is one that Rousseau is fond of producing, it is not surprising that he stole the passage for use in the *Discours sur l'origine de l'inégalité*. The technique of criticizing French society through the eyes of supposedly impartial foreign observers becomes a favorite device in the eighteenth century; the essay *Des cannibales* makes us think of the *Lettres persanes* and *L'Ingénu*.

Actually, such "revolutionary" passages are rare in the *Essais*, for the author's basic instincts are conservative. But he feels a deep sympathy with the common people. This is the result of a deliberate policy followed by his father when Michel was a child. The infant was sent out to nurse in a peasant family and kept there for a number of years, so that he became accustomed to the humblest way of life. Forever afterward Montaigne felt at home with peasants and genuinely liked them.[7] An important message of the *Essais* is that we should admire the courage and wisdom of working people:

Regardons à terre les pauvres gens que nous y voyons espandus, la teste penchante apres leur besongne, qui ne sçavent ny Aristote ny Caton, ny exemple, ny precepte: de ceux là tire nature tous les jours des effects de constance et de patience, plus purs et plus roides que ne sont ceux que nous estudions si curieusement en l'escole.[8]

To be sure, Montaigne thought of himself as an aristocrat, and his feeling of responsibility toward the poor is in reality a sense of *noblesse oblige*. The

6. I, 31, 277.   7. Cf. III, 13, 428.   8. III, 12, 345.

leftists cannot claim him for their own. Despite the passages we have just
seen, such political propaganda as may exist in the *Essais* is mainly conservative. Having lived through the horrors of the religious wars, Montaigne
is suspicious of reformers and is anxious to make the reader share his dislike
of innovations in the structure of society:

Il y a grand doute, s'il se peut trouver si evident profit au changement d'une
loy receue, telle qu'elle soit, qu'il y a de mal à la remuer: d'autant qu'une police,
c'est comme un bastiment de diverses pieces jointes ensemble, d'une telle liaison,
qu'il est impossible d'en esbranler une, que tout le corps ne s'en sente.[9]

And, a little further along, even more emphatically:

Je suis desgousté de la nouvelleté, quelque visage qu'elle porte, et ay raison, car
j'en ay veu des effets tres-dommageables.[10]

The *Apologie de Raymond Sebond* is generally regarded as representing
the skeptical crisis in Montaigne's thought. In any case, it is primarily concerned with problems of epistemology. It may seem strange to mention it
in the course of a discussion of moral purpose in the baroque style. Actually,
I think that most critics, in their concern with Montaigne's Pyrrhonism, have
tended to overlook the beginning and the end of this essay. At the very
outset, Montaigne explains why he is interested in Sebond's *Natural Theology*.
A friend of the family, Pierre Bunel, had given a copy to Montaigne's
father, and the latter, shortly before his death, requested his son to translate
the barbarous Spanish Latin text into French. The author of the *Apologie*
makes it clear that he considers Sebond's book valuable and timely:

. . . [et Pierre Bunel] le luy recommanda comme livre tres-utile et propre à
la saison en laquelle il le luy donna; ce fut lors que les nouvelletez de Luther
commençoyent d'entrer en credit et esbranler en beaucoup de lieux nostre
ancienne creance. En quoy il avoit un tresbon advis, prevoyant bien, par discours
de raison, que ce commencement de maladie declineroit aysement en un execrable
atheisme . . .[11]

We know that Montaigne dislikes "nouvelletez" and is anxious to combat
them. I think that insufficient importance has been attached to the fact that
the essay is, after all, entitled an *Apologie*. Even if large sections of it, by
attacking human reason, seem to attack the very method employed by
Sebond to demonstrate the validity of Christianity, it is surely significant
that Montaigne's declared intention is to defend the Spanish theologian. In
this connection, Professor Frame has made a valuable contribution [12] to our
understanding of the *Apologie* by pointing out the following crucial passage:

---

9. I, 23, 151.   10. I, 23, 152.   11. II, 12, 147.
12. In his *Montaigne's Discovery of Man. The Humanization of a Humanist*, New York,
Columbia University Press, 1955.

. . . ce dernier tour d'escrime icy, il ne le faut employer que comme un extreme remede. C'est un coup desesperé, auquel il faut abandonner vos armes pour faire perdre à vostre adversaire les siennes . . .[13]

In other words, what follows is a last resort. In the ensuing and final third of the essay, Montaigne goes further than ever before in demonstrating the perpetual variations and contradictions of human reason, its inability to determine moral law, and the imperfections of our senses. But he has warned us that this is a fencing trick; his object is to deprive his adversary of weapons. Now the adversary is the person who attacks Sebond; therefore, by his own admission, Montaigne really is trying to defend the *Theologia naturalis*. When he refers to atheism as execrable, he means it, and it is not merely being prudent or hypocritical. Atheism is a dangerous *nouvelleté* which threatens the very structure of society, and Montaigne is determined to campaign against it. The last page of the *Apologie* contains positive affirmations of religious faith:

Parquoy il faut conclurre que Dieu seul est,

and

Il [i.e. l'homme] s'eslevera si Dieu lui preste extraordinairement la main; il s'eslevera, abandonnant et renonçant à ses propres moyens, et se laissant hausser et soubslever par les moyens purement celestes.

C'est à nostre foy Chrestienne, non à sa vertu Stoïque, de pretendre à cette divine et miraculeuse metamorphose.[14]

I see nothing precautionary or insincere in these statements; on the contrary, they appear to me to proceed as logical conclusions from the whole argument of the *Apologie*. It is somewhat surprising to think of Montaigne as a religious propagandist, but this element is occasionally present in the *Essais*. To be sure, he is not an especially devout man, and the religious propaganda, where it exists, is a form of political propaganda; the message is one of conservatism: it is exceedingly dangerous to tamper with the structure of society. However, deeper than the religious or political intentions of this book is its humanistic message: "Chaque homme porte la forme entiere de l'humaine condition." It is this conviction which makes Montaigne occasionally depart from his conservatism, and express vehement sympathy for oppressed classes or peoples. Inevitably we must come back to the truism that Montaigne is not only a literary artist, he is a moralist also.

3. EMPHASIS AND EXAGGERATION

My next baroque category is emphasis and exaggeration. Montaigne hints that he is aware of this characteristic of his style when he confesses that he has sometimes heightened the colors of his self-portraiture. Also, when he declares that he would rather shock than bore us, he is warning us to be prepared for a certain amount of exaggeration. But this latter trait can be more appropriately discussed under other categories—those of horror and surprise. As a matter of fact, many of the categories are intimately related. When M. Jean Rousset gives to his recent book, *La Littérature de l'âge baroque en France,* the subtitle *Circé et le paon,* his peacock symbol represents the baroque love of ostentation; this has connections both with what I call "emphasis and exaggeration" and what I call "theatricality." A good example of baroque exaggeration may be seen in the sixth picture of Rubens' Medici series: the "Presentation of the Portrait." Henri IV, in full armor, stands in a beautiful landscape and gazes ecstatically at the portrait of Marie, which is held aloft by Hymen and Cupid. In the heavens, attended by the eagle and the peacock, are Jupiter and Juno, who gaze benignly down upon the scene. This is of course an extravagant glorification of a political and unromantic marriage. If we wish to appreciate how exaggerated this treatment of the subject is, we have only to transpose it into modern terms, and imagine for a moment a similar representation of the betrothal of the head of any twentieth-century state.

In this section I wish to limit myself to three forms of exaggeration found in Montaigne's style: hyperbole pure and simple, the fondness for exclamatory sentences, and heaping or asyndeton.

Hyperbole is extremely frequent in the *Essais.* In the following examples the writer has chosen to express himself more forcefully than the idea really requires. I do not mean by this to imply any aesthetic condemnation, or to suggest that I consider the emphasis a fault; on the contrary, the literary effectiveness of these passages, so striking that they linger long in the memory, derives directly from the exaggeration. In each case I shall present first the idea, in its barest and simplest form, and then Montaigne's expression of it.

Despite all philosophical theories, it is difficult to deny the evidence of our senses, particularly with regard to pain:

Ferons-nous croire à nostre peau que les coups d'estriviere la chatouillent? Et à nostre goût que l'aloé soit du vin de Graves? [1]

I want to be known exactly as I am, neither better nor worse:

Je reviendrois volontiers de l'autre monde pour dementir celuy qui me formeroit autre que je n'estois, fut-ce pour m'honorer. [2]

In my early education, the very first things I learned were about Rome:

1. I, 14, 65.   2. III, 9, 267.

J'ay eu connoissance des affaires de Romme, long temps avant que je l'aye eue de ceux de ma maison: je sçavois le Capitole et son plant avant que je sceusse le Louvre, et le Tibre avant la Seine.[3]

It is foolish to train oneself to bear hardships before they actually occur:

. . . certes c'est fiévre, aller dés à cette heure vous faire donner le fouet, parce qu'il peut advenir que fortune vous le fera souffrir un jour, et prendre vostre robe fourrée dés la S. Jean parce que vous en aurez besoing à Noel? [4]

Since uneducated people seem able to face pain and death more bravely than others, ignorance may be an advantage:

Pour Dieu, s'il est ainsi, tenons d'ores en avant escolle de bestise.[5]

I love my own freedom so much that I am impatient of any restraint:

Je suis si affady apres la liberté, que qui me deffendroit l'accez de quelque coin des Indes, j'en vivroys aucunement plus mal à mon aise.[6]

It is unhealthy to be too intellectual or too learned:

O que c'est un doux et mol chevet, et sain, que l'ignorance et l'incuriosité, à reposer une teste bien faicte.[7]

A classical writer, in all these cases, would have sought methods of expression more exactly proportioned to the ideas. I think that we may be grateful that the baroque temperament of Montaigne was not obsessed with the concept of *la mesure*. A classical writer would also have been considerably less concrete; but here I am anticipating another category to be discussed later.

It should be noted that two of the above examples—numbers 5 and 7—are really exclamatory sentences. Also, in a way the two questions in the first example come very close to being exclamations. But Montaigne is fairly liberal in the actual use of exclamation points. Suffering from kidney stones, he cries out against stoical philosophy, saying:

Pourveu que le courage soit sans effroy, les parolles sans desespoir, qu'elle se contente! Qu'importe que nous tordons nos bras pourveu que nous ne tordons nos pensées! [8]

And at the end of his life, in an even more complete repudiation of preconceived ideas, he exclaims:

Pour Dieu, que la medecine me face un jour quelque bon et perceptible secours, voir comme je crieray de bonne foy:

Tandem efficaci do manus scientiae! [9]

3. III, 9, 285.   4. III, 12, 359.   5. III, 12, 362.
6. III, 13, 389.   7. III, 13, 391.   8. II, 37, 577.
9. III, 13, 399.

Throughout his life after the death of La Boétie, he continued to long for a great friend. In fact, one of his reasons for writing is that he hopes to find a friend:

O un amy! Combien est vraye cette ancienne sentence, que l'usage en est plus necessaire et plus doux que des elemens de l'eau et du feu![10]

And for a cascade of exclamatory sentences, the reader is referred to the essay *Des coches,* where Montaigne pours forth his indignation against the Spanish methods of conquest.[11]

One of Montaigne's favorite methods of achieving emphasis is by heaping up words. This may take the form of asyndeton—or it may merely be a long list. The effect is one of massiveness, comparable, I think, to the multiplication of columns or decorative motifs on a baroque façade. The triple columns on either side of the main door of SS. Vincenzo ed Anastastio, near the Trevi fountain in Rome, and, on the upper story, the triple columns and pediments, are an emphatic exaggeration of what normal decoration would seem to require; yet they give added mass, and give to the building its essential character. The long row of fantastic animals on the façade of Santa Croce in Lecce is perhaps superfluous; in any case, by usual standards of taste there are too many of them; but they create a distinctive style and rhythm. In the examples of heaping to be found in the *Essais,* the fundamental meaning of each passage would be amply expressed by one or two words, or one or two examples; instead, the author has chosen to make a long list for emphasis, and just for the exuberant fun of it.

In the *Apologie* Montaigne is arguing that we are wrong to assume that animals have no way of communicating with each other. Human beings, who attempt to arrogate to themselves the privilege of language, often resort to signs and gestures. It is quite plausible to conclude that animals may have a sign language. As for us, what do we do with our hands?

. . . nous requerons, nous promettons, appellons, congedions, menaçons, prions, supplions, nions, refusons, interrogeons, admirons, nombrons, confessons, repentons, craignons, vergoignons, doubtons, instruisons, commandons . . .[12]

and here I interrupt the list—there are twenty-nine more verbs in addition to those I have just quoted. Immediately following is a list of expressive gestures of the head:

. . . nous convions, nous renvoyons, advouons, desadvouons, desmentons, bienveignons, honorons, venerons . . .

—twenty-one in all. Such lists are unnecessary for making clear the intellectual content of the passage; the emphasis they lend is excessive, and they

---

10. III, 9, 264–5.   11. See especially III, 6, 168.   12. II, 12, 167.

are to be justified only in terms of decoration. Since here we are dealing with verbs, which suggest motion, the total effect is that characteristically baroque one of mass combined with movement. The section of the *Apologie* from which the paragraph comes is an example of the same technique on a larger scale; for fifty pages Montaigne accumulates evidence of intelligence in animals: the building of swallows' nests, the Thracian fox who tests the thickness of ice by ear, goats and turtles who cure their illnesses with the appropriate herbs, elephants who extract javelins from each other's bodies so skillfully as to avoid all pain, birds who learn how to talk, oxen who consent to turn a wheel precisely one hundred times—the catalogue goes on and on. The examples are picturesque and amusing—and when fifty pages of them are piled up, it produces a considerable impression of weight. Alone, they constitute over a fifth of the entire *Apologie*—a disproportionate amount when we consider that the idea illustrated is relatively unimportant in the development of the essay as a whole. Here the baroque artist completely overshadows the moralist and thinker.

Later in the *Apologie* we have the same procedure all over again: this time the author is listing examples of the imperfections of our senses. One after another, they come in rapid succession: echoes in a valley make the sound of a trumpet appear to come from ahead of us instead of behind; if we cross our fingers while handling a bullet, we get the impression of two instead of one; the somber vastness of churches and the sound of religious music act powerfully upon the most skeptical soul; a philosopher suspended in a cage between the towers of Notre Dame, though perfectly safe, would be overcome by dizziness; and so on.

Or again, there is the catalogue of extraordinary customs in the essai *De la coutume*. There are countries *where,* says Montaigne—and fifty sentences begin with the word "où"; I select a section almost arbitrarily:

Où l'on pleure la mort des effans, et festoye l'on celle des vieillards. Où ils couchent en des licts dix ou douze ensemble avec leurs femmes. Où les femmes qui perdent leurs maris par mort violente se peuvent remarier, les autres non. Où l'on estime si mal la condition des femmes, qu'on y tue les femelles qui y naissent, et achepte l'on des voisins des femmes pour le besoing. Où les maris peuvent repudier sans alleguer aucune cause, les femmes non pour cause quelconque. Où les maris ont loy de les vendre si elles sont steriles.[13]

The point of departure for all this is Montaigne's idea that we cannot conceive of any fancy so crazy as not to be the basis of a custom in some part of the world. With fifty illustrations, the writer drives the point relentlessly home. Each illustration is an interesting picture, but after we have seen them

13. Cf. I, 23, 142–5.

all, there comes upon us some of the feeling of fatigue experienced after a day of walking through the Louvre.

Less overwhelming, but utilizing also the technique of exaggeration through accumulation, are some of Montaigne's comments on Roman circuses in the essay *Des coches*. Money spent in this way was largely wasted:

L'emploitte me sembleroit bien plus royale, comme plus utile, juste et durable, en ports, en havres, fortifications et murs, en bastiments somptueux, en eglises, hospitaux, colleges, reformation de rues et chemins . . .[14]

Four adjectives: royal, useful, just, and enduring. Ten constructive examples of the use of public money. A similar heaping of words expresses Montaigne's sympathy for the natives of the New World:

Mais, quant à la devotion, observance des loix, bonté, liberalité, loyauté, franchise, il nous a bien servy de n'en avoir tant qu'eux: ils se sont perdus par cet avantage, et vendus, et trahis eux mesme. Quant à la hardiesse et courage; quant à la fermeté, constance, resolution contre les douleurs et la faim et la mort, je ne craindrois pas d'opposer les exemples que je trouverois parmy eux aux plus fameux exemples anciens que nous ayons aus memoires de nostre monde par deçà.[15]

As for the corruption of Montaigne's own age and country,

. . . les uns y conferent la trahison, les autres l'injustice, l'irreligion, la tyrannie, l'avarice, la cruauté, selon qu'ils sont plus puissans; les plus foibles y apportent la sottise, la vanité, l'oisiveté, desquels je suis.[16]

As a concluding example of the emphasis and exaggeration of Montaigne's style, I should like to offer the celebrated description of those who make no effort to prepare for death. It combines the three elements we have been studying here, and also possesses some baroque characteristics which I shall take up later: theatricality, movement, and concreteness of imagery. It should be noted that the two interrogative sentences may more properly be regarded as exclamatory:

Ils vont, ils viennent, ils trottent, ils dansent, de mort nulles nouvelles. Tout cela est beau. Mais aussi quand elle arrive, ou à eux, ou à leurs femmes, enfans et amis, les surprenant en dessoude et à descouvert, quels tourmens, quels cris, quelle rage, et quel desespoir les accable? Vites-vous jamais rien si rabaissé, si changé, si confus? [17]

And Montaigne terms this whole attitude "nonchalance bestiale." Later he came to regard this epithet as not only hyperbolic but completely unjustified, for in the essay *De la phisionomie* nonchalance toward death is highly recom-

14. III, 6, 157.   15. III, 6, 166.   16. III, 9, 217.   17. I, 20, 106.

mended. The first sentence of this quotation is interesting because of the asyndeton: four verbs in rapid juxtaposition, and no connective to introduce "de mort nulles nouvelles." The only sentence which does not contain a heaping of words is "Tout cela est beau"; and this brings out, by contrast, the massive accumulations in the others. It also interrupts, for a moment, the precipitate movement of the passage, and helps prepare the *coup de théâtre* of the latter part. We have here a truly extraordinary concentration of baroque aspects.

4. HORROR

Horror, whether of style or content, is a characteristic perhaps more frequently met with in other baroque artists than in Montaigne: Callot, in "Les Misères et les malheurs de la guerre," depicts the ravaging of Lorraine by the troops of Richelieu; Rubens, in the "Martyrdom of St. Livinus," shows that saint having his tongue cut out; Caravaggio, with striking chiaroscuro, dramatizes the martyrdoms of St. Peter and St. Matthew; Agrippa d'Aubigné, in "Misères," accumulates scenes of savagery from the religious wars. We know, of course, that Montaigne lived in the same disastrous epoch as that described in "Misères"; yet, despite occasional remarks which reveal that the author of the *Essais* lived in constant fear of having his house attacked, the prevailing impression tends to be that of a wise and tolerant gentleman who accepts the world with good humor. The impression is not altogether accurate: in Montaigne there is more *angoisse,* more moral indignation, and even more simple curiosity about horror than one thinks.

In the essay *Que le goust des biens et des maux depend en bonne partie de l'opinion que nous en avons,* written in Montaigne's stoical period, there is an accumulation of grotesque examples of human suffering. To be sure, they reinforce the author's main argument (we have noted his lack of restraint in heaping up illustrations) but, with their wealth of painful detail, they betray a certain interest in the subject for its own sake. The episode of the Spartan boy who hid a stolen fox under his cloak and had his belly eaten away rather than reveal his pain—a story mercilessly satirized by Anouilh in *La Valse des toréadors*—is familiar to all school children, and it is inevitable that a humanist scholar should know it, but Montaigne proceeds to follow it up with other cases of physical courage. He cites the story of Scevola who, failing in his attempt to assassinate an enemy king, chose a singular way to demonstrate his own bravery:

Et pour montrer quel il estoit, s'estant faict apporter un brasier, veit et souffrit griller et rostir son bras, jusques à ce que l'ennemy mesme en ayant horreur commanda oster le brasier.[1]

1. I, 14, 71.

The catalogue continues:

> Quoy, celuy qui ne daigna interrompre la lecture de son livre pendant qu'on l'incisoit? Et celuy qui s'obstina à se mocquer et à rire à l'envy des maux qu'on luy faisoit: de façon que la cruauté irritée des bourreaux qui le tenoyent, et toutes les inventions des tourmens redoublez les uns sur les autres luy donnerent gaigné. . . . Quoy? un gladiateur de Caesar endura tousjours riant qu'on lui sondat et detaillat ses playes . . . Meslons-y les femmes. Qui n'a ouy parler à Paris de celle qui se fit escorcher pour seulement en acquerir le teint plus frais d'une nouvelle peau?

This is, of course, an example of what I have termed "heaping." An author who indulges in this practice reveals, by exceeding the normal requirements of expression, that he enjoys the items heaped up for their own sake. This is a charge which, I feel, Montaigne cannot escape here.

Elsewhere, Montaigne exhibits interest in the man-eating activities of the cannibals:

> . . . il attache une corde à l'un des bras du prisonnier . . . et donne au plus cher de ses amis l'autre bras à tenir de mesme; et eux deux, en presence de toute l'assemblée, l'assomment à coups d'epée. Cela faict, ils le rostissent et en mangent en commun et en envoient des lopins à ceux de leurs amis qui sont absents.[2]

The victim is tied, stabbed to death, roasted, and eaten; this in itself constitutes a sufficiently gruesome scene, but what I regard as significantly baroque is the added detail: bits of meat are sent off to absent friends. But then Montaigne, having had the amusement of horrifying us, proceeds to defend his cannibals by pointing out that Europeans can sometimes be even more barbarous; presumably he has in mind the autos-da-fé of the Spanish Inquisition and of the Ligue:

> Je pense qu'il y a plus de barbarie à manger un homme vivant qu'à le manger mort, à deschirer, par tourmens et par geénes, un corps encor plein de sentiment, le faire rostir par le menu, le faire mordre et meurtrir aux chiens et aux pourceaux (comme nous l'avons, non seulement leu, mais veu de fresche memoire, non entre des ennemis anciens, mais entre des voisins et concitoyens, et, qui pis est, sous pretexte de piété et de religion) que de rostir et manger apres qu'il est trespassé.

This protest against the torture of heretics shows us once more that Montaigne, in writing the *Essais,* was animated by a moral purpose. However, the moral indignation is not unalloyed with a certain morbid interest in the details of executions. Actually, during his trip to Rome, he had the occasion to witness an execution; and while the incident is mentioned os-

2. I, 31, 270.

tensibly because it provides an interesting illustration of mob psychology, the mere facts of choosing to watch and to describe such an event reveal a significant aspect of the author's sensibility:

Je me rencontray un jour a Rome sur le point qu'on defaisoit Catena, un voleur insigne. On l'estrangla sans aucune emotion de l'assistance; mais quand on vint à le mettre en quartiers, le bourreau ne donnoit coup, que le peuple ne suivit d'une vois pleintive et d'une exclamation, comme si chacun eut presté son sentiment à cette charongne.[3]

The essay in question (*De la cruauté,* II, 11) is one of three in the second book where Montaigne condemns judicial cruelty and torture—the others being II, 5, *De la conscience,* and II, 27, *Couardise mere de cruauté.* The sentiments expressed in these chapters do great honor to Montaigne's humanity, and he shows himself far in advance of his age. Very few contemporaries of Montaigne, I imagine, were disturbed by cruelty in daily life or in judicial procedure. Full credit must be given to this author's vision and moral sense; yet, when he concludes the essay *De la conscience* with the following anecdote, the artist's desire to fascinate us through horror is blended with the moralist's aim to instruct us through moral indignation:

Une femme de village accusoit devant un general d'armée, un grand justicier, un soldat pour avoir arraché à ses petits enfans ce peu de bouillie qui luy restoit à les substanter, cette armée ayant ravagé tous les villages à l'environ. De preuve, il n'y en avoit point. Le general, apres avoir sommé la femme de regarder bien à ce qu'elle disoit, d'autant qu'elle seroit coupable de son accusation si elle mentoit, et elle persistant, il fit ouvrir le ventre au soldat pour s'esclaircir de la verité du faict. Et la femme se trouva avoir raison. Condemnation instructive.[4]

With this scene we find ourselves in the savage civil-war world of d'Aubigné's "Misères," where dying peasants' brains ooze out on the doorstep, and pregnant women, beaten to death, rot on the ground. We cannot deny d'Aubigné's sincere moral purpose when he seeks to arouse us to the horrors of religious war, but we cannot help noticing the poet's enthusiasm for depicting scenes of horror. In *Couardise mere de cruauté,* and also in *De trois bonnes femmes* (II, 35), Montaigne gives us examples of high moral courage in the face of a tyrant's cruelty: Theoxena, to escape the ferocity of Philip of Macedonia, encourages her children to stab themselves and then, with her husband, commits suicide by leaping into the sea; and there is the story told by Pliny of Arria and Paetus, persecuted by Nero: the husband was lacking in resolution until his wife, having stabbed herself, handed him the dagger saying, "Paete, non dolet." These chapters contain a kind of humanistic martyrology comparable to d'Aubigné's Christian one in "Les

3. II, 11, 137.   4. II, 5, 53.

Feux." The basic aim, in both cases, is moral instruction, but both writers linger lovingly over the horrifying details.

There are other scenes of martyrdom in *Des coches*. As in d'Aubigné's "Les Feux," the executioners are Catholics, but the victims are not Protestants—they are the pagan king of Mexico and a nobleman of his court:

> . . . ils condamnerent le Roy mesme et l'un des principaux seigneurs de sa court a la geine en presence l'un de l'autre. Ce seigneur, se trouvant force de sa douleur, environné de braziers ardens, tourna sur sa fin piteusement sa veue vers son maistre, comme pour luy demander mercy de ce qu'il n'en pouvoit plus. Le Roy, plantant fierement et rigoureusement les yeux sur luy, pour reproche de sa lascheté et pusillanimité, luy dict seulement ces mots, d'une voix rude et ferme: Et moy, suis-je dans un bain? suis-je plus à mon aise que toy? Celuy-là, soudain apres, succomba aux douleurs, et mourut sur la place. Le Roy, a demy rosty, fut emporté de là. . . . Ils le pendirent depuis . . .[5]

Baroque art has sometimes been represented as essentially an art of the Counter Reformation. It is true of course that many of the greatest painters of the period were in the service of the Roman church, and the martyrdoms they depict—Ribera of St. Bartholomew, Rubens of St. Livinus, Poussin of St. Erasmus, Caravaggio of St. Matthew—are illustrations of Catholic doctrine; but the baroque style transcends religious limits. The essential criterion of the style is not the espousal of a particular religious cause; more fundamental than this is the peculiar conjunction of moral purpose, horror, and martyrdom. The moral purpose may, as in the case of d'Aubigné, be the furtherance of Protestantism; or it may, as with Montaigne, be a denunciation of Roman Catholic excesses. What d'Aubigné and Montaigne share in common with the above painters is the curious blending of moral indignation with a vivid and detailed depiction of horror.

Intimately connected with this artistic attitude is the writer's love of shocking the reader. It would be possible to consider under the present category Montaigne's propensity for startling the reader with brutally crude expressions, contrary to later ideas of *bienséance:* "j'aimerais mieux poindre que lasser." But this trait is really closer to "surprise" than to "horror"—even if some readers of the *Essais* feel "horrified" by vulgarity.

5. INCARNATION

"Incarnation" is essentially a theological term. The best exposition of its meaning is to be found in the first chapter of St. John, from "In the beginning was the Word" to "And the Word was made flesh." The stylistic trait which I wish to discuss here, while not in itself religious, possesses a strong analogy with the dogma of the Incarnation. I refer to the baroque

5. III, 6, 171.

tendency to express intangible ideas in concrete form. Instead of abstractions, we have images which appeal to the senses. Through the creative activity of the baroque artist, ideas take on physical being. This characteristic, so different from anything to be encountered in Descartes or strict classicists, is especially noticeable in the works of d'Aubigné, St. François de Sales, or Sir Thomas Browne. It is also conspicuous in the *Essais* of Montaigne. Under this category of incarnation I would include the following aspects: imagery, which though expressing abstract ideas retains its full physical effect; vividness of realistic detail; a fondness for color and lighting effects, especially redness, radiance, and chiaroscuro; multiple-sense imagery (that is, the simultaneous appeal to several senses, as sound, sight, and smell, at once); and the use of erotic imagery to express religious ecstasy. It is the first two of these which are particularly frequent in Montaigne; the others, though occasionally present, are not nearly so important in the *Essais* as, for example, in the *Introduction à la vie dévote*.

In order to illustrate how, in the *Essais,* ideas become incarnate, I shall preface each example with an abstract statement of the thought. This will show, I think, that Montaigne must be regarded as an artist as well as a thinker. In the beginning, to be sure, was the word—but the peculiar quality of Montaigne is that he has made the word become flesh. As a result (to continue the paraphrase of St. John) the word dwells among us; we the ordinary, unphilosophical readers are able to perceive the grace and truth of the *Essais*. The baroque work of art emerges before us—a moral purpose given sensuous expression.

In a teacher, good judgment is more important than encyclopaedic knowledge:

. . . je voudrois aussi qu'on fut soigneux de luy choisir un conducteur qui eust plutost la teste bien faicte que bien pleine . . .[1]

The student should learn to admit being wrong in an argument:

Qu'on l'instruise sur tout à se rendre et à quitter les armes à la verité, aussi tost qu'il l'appercevra: soit qu'elle naisse és mains de son adversaire, soit qu'elle naisse en luy-mesme par quelque ravisement.[2]

Virtue is not unpleasant and hard to attain:

Elle [i.e. la philosophie] a pour son but la vertu, qui n'est pas, comme dit l'eschole, plantée à la teste d'un mont coupé, rabotteux et inaccessible. Ceux qui l'ont approchée, la tiennent, au rebours, logée dans une belle plaine fertile et fleurissante, d'où elle void bien souz soy toutes choses; mais si peut on y arriver, qui en sçait l'addresse, par des routtes ombrageuses, gazonnées et doux fleurantes, plaisamment et d'une pante facile et polie, comme est celle des voutes celestes.[3] [Here the concept has become a landscape. In painting the picture, Montaigne

1. I, 26, 193.   2. I, 26, 199.   3. I, 26, 207.

has appealed to other senses than sight alone: muscular effort is suggested by the rugged, inaccessible mountain, and coolness by the shady roads. Smell is implied by the epithet "doux fleurantes."]

A picture of pedantic scholars who have no real love of wisdom:

. . . des asnes chargez de livres.[4]

A description of the complete spiritual union of true friendship:

En l'ámitié dequoy je parle, elles (les ames) se meslent et confondent l'une en l'autre, d'un melange si universel, qu'elles effacent et ne retrouvent plus la couture qui les a jointes.[5] [The word "couture" is the characteristic one here.]

Laws and customs differ widely from one country to another:

Quelle verité que ces montagnes bornent, qui est mensonge au monde qui se tient au delà?[6]

We cannot define our own consciousness:

Et si, de fortune, vous fichez vostre pensée à vouloir prendre son estre, ce sera ne plus ne moins que qui voudroit empoigner l'eau . . .[7]

Reason can prove directly contradictory things:

La raison humaine est un glaive double et dangereux.[8]

We become unreasonably angry when people point out our mistakes and faults:

Au lieu d'y tendre les bras, nous y tendons les griffes.[9]

I feel that I have escaped the moral corruption of my era:

Encore qu'il s'advenoit, comme disent aucuns jardiniers, que les roses et violettes naissant plus odoriferantes pres des aux et des oignons, d'autant qu'ils sucent et tirent à eux ce qu'il y a de mauvaide odeur en la terre, aussi que ces depravées natures humassent tout le venin de mon air et du climat et m'en rendissent d'autant meilleur et plus pur par leur voisinage que je ne perdisse pas tout.[10] [The metaphor, with its olfactory images taken from gardening, is similar to many found in the *Introduction à la vie dévote*.]

Reform of one's character late in life is inappropriate ("Il vaut quasi mieux jamais que si tard devenir honneste homme"):

Moustarde apres disner.[11]

Premature preparation for hardship is folly:

[C'est fiévre de] prendre vostre robe fourrée dés la S. Jean parce que vous en aurez besoing à Noel.[12] [We have already noted this passage as an example of

4. I, 26, 228.	5. I, 28, 242.	6. II, 12, 338.	7. II, 12, 367.
8. II, 17, 439.	9. III, 8, 186.	10. III, 9, 251.	11. III, 10, 304.
12. III, 12, 359.			

emphasis and exaggeration; but it is no less remarkable for its concrete imagery. The next quotation likewise belongs to both categories.]

A lack of intellectual curiosity is pleasant and healthy:

O que c'est un doux et mol chevet, et sain, que l'ignorance et l'incuriosité, à reposer une teste bien faicte.[13] [It should perhaps be pointed out that "chevet" means "pillow"; the image appeals strongly to the sense of touch.]

My essays may be useful to the reader, since I have tried so many things before him:

Pour qui en voudra gouster, j'en ay faict l'essay, son eschançon.[14] [In other words, just as the cupbearer tests all food and drink for poison before serving them to the king, so I test the experiences of life before passing them on to my reader.]

The above is only a very fragmentary list of specimens of Montaigne's concreteness. Actually, the majority of the examples I give to illustrate my other categories could also find a place here, for Montaigne's style is nearly always incarnational. Granted this permanent feature of his writing, it has seemed more instructive to present quotations which are noteworthy for moral indignation, hyperbole, horror, theatricality, metamorphosis, etc. in the more specifically appropriate categories.

6. THEATRICALITY AND ILLUSION

Although Montaigne's book is a collection of philosophical and moral essays, it is somewhat surprising to observe that its author displays a decided taste for theatrical scenes. But in the baroque age the dramatic and spectacular are by no means limited to the theater. Take, for example, one of the greatest paintings of Caravaggio, the "Calling of St. Matthew." The publicans are seated at a table in a dark room, counting their money. On the extreme right, Christ has just entered the room; and from the same direction, a strong beam of light penetrates the darkness. It picks out the face of Christ and His hand as He points to Matthew, and illuminates the realistic faces of the men at the table; some are surprised, while others indifferently go about their business. But Matthew, who is the focus both of Christ's gesture and of the spotlight, looking up with incredulous awe, seems to be saying "Who, me?" It is a turning point in a man's life, coming with dramatic suddenness while he is engaged in worldly affairs. The drama is all the more forceful because the scene is painted with great naturalism; the theatrical quality comes principally from gestures and lighting—as it would indeed if this were taking place on a stage. Or let us consider a baroque picture of a very different kind: Rubens' "Landing of Marie of Medici at Marseille."

13. III, 13, 391.   14. III, 13, 400.

This is pure pageantry, and makes one think of a scene from a Wagnerian opera: the splendidly ornate ship lies alongside the porticoed quay; Marie, in gorgeous robes, accompanied by the Duchess of Mantua, progresses triumphantly down the gangplank, while a helmeted allegorical figure of France bows to welcome her. Overhead flies the winged goddess of Fame, blowing trumpets, while in the waves beneath, three buxom sea nymphs writhe in joyous dance. And—thinking of baroque architecture—the great squares of Rome are above all theatrical, perhaps because we so often come upon them suddenly from a narrow street (the Piazza San Pietro, though it no longer presents itself to us in this way, was originally so designed; and the Piazza Navona still produces this impression); perhaps also because they seem like huge outdoor stages for a spectacle (the Piazza Navona was originally a Roman circus, and the Piazza San Pietro is still the setting for great gatherings during religious festivals).

One might not expect the spectacular to play a part in a work as personal and intimate as the *Essais*. However, we have just seen that Montaigne's style, regardless of his subject matter, tends to be sensuous and concrete; and often the images and metaphors expand into theatrical scenes. Here, for example, is a passage which we have already studied because of its heaping technique:

Ils vont, ils viennent, ils trottent, ils dansent, de mort nulles nouvelles. Tout cela est beau. Mais aussi quand elle arrive, ou à eux, ou à leurs femmes, enfans et amis, les surprenant en dessoude et à decouvert, quels tourmens, quels cris, quelle rage, et quel desespoir les accable?[1]

This is a vivid scene in a play. The sudden arrival of death, bursting unexpectedly upon the daily round of human activities, is as dramatically powerful as the entry of Christ into the publicans' room in Caravaggio's picture. And Montaigne continues, by means of little dramatic vignettes, to develop his theme of psychological preparation for death:

Au broncher d'un cheval, à la cheute d'une tuille, à la moindre piqueure d'espleingue, remachons soudain: Et bien, quand ce seroit la mort mesme? et là dessus, roidissons nous et efforçons nous. Parmy les festes et la joye, ayons toujours ce refrein de la souvenance de nostre condition . . .[2]

The passage also illustrates two other baroque characteristics, one already discussed and the other yet to come: concreteness and movement. Again:

. . . que la mort me treuve plantant mes chous, mais nonchalant d'elle, et encore plus de mon jardin imparfait.[3]

1. I, 20, 106.   2. I, 20, 107.   3. I, 20, 111.

Because of their mixture of concreteness, movement, and drama, such passages may be regarded as little theatrical scenes.

The various episodes of horror and martyrdom which I have discussed—the general who ordered the soldier's stomach opened up to see whether he had eaten the porridge; the torture of the king of Mexico; the heroic suicides of Theoxena and Arria—are all conceived dramatically. In a sense, the essay *De trois bonnes femmes* may be said to consist of three dramas, in each of which a wife is the heroine. Montaigne thinks of these three stories as "plaisans et tragiques"; in all fairness, therefore, we should admit that, in addition to his morbid curiosity about the horrible, he has a strong sense of the theatrical.

He is at times inclined toward self-dramatization. Needless to say, the troubled and violent times in which he lived gave him an ample excuse for describing his situation theatrically:

Je me suis couché mille fois chez moy, imaginant qu'on me trahiroit et assomeroit cette nuict là . . .[4]

As an example of the dangers to which he was exposed, he tells us the story of an attempted plot to capture his house. A neighbor knocked at his door, claiming to be pursued by enemies, and asking for asylum. While Montaigne was comforting and refreshing his guest—

Tantost apres, voylà quatre ou cinq de ses soldats qui se presentent en mesme contenance et effroy, pour entrer; et puis d'autres et d'autres encore apres, bien equipez et bien armez, jusques à vingt cinq ou trante, feignants avoir leur ennemy aux talons.

Montaigne decided that the best defense was to show neither suspicion of treachery nor fear. He remained quietly in his living room, talking to the chief, while the soldiers waited on horseback in the courtyard.

Souvant depuis il a dict, car il ne craignoit pas de faire ce compte, que mon visage et ma franchise luy avoient arraché la trahison des poincts. Il remonta à cheval, ses gens ayants continuellement les yeux sur luy pour voir quel signe il leur donneroit, bien estonnez de le voir sortir et abandonner son avantage.[5]

The episode is vividly described, and suspense maintained throughout; it is not until the very end that we know that the author and his house escaped all harm. There is a similar dramatic technique in his account of being held up for ransom during a journey through a guerrilla-infested region. Montaigne pleaded his limited means and his neutrality in the civil war:

4. III, 9, 250.   5. III, 12, 372–4.

Apres deux ou trois heures que nous eusmes esté là et qu'ils m'eurent faict monter sur un cheval qui n'avoit garde de leur eschaper, et commis ma conduitte particuliere à quinze ou vingt harquebousiers, et dispersé mes gens à d'autres, ayant ordonné qu'on nous menast prisonniers diverses routes, et moy déjà acheminé à deux ou trois harquebousades de là, . . . voicy une soudaine et tres-inopinée mutation qui leur print. Je vis revenir à moy le chef avec parolles plus douces, se mettant en peine de recercher en la troupe mes hardes escartées, et m'en faisant rendre selon qu'il s'en pouvoit recouvrer, jusques à ma boyte. Le meilleur present qu'ils me firent ce fut en fin ma liberté . . .[6]

The scene builds up to a dramatic climax when Montaigne is led off under armed escort; just at the moment when we expect the worst to happen, the "sudden and unexpected change" occurs.

The description of Montaigne's wanderings during the plague, though less sensational, presents a somber and dramatic picture. Again one thinks of Caravaggio or Callot:

J'eus à souffrir cette plaisante condition que la veue de ma maison m'estoit effroiable. Tout ce qui y estoit estoit sans garde, et à l'abandon de qui en avoit envie. Moy qui suis si hospitalier, fus en tres penible queste de re-traicte pour ma famille; une famille esgarée, faisant peur à ses amis et à soy-mesme, et horreur où elle cerchast à se placer, ayant à changer de demeure soudain qu'un de la troupe commençoit à se douloir du bout du doigt.[7]

To speak of theatricality is to speak of illusion. The art of the theater is not only spectacle and suspense—it is above all the creation of illusion. This is true of drama in general, and especially so of two baroque plays which we shall study in these pages, Corneille's *L'Illusion comique* and Rotrou's *Saint Genest,* for they approach the whole problem of illusion with extreme self-consciousness. No less aware of the delight of deceiving the spectator was Pietro da Cortona when, by extending the façade of Santa Maria della Pace over the private houses on either side, he made this small Roman church appear nearly three times as large as it actually is. By similar devices, the provincial town of Lecce in the heel of Italy, with medium-sized churches and medium-sized palaces, is baroquely made to appear a capital with huge churches and impressive palaces. Thus, when I speak of the theatricality of the *Essais,* even more than the author's love of spectacle and suspense I mean his fascination with the problems of illusion. It may be objected that here I am speaking of an intellectual interest of Montaigne's rather than of a stylistic trait, but the baroque is a matter of content and spirit as well as of form and style. There is such a thing as the baroque mind; by his enjoyment of the contrast between appearance and reality, Montaigne reveals his baroque mind.

6. III, 12, 375.   7. III, 12, 355.

As might be expected, the criticism of the human senses in the *Apologie* is much concerned with this question. Under certain circumstances, a single bullet may feel like two:

A manier une balle d'arquebouse soubs le second doigt, celuy du milieu estant entrelassé par dessus, il faut extremement se contraindre, pour advouer qu'il n'y en ait qu'une, tant le sens nous en represente deux.[8]

Here the contrast between illusion and reality is a physical problem of minor importance; but Montaigne raises more serious issues: perhaps the religious impression we receive upon entering a church is an illusion caused by our senses.

[Il n'est] ame si revesche qui ne se sente touchée de quelque reverence à considerer cette vastité sombre de nos Eglises, la diversité d'ornemens et ordre de nos ceremonies, et ouyr le son devotieux de nos orgues, et la harmonie si posée et religieuse de nos voix.[9]

By the use of the word "revesche" Montaigne indicates, it seems to me, sympathetic approval of the emotion we feel when we enter a French Gothic church or attend a High Mass; but intellectually he raises the question as to whether our senses are deceiving us. As an artist, and possibly as a Christian also, he admires the theatrical technique which moves us; nevertheless, he is fully aware of the illusion which may be involved. At times we may know perfectly well that illusionistic techniques are contributing to our pleasure. For example, even though we are seldom deceived by a woman's make-up, we find her appearance more agreeable because of it:

Nous avons beau sçavoir que ces tresses sont empruntées d'un page ou d'un laquais; que cette rougeur est venue d'Espaigne, et cette blancheur et polisseure de la mer Oceane, encore faut il que la veue nous force d'en trouver le subject plus aimable et plus agreable, contre toute raison.[10]

As a further and more powerful example of the way in which we are emotionally and physically influenced by illusions which our reason knows to be false, Montaigne gives us his famous philosopher hung in a cage between the towers of Notre Dame:

Qu'on loge un philosophe dans une cage de menus filets de fer clersemez, qui soit suspendue au haut des tours nostre Dame de Paris, il verra par raison evidente qu'il est impossible qu'il en tombe, et si ne se sçauroit garder (s'il n'a accoustumé le mestier des recouvreurs) que la veue de cette hauteur extreme ne l'espouvante et ne le transisse.[11]

Often, of course, the illusion deceives our reason as well as our senses. This is particularly likely to happen when we consider people in high office.

8. II, 12, 356.   9. Ibid.   10. II, 12, 357.   11. II, 12, 358.

Just because their appearance is impressive and their position important, we assume—erroneously—that their thoughts and motives are lofty. I refrain from contemporary political allusions, but the reader can make his own:

Considerant l'importance des actions des princes et leur pois, nous nous persuadons qu'elles soyent produites par quelques causes aussi poisantes et importantes: nous nous trompons: ils sont menez et ramenez en leurs mouvemens par les mesmes ressors que nous sommes aux nostres. La mesme raison qui nous fait tanser avec un voisin, dresse entre les Princes une guerre; la mesme raison qui nous faict foiter un lacquais, tombant en un Roy, luy faict ruiner une province.[12]

In all these passages, I feel that attention should be called to something that properly belongs in an earlier category: the concreteness of the imagery. The person entering the church has many senses assailed: it is vast and dark, the organ is playing and there is choral singing, the liturgy is visually beautiful as well. The woman's false hair comes from a page or a lackey, her rouge from Spain, her powder and cream from the ocean. The philosopher is not suspended in some indefinite high spot, but specifically between the towers of Notre Dame. Finally, the irritability of the sovereign is compared to that of Montaigne and his neighbors, or to their ill-humor when they whip a servant. Nothing is vague and abstract; all is specific and tangible.

At times disguise, which ordinarily fascinates Montaigne, disgusts him —in particular, he has no patience with the art of feigning piety. There is a passage in *Du repentir* which anticipates *Tartuffe*:

Je ne trouve aucune qualité si aysée à contrefaire que la devotion, si on n'y conforme les meurs et la vie: son essence est abstruse et occulte; les apparences, faciles et trompeuses.[13]

But to return to the question of public office, Montaigne himself, who had been both magistrate and mayor of Bordeaux, was acutely aware of the difference between the inward and the outward man. He insists strongly upon the distinction—this time without moral overtones, so that his emphasis is upon the theatricality rather than on the morality of the problem. In playing a public part, we should not lose sight of ourselves:

Du masque et de l'apparence il n'en faut pas faire une essence réelle, ny de l'estranger le propre. C'est assez de s'enfariner le visage, sans s'enfariner la poictrine.[14]

The image, which derives so directly from the stage, is significant. And he concludes by saying:

Le Maire et Montaigne ont toujours esté deux, d'une separation bien claire.

12. II, 12, 197.   13. III, 2, 38.   14. III, 10, 306.

In other words, it is all a game, and while hypocrisy is reprehensible, the theatrical art is fun. After all, the spectacles presented by the Romans in the Colosseum arouse his admiration rather than his disapproval, even if at times he feels that the money might have been more usefully spent:

C'estoit pourtant une belle chose, d'aller faire apporter et planter en la place aus arenes une grande quantité de gros arbres, tous branchus et tous verts, representans une grande forest ombrageuse, despartie en belle symmetrie, et, le premier jour, jetter la dedans mille austruches, mille cerfs, mille sangliers et mille dains, les abandonnants a piller au peuple; le lendemain, faire assommer en sa presence cent gros lions, cent leopards, et trois cens ours, et pour le troisiesme jour, faire combatre à outrance trois cens paires de gladiateurs . . .[15]

In part this belongs to the category of horror, but the continuation is pure theatricality:

. . . faire premierement, par art, entr'ouvrir et fendre en crevasses representant des autres qui vomissoient les bestes destinées au spectacle, et puis secondement l'inonder d'une mer profonde, qui charrioit force monstres marins, chargée de vaisseaux armez, à representer une bataille navalle . . .[16]

And, as a further specimen of the theatrical art:

Quelquefois on y a faict naistre une haute montagne plaine de fruitiers et arbres verdoyand, rendans par son feste un ruisseau d'eau, comme de la bouche d'une vive fontaine. Quelquefois on y promena un grand navire qui s'ouvroit et desprenoit de soy-mesme, et, apres avoir vomy de son ventre quatre ou cinq cens bestes à combat, se resserroit et s'esvanouissoit, sans aide.[17]

Some readers of the *Essais* may be surprised at discovering Montaigne's childlike delight in re-imagining the spectacles of the Colosseum; but if we look at his *Journal de voyage,* we shall have no doubt as to the reality of this enthusiasm. Montaigne, who on his trip to Italy shows little interest in Raphael or Michelangelo, is fascinated by the spectacular wonders of the gardens of Italy. He likes devices which put on a good show. One of his favorite places is the Villa d'Este at Tivoli, with its theatrically spouting fountains and its grand staircases whose handrails are cascades of water; he loves its fake grottoes and festive avenues of overflowing spray. It is not a coincidence that, in the period in which he visited Rome, the papal architects were everywhere busy erecting the fountains which make the great charm of the city: the Fontana della Barcaccia by Bernini's father in the Piazza di Spagna, or the lovely Fontana delle Tartarughe (1585) with the graceful youths pushing the turtles into the upper basin.

There remains to be discussed one further aspect of theatricality. Baroque artists, in thinking of their work in terms of theater, necessarily have in mind the spectator. Bernini's St. Teresa and her angel, lighted by a hidden

15. III, 6, 161.   16. III, 6, 162.   17. III, 6, 163.

window and framed on a stage, is conceived with respect to onlookers; the fact is underlined by the sculptured audience in high relief on either side of the north transept of Santa Maria della Vittoria. It is an anticipation, nearly three centuries ahead of time, of impressionism: the particular way in which the beholder looks at the work of art is regarded as having great importance. Or, let us consider a painting recently discussed in this section: Caravaggio's "Calling of St. Matthew." We come upon the great event in St. Matthew's life almost by accident: Nothing is posed and planned. In Raphael's great Stanze frescoes, on the other hand, all is symmetrically arranged: the view we have of the "Disputa" or the "School of Athens" is obviously the one right way of looking at them. Similarly, there is a single significant aspect of the garden façade of Versailles: we must stand in the central axis, so that both wings of the palace extend symmetrically on either side of Louis XIV's bedchamber, and all avenues of the park radiate with a geometrical equilibrium. But in Caravaggio's painting, we feel that another aspect might have been interesting also; in any case, the particular view we have, dramatic as it is, is only one of many possible glimpses. Baroque architecture and town planning, as a rule, avoid suggesting that there is one best way of looking at a building or group of buildings. No single photograph of the Piazza Navona will ever be satisfactory; it is by walking through this extraordinary square, and allowing its aspects to strike us in varied sequence, that we appreciate its meaning. It is just so with the art of Montaigne. In order to appreciate the *Essais* fully, we must take delight in all the various and often contradictory things he has to say on a single subject. Sometimes these statements are divergent because they represent, chronologically, different stages of Montaigne's opinion on a single subject; and we know that he scorned to repudiate his past. But often, in the midst of passages composed at one same time, there is a picturesque proliferation of different points of view. It seems as if Montaigne took delight in examining an idea from varying angles. This is, I think, one reason for the multiplication, in the essay *De la coutume* or in the *Apologie,* of illustrations of strange customs. There is a basic idea—social usages are crazy—and then the author proceeds to demonstrate this in multitudinous aspects. The same is true in the *Apologie* when Montaigne wishes to point out the intelligence of animals or the fallibility of the human senses. We have a cascade of examples, all very concrete and pictorial, which create massive emphasis as they heap themselves up; but also each individual case gives us a different perspective of the concept. Each perspective is considered significant; just as the idea without concrete examples would be felt to be bare, so the single point of view would appear deficient in picturesqueness and life. This stylistic procedure is a frequent one with St. François de Sales. I think we may conveniently term it "multiple-aspect imagery." A characteristic sign is the multiplication of semicolons; the author keeps playing with his idea, returning to look at it in different ways, restating it with different images.

Here are a few examples, taken almost at random from the Book III. In the essay *Du repentir* Montaigne tells us that he follows his own judgment and conscience rather than listening to other people's criticisms:

J'ay mes loix et ma court pour juger de moy, et m'y adresse plus qu'ailleurs. Je restrains bien selon autruy mes actions, mais je ne les estends que selon moy. Il n'y a que vous qui sçache si vous estes lache et cruel, ou loyal et devotieux; les autres ne vous voyent poinct, ils vous devinent par conjectures incertaines; ils voyent non tant vostre nature que vostre art. Par ainsi ne vous tenez pas à leur sentence; tenez vous à la vostre.[18]

This passage is a succession of brief clauses; for the most part, the author has dispensed with conjunctions. There is no progression of thought here; Montaigne is circling around his idea, giving us a series of interesting views. As in the case of baroque architecture, the frontal view is not the only important one; on the contrary, each new angle presents us with an unexpected picturesqueness. Such a procedure places great emphasis on the spectator and his position; that is why I feel that multiple-aspect imagery is intimately related to the problem of illusion, and to the art of the theatre. Here, the writer begins by saying that he has his own private law court to judge his actions. He then pauses, retreating a little to a new position, and concedes that he does pay attention to the opinions of other people, insofar as negative restraints are concerned; however, his positive actions all proceed from his own temperament and judgment. There is another pause, while the writer again shifts his viewpoint slightly. You alone, he declares, know the real truth about your inmost moral nature; other people have to base their opinion of you on uncertain guesswork. The semicolon introduces a new perspective: all the world is a stage, we are actors, and our fellow men see our histrionic art, but not our true personality. Thus theatricality and illusion are a fundamental element of life—as well as of Montaigne's style. In the final sentence, we have a maxim: Obey your own judgment and not that of other people. The same idea has already been expressed, but as a simple statement of what Montaigne himself does; here it is an imperative, addressed to mankind at large. The final view is a panoramic one.

Or consider this paragraph from *L'Art de conferer*. The topic is, in a sense, complementary to the one which Montaigne had discussed in *Du repentir*. There he had advised us to allow our own conscience to be our guide, and not to worry too much about the opinion of the world. Here, on the other

18. III, 2, 31.

hand, he is recommending that we accept criticism with good grace. The passages are about a hundred and fifty pages apart—it is I, and not Montaigne, who make the juxtaposition—but if we consider each one as a whole, and compare the two, we have in reality two different and equally interesting perspectives of the same problem. However, my main concern is with the internal organization of the following paragraph:

> Les contradictions donc des jugemens ne m'offensent ny m'alterent; elles m'esveillent seulement et m'exercent. Nous fuyons à la contradiction, il s'y faudroit presenter et produire, notamment quand elle vient par forme de conference, non de rejance. A chaque opposition, on ne regarde pas si elle est juste, mais, à tort ou à droit, comment on s'en deffera. Au lieu d'y tendre les bras, nous y tendons les griffes. Je souffrirois estre rudement heurté par mes amis: Tu es un sot, tu resves. J'ayme, entre les galans hommes, qu'on s'exprime courageusement, que les mots aillent où va la pensée. Il nous faut fortifier l'ouie et la durcir contre cette tandreur du son ceremonieux des parolles. J'ayme une societé et familiarité forte et virile, une amitié qui se flatte en l'aspreté et vigueur de son commerce, comme l'amour, és morsures et esgratigneures sanglantes.[19]

Montaigne starts off by declaring that, in conversation, it does not offend him to be contradicted. After the semicolon, he looks at the idea in another way: "On the contrary," he says, "contradiction wakes me up and trains my mind." Then he thinks of the idea in terms of human nature in general: we all run away from intellectual opposition. Now comes a comma (note the absence of any grammatical connective). We ought to seek out opposing points of view. The clause introduced by "notamment" constitutes a slight concession, a few steps backward to see another aspect: lively discussion is stimulating, but of course it is disagreeable to be lectured by somebody else. Next he analyzes the attitude of most people during an argument: they seek to destroy opposition rather than see whether it is justified. There follows the image of arms and claws which I have already discussed elsewhere; this metaphor is not mere decoration but a fresh and picturesque approach from a slightly different point of view. Now the writer shifts his position somewhat—"we" gives place to "I": *I* allow my friends to criticize my ideas frankly and roughly. He moves on to tell us what kind of conversation he enjoys among gentlemen and friends; it is characterized by courage and sincerity. A new shift occurs; we go back from "I" to "we," and two new reflections occur: it is good for us to train ourselves not to be too sensitive; formal language tends too much to protect our sensibilities. Returning to himself, Montaigne describes the kind of human relationships he enjoys: strong, virile informality, marked by vigorous give-and-take. The final clause opens up new perspectives: a rough-and-tumble friendship is the

19. III, 8, 186.

most satisfactory, just as love-making is best when accompanied by deep bites and scratches. During this whole passage the writer has been playing with a single basic idea, but he has shown us all its lively facets; the delight in such picturesque complexity is typically baroque.

As a final example of multiple-aspect imagery, I should like to propose a passage from *De la vanité,* where the author condemns excessive rigorism in moral standards. This is from the "down-to-earth" period of his philosophy, antistoical and antipuritanical in spirit:

A quoy faire ces poinctes eslevées de la philosophie sur lesquelles aucun estre humain ne se peut rasseir, et ces regles qui excedent nostre usage et nostre force? Je voy souvent qu'on nous propose des images de vie, lesquelles ny le proposant ny les auditeurs n'ont aucune esperance de suyvre ny, qui plus est, envie. De ce mesme papier où il vient d'escrire l'arrest de condemnation contre un adultere, le juge en desrobe un lopin pour en faire un poulet à la femme de son compaignon. Celle à qui vous venez de vous frotter illicitement, criera plus asprement tantost, en vostre presence mesme, à l'encontre d'une pareille faute de sa compaigne que ne feroit Porcie. Et tel condamne des hommes à mourir pour des crimes qu'il n'estime point fautes. J'ay veu en ma jeunesse un galant homme presenter d'une main au peuple des vers excellens et en beauté et en desbordement, et de l'autre main en mesme instant la plus quereleuse reformation theologienne de quoy le monde se soit desjeuné il y a longtemps.[20]

The opening sentence is a protest against inhumanly lofty codes of moral conduct; ethical rules should have due consideration for man's actual capabilities. Then we have a little scene: the preacher or lecturer recommending a way of life which neither he nor his audience has any hope of being able to follow. The words 'ny, qui plus est, envie" introduce another aspect of the question: when moralists sing the praises of stoicism or puritanism, they do not even have the desire to live up to such standards. And so we are led to think of the subject in another light, that of hypocrisy. Viewed from a certain perspective, moral rigorism looks like hypocrisy. The illustrations are presented dramatically; they are good examples of Montaigne's theatrical technique, as described in the beginning of this section. A judge has just sentenced a man for adultery, and tears off an end of the sheet of paper to write a love letter to a friend's wife. (We are reminded, inevitably, of *Measure for Measure.*) Your mistress, in your very presence, virtuously denounces the morals of another woman. After these vivid scenes, we move on to another facet of the problem: the cruel and unrealistic severity of many laws. It may frequently happen that a judge is legally obliged to impose sentences of which his judgment and conscience disapprove; the punishment of death may be mandatory for actions which he does not even con-

20. III, 9, 275.

sider to be wrong. Finally, not only is there this dichotomy between private and public morals, but a man may often, before the face of the world, engage in activities which, according to a consistent moral standard, appear mutually exclusive: in Montaigne's youth there was a gentleman who was equally famous for his licentious poetry and his severe projects for religious reform. Everything depends upon the way you look at things: so affirms the philosophy of Montaigne, but his style, with its theatricality, interest in illusion, and multiple-aspect imagery, implies this with equal force.

7. CONTRAST AND SURPRISE

A discussion of multiple-aspect imagery brings us very naturally to the next baroque category: contrast and surprise. Often, as he circles around a subject, Montaigne seeks to give us contrasting points of view, or to surprise us with an unexpected aspect. The categories overlap, as in the case of Montaigne's cat:

> Quand je me joue à ma chatte, qui sçait si elle passe son temps de moy plus que je ne fay d'elle.[1]

The two ways of looking at the question are set off against each other, antithetically. Antithesis is a favorite device in the *Essais*. Let us look at a few examples:

> Il nous faut abestir pour nous assagir, et nous esblouir pour nous guider.[2]

> Quelle verité que ces montaignes bornent, qui est mensonge au monde qui se tient au delà? [3]

> Plustost lairrois je rompre le col aux affaires que de tordre ma foy pour leur service.[4]

In referring to the fact that, in moments of pain or danger, a calm and dignified demeanor is far less important than our inward state of mind, he says:

> Qu'importe que nous tordons nos bras pourveu que nous ne tordons nos pensées! [5]

The above exclamatory sentence, already quoted, is also a good example of the concreteness of Montaigne's imagery.

He expresses his conservative yet individualistic morality. The reader will recognize this sentence, which forms a part of one of the multiple-aspect passages:

> Je restrains bien selon autruy mes actions, mais je ne les estends que selon moy.[6]

1. II, 12, 165.	2. II, 12, 220.	3. II, 12, 338.
4. II, 17, 429.	5. II, 37, 577.	6. III, 2, 31.

In one of the many passages where he reveals his distaste for a gloomy outlook on life, he says:

Je hay un esprit hargneux et triste qui glisse par dessus les plaisirs de sa vie et s'empoigne et paist aux malheurs . . .[7]

(Incidentally, after this antithesis Montaigne illustrates the idea further with two picturesque comparisons: flies cling to a rough rather than a smooth surface, and cupping-glasses draw out the bad blood.)

Elsewhere he gives us, in rapid succession, three antitheses to express the paradox of our attitudes toward birth and death. Conception and accouchement are regarded as vaguely disgraceful, whereas the slaughter of the battlefield is glorious:

Chacun fuit à le voir naistre, chacun suit à le voir mourir. Pour le destruire, on cerche un champ spacieux en pleine lumiere; pour le construire, on se musse dans un creux tenebreux et contraint. C'est le devoir de se cacher et rougir pour le faire; et c'est gloire, et naissent plusieurs vertus de le sçavoir deffaire.[8]

Royal grandeur, Montaigne observes, is largely a matter of theatricality and illusion. In the presence of a king, what we really worship is the throng of worshipers. But we should maintain a careful distinction between outward and inward submission:

Ma raison n'est pas duite à se courber et flechir, ce sont mes genoux.[9]

An expression of the optimism of Montaigne:

Il faut estendre la joye, mais retrencher autant qu'on peut la tristesse.[10]

His independent spirit:

Mon opinion est qu'il se faut prester à autruy et ne se donner qu'à soy-mesme.[11]

We should not be taken in by the roles we are forced to play (again theatricality!):

C'est assés de s'enfariner le visage, sans s'enfariner la poictrine.[12]

The difficult situation caused by his neutrality in the civil wars:

Je fus pelaudé à toutes mains: au Gibelin j'estois Guelphe, au Guelphe Gibelin . . .[13]

The contrast between his own way of life and that of his servants:

Regardez la difference du vivre de mes valets à bras à la mienne: les Scythes et les Indes n'ont rien plus esloigné de ma force et de ma forme.[14]

7. III, 5, 82.   8. III, 5, 126.   9. III, 8, 201.   10. III, 9, 262.
11. III, 10, 295.   12. III, 10, 306.   13. III, 12, 350.   14. III, 13, 404.

His personal reaction to heat and cold:

L'aspreté de l'esté m'est plus ennemie que celle de l'hyver . . .[15]

People who try to be superhuman always fail:

C'est folie; au lieu de se transformer en anges, ils se transforment en bestes.[16]

This, I think, constitutes a fair assortment of antitheses from the *Essais*. It may be objected that antithesis is so fundamental a rhetorical device that it can scarcely be used as a criterion of the baroque. This, of course, is true; in the history of literature, there has probably never been a time when writers did not express themselves in contrasts, and the romantics especially were fond of this figure. Perhaps the easiest way to parody Victor Hugo would be to use as many sensational antitheses as possible. I maintain, however, that most of the examples I have given here are not mere banal rhetorical ornamentation; they correspond to a basic exigency of the author's spirit. We have seen that he likes to look at the world from a variety of angles; similarly, he delights in contrasts and oppositions. For Montaigne reality is not monolithic: it is complex and often contradictory. Paradox, for the baroque writer, is not only enjoyable in itself, it is also a way of arriving at the truth; and the truth, as Oscar Wilde has remarked, is neither pure nor simple. Then, as is the case with virtually all these baroque categories, the antithetical spirit alone does not determine the style; it becomes significant when appearing in conjunction with other characteristics, such as theatricality, multiple-aspect imagery, concreteness, movement, and the like.

Another way of understanding the style of Montaigne is to realize that his art is one of surprises. In this, he agrees with Marino's opinion that no poet is worthy of the name unless he is able to amaze his readers. Be this as it may, it is certain that many of Montaigne's most striking effects derive from their unexpectedness. When he tells us that he has an intense love of personal freedom, we do not quite expect the declaration that it would make him uncomfortable to be excluded from a remote corner of India. We are startled also to hear that whenever he goes to bed he wonders whether the house will be attacked during the night. The catalogues of curious customs which appear in various parts of the *Essais* are not only examples of emphasis through heaping and of multiple-aspect imagery; the customs themselves are meant to amaze us—as, for instance, that in one country it should be regarded as an act of piety to eat one's father. "When I play with my cat," he begins; and the conclusion is all the more amusing because unexpected. Illusion delights him because, by unmasking it, he can present us with a surprising reality. Throughout the *Essais* he keeps showing us that the world is not as

15. III, 13, 435.   16. III, 13, 449.

we think it is. Some minds take pride in a kind of omniscient calm, liking to feel that they have foreseen every possible contingency. Such are many classical writers: for them it is the mark of the intelligent and civilized man to believe that there is nothing new under the sun. Not so Montaigne: he is never so happy as when he has just discovered some new strange aspect of life; and he wants his reader to share the same sense of wonder. Antithesis, as a rhetorical figure, pleases him because it produces surprise. When the author tells us that we hide ourselves to conceive children but come out into the open in order to kill men, our reaction is one of mingled shock and amusement. And here I should like to discuss for a moment one of Montaigne's surprise techniques; believing as he does that it is better to shock the reader than to bore him, he often violates la bienséance with a startling, crude word:

> Et les Roys et les philosophes fientent, et les dames aussi.[17]

This is not just polissonnerie, though there are plenty of examples of that also in the *Essais,* particularly in the *Vers de Virgile;* it is rather an attempt to arouse our attention through shock. The basic idea is that all human beings, however exalted, distinguished, or refined, are alike subject to physical contingencies. The thought is not remarkably original, but the word "fientent" arrests our attention, and we are likely to remember the surprise we felt upon first reading the sentence. Similar in technique, and in content, is one of the last sentences in the *Essais:*

> Et au plus eslevé throne du monde si ne sommes assis que sus nostre cul.[18]

8. MOVEMENT AND METAMORPHOSIS

Whenever I read the *Essais,* I am struck by one aspect of its style best expressed by the almost untranslatable French verb *grouiller.* This book is a collection of philosophical essays, not a novel of action, and yet its pages teem and swarm with movement. If the reader will think back over some of the passages I have quoted, he will realize how alive they are with verbs and motion. One page of the *Apologie,* which describes the infinite variety of human gestures, contains in rapid succession a list of seventy verbs. The careless fools who avoid thinking about death are depicted as madly rushing around ("Ils vont, ils viennent, ils trottent, ils dansent"). When the author wishes to express the idea that inner peace of soul is more important than outward decorous calm, he instinctively resorts to images of writhing movement ("Qu'importe que nous tordons nos bras pourveu que nous ne tordons nos pensées!"). His fundamental optimism is expressed not statically but

17. III, 13, 407.   18. III, 13, 450.

dynamically ("Il faut estendre la joye, mais retrencher autant qu'on peut la tristesse").

The world, for Montaigne, is in a constant state of flux. The custom of the country, for example (though in general he recommends that we follow it), is not an altogether satisfactory guide to moral conduct:

> Que nous suyvons les loix de nostre pays? c'est à dire cette mer flotante des opinions d'un peuple ou d'un Prince, qui me peindront la justice d'autant de douleurs et la reformeront en autant de visages qu'il y aura en eux de changemens de passion? [1]

Montaigne here is insisting not so much on the infinite variety of human customs (an idea which he stresses at great length in a number of other places) as on the fact that moral standards keep changing: the key words here are "reformeront" and "changemens." The image of the fluctuations of the sea is also essential: it corresponds to Montaigne's vision of civilization. But not only is society like an ever moving sea; the body and soul of the individual man are constantly changing also:

> Il est certain que nostre apprehension, nostre jugement et les facultez de nostre ame en general souffrent selon les mouvemens et alterations du corps, qui sont continuelles.[2]

Above all, these fluctuations exist in Montaigne himself. When he is healthy and the weather is fine, he feels that he is a good man; on the contrary, if he has a corn on his toe the world and his own personality seem disagreeable:

> Il se faict mille agitations indiscretes et casuelles chez moy.[3]

The *Essais* are, of course, a record of these changes in Montaigne's personality and thought; this is a subject to which we shall return later.

The most explicit statement of this whole attitude on Montaigne's part— and, incidentally, the best definition of what "movement and metamorphosis" means as a baroque category—is to be found in the opening paragraph of *Du repentir:*

> Le monde n'est qu'une branloire perenne. Toutes choses y branlent sans cesse: la terre, les rochers du Caucase, les pyramides d'Aegypte, et du branle public et du leur. La constance mesme n'est autre chose qu'un branle plus languissant. Je ne puis asseurer mon objet. Il va trouble et chancelant, d'une yvresse naturelle. Je le prens en ce point, comme il est, en l'instant que je m'amuse à luy. Je ne peints pas l'estre. Je peints le passage . . .[4]

Montaigne and other baroque artists do not conceive of the world as static. Even those things which appear most stable—pyramids and mountains—are in reality undergoing constant evolution. Stability itself is an illusion; actu-

1. II, 12, 338.   2. II, 12, 317.   3. II, 12, 319.   4. III, 2, 27.

ally it is an extremely slow form of change. (Here we meet again the other baroque categories of illusion and of contrast.) Montaigne, who is the subject of his own book, proceeds with a confused and staggering gait, in a natural drunkenness. And we have the concluding epigram, which sums up so well this aspect of the baroque: "I do not paint being, I paint transformation."

A glance at several important baroque works of painting, sculpture, and architecture will show that they too are deeply concerned with movement, fluctuation, transformation, and even drunken staggering. For an example of the last of these, pure and simple, I refer the reader to Rubens' "Kermesse." Here indeed is a picture which teems and swarms with life. The peasants, as they eat, drink, dance, or rush off into the bushes, are whirling with an "yvresse naturelle." Any of Callot's larger engravings—the "Disasters of War" or the "Temptation of St. Anthony"—are similarly *grouillants*. And as for "le passage" rather than "l'estre," probably the greatest representation in art of a metamorphosis is Bernini's "Apollo and Daphne": as the god rushes forward to seize the girl, she is in the process of changing into an olive tree—part of her soft flesh has become bark, and leafy branches in strategic places hinder Apollo's embrace. One would think a church façade a relatively stable thing, but Borromini succeeds in giving it a "branle languissant": in San Carlo alle Quattro Fontane, concavities and convexities alternate to form an undulating rhythm. Pietro da Cortona has achieved a similar effect in Santa Maria della Pace: the semicircular portico swells forth from a receding amphitheatre. It has often been said that baroque façades are Renaissance ones reflected on the rippling surface of a fountain's pool. If this be so, the whole city of Lecce, with its dozen baroque churches and fifty baroque palaces, appears like a shimmering reflection. Contrary to popular belief, such tremulous façades are not totally absent in France: the Chapel of the Visitation in Nevers, erected by St. François de Sales, is an example, and particularly so are the fantastic façade and tower of the former abbey at St.-Amand-les-Eaux, near Valenciennes. Pushing farther north, into Belgian Flanders, one should mention the extraordinary pulpits—*chaires de vérité* as they are called there—of the parish churches of Malines. Here, as in Bernini's "Apollo and Daphne," the pulpit, by imperceptible gradations, changes itself into a leafy tree, swarming with saints and angels; the whole structure teems with metamorphosis, growth, and life. But in this category of movement and metamorphosis, perhaps the most characteristic invention is the Roman fountain—that very fountain which so often reflects a quivering baroque façade, as Bernini's "Fountain of the Rivers" does that of Borromini's Sant'-Agnese, making it even more baroque. A period which enjoyed and demanded such structures as this, or the same artist's Triton fountain, visualized and enjoyed the world as a "branloire perenne"; and even if a fountain is not quite a "mer flottante," it satisfies some of the same exigencies of the spirit. We can be thankful, I think, that in Rome no rigidly formulated classicism arrested this development; and Romans, still fascinated by movement and metamorphosis, continued in the eighteenth and nineteenth centuries to create such spirited torrents of moving water as the Trevi fountain, with its illusionistic rocks and grottoes, or the tremendous domelike geyser of the fountain in Piazza dell'Esedra, which dates from less than seventy years ago. As Blake observes, "The cistern contains, the fountain overflows." [5] It may be objected that French classicism knew fountains too—as in Le Nôtre's gardens of Versailles; to this I can only reply that the fountains of Versailles or Vaux-le-Vicomte, compared to the Roman ones, represent a kind of *baroque dompté* (this indeed has often been given as a definition of French classicism itself, and the evolution of Corneille's style would tend to confirm this)—and besides, no more than antithesis or imagery can fountains be regarded as the exclusive possession of the baroque. They are, however, symptomatic of the baroque spirit.

That Montaigne tended to see phenomena in terms of metamorphosis is apparent in his remarks on the influence of habit and custom. He does not look upon customs as static things; on the contrary, they are powerful forces, which mold our life, strengthening our capabilities in some respects and weakening them in others:

> C'est à la coustume de donner forme à nostre vie, telle qu'il luy plaist; elle peut tout en cela: c'est le breuvage de Circe, qui diversifie notre nature comme bon luy semble.[6]

The passage from which this comes stresses the diversity of customs in different parts of the world (stoves in Germany, fireplaces in France, featherbeds in Germany, mattresses in Italy) but Montaigne is also at pains to show that people in different countries are basically changed by their customs. In the essay *De la coustume* itself, he tells us an anecdote to illustrate this transforming power:

> Celuy me semble avoir tres-bien conceu la force de la coustume, qui premier forgea ce conte, qu'une femme de village, ayant apris de caresser et porter entre ses bras un veau des l'heure de la naissance, et continuant tousjours à la faire, gaigna cela par l'accoutumance, que tout grand beuf qu'il estoit, elle le portoit encore.[7]

(This experiment was actually tried a number of years ago in the Middle West, and its progressive stages photographed in a number of magazines. I regret to say, for Montaigne's sake, that it failed, though it succeeded for

---

5. Cf. *Proverbs of Hell*.   6. III, 13, 400.   7. I, 23, 137.

a remarkably long time; a certain point was eventually reached when the farm hand could no longer hold the ox in his arms.)

With regard to education, Montaigne is principally interested in its transforming effect. His principal criticism of pedantry, after all, is that it does not make the scholar a better person:

> Mais s'il est devenu meilleur ou plus advisé, c'estoit le principal, et c'est ce qui demeure derriere.[8]

Mediaeval systems of education—and perhaps also the encyclopaedic brainstuffing of Rabelais—are condemned because of their corrupting influence:

> Je ne veux pas corrompre son esprit à le tenir à la gehene et au travail, à la mode des autres; quatorze ou quinze heures par jour, comme un portefaiz.[9]

Finally, the whole aim of education is to transform man, to make him wiser and better:

> Le guain de nostre estude, c'est en estre devenu meilleur et plus sage.[10]

The key word here is "devenu."

Throughout the *Essais,* we can detect Montaigne's great interest in "becoming." Frequently, it is the forces of deterioration which arouse his concern. As we know, he tends to regard social and religious innovations as dangerous, because they lead to a weakening of the structure of civilization. Protestantism, for example, is just such a deteriorating force. Out of it, he fears, atheism will gradually develop:

> . . . les nouvelletez de Luther commençoyent d'entrer en credit et esbranler en beaucoup de lieux nostre ancienne creance. En quoy il [i.e. the family friend who brought Raymond de Sebond to the attention of Montaigne and his father] avoit un tresbon advis, prevoyant bien, par discours de raison, que ce commencement de maladie declineroit aysément en un execrable atheisme . . .[11]

This, actually, is the point of departure for the whole *Apologie.* It is interesting to observe that Montaigne here anticipates the leading idea of Bossuet's *Variations du Protestantisme:* the Protestant appeal to the individual conscience leads inevitably to a multiplication of religious sects; eventually every man will have his own religion; the final stage of this evolution will be atheism. As a matter of fact, the atheists have gone to work on Sebond's *Natural Theology,* distorting its sense to their own ends:

> On couche volontiers le sens des escris d'autrui à la faveur des opinions qu'on a prejugées en soy: et un atheiste se flate à ramener tous autheurs à l'atheisme, infectant de son propre venin la matiere innocente.[12]

---

8. I, 25, 174.   9. I, 26, 211.   10. I, 26, 195.
11. II, 12, 147.   12. II, 12, 159.

And so it does no good to attempt to solve religious problems by referring to the literal text of the Bible:

> Et ceux là se moquent, qui pensent appetisser nos debats et les arrester en nous r'appelant à l'expresse parole de la Bible. D'autant que nostre esprit ne trouve pas le champ moins spatieux à contreroller le sens d'autruy qu'à representer le sien, et comme s'il y avoit moins d'animosité à gloser qu'à inventer.[13]

For the writings of Luther have merely begotten further commentaries and disputes:

> J'ay veu en Allemagne que Luther a laissé autant de divisions et altercations sur le doubte de ses opinions, et plus, qu'il n'en esmeut sur les escritures sainctes.[14]

Religious and intellectual activity are, as Montaigne says, like the many-headed hydra: new heads are reborn as soon as the old ones are cut off. Books produce commentaries, and the commentaries themselves lead to further commentaries:

> Il y a plus affaire à interpreter les interpretations qu'à interpreter les choses, et plus de livres sur les livres que sur tout autre sujet: nous ne faisons que nous entre-gloser. Tout fourmille de commentaires; d'auteurs, il en est grand cherté.[15]

This constitutes a fairly accurate description of scholarly activity. The three volumes of the *Essais* have given birth to hundreds of volumes of interpretation. As I sit here writing about Montaigne, I myself am contributing to the "fourmillement"; and if somebody else reviews my book, he is carrying on the swarming, growing, hydra-headed process.

During his trip to Italy, Montaigne was painfully affected by meeting with the mad Tasso. It is for him an example of the way in which genius can evolve into insanity:

> Quel saut vient de prendre, de sa propre agitation, et allegresse, l'un des plus judicieux, ingenieux et plus formés à l'air de cette antique et pure poesie, qu'autre poëte Italien aye de long temps esté? N'a il pas dequoy sçavoir gré à cette exacte et tendue apprehension de la raison qui l'a mis sans raison? à la curieuse et laborieuse queste des sciences qui l'a conduit à la bestise? à cette rare aptitude aux exercices de l'ame, qui l'a rendu sans exercice et sans ame? J'eus plus de despit encore que de compassion, de le voir à Ferrare en si piteux estat, survivant à soy-mesmes, mesconnoissant et soy et ses ouvrages, lesquels, sans son sceu, et toutesfois à sa veue, on a mis en lumiere incorrigez et informes.[16]

In this passage, which is, incidentally, a noteworthy example of the heaping technique, the questions are in reality exclamations. The verbs express transformations: to jump, to blind, to lead, to render. The fact that Montaigne, on seeing the poet, felt chagrin rather than pity shows that he is principally

13. III, 13, 380.　　14. III, 13, 386.　　15. III, 13, 385.　　16. II, 12, 219.

struck by the *deterioration* of a great mind: it is the *change* which has taken place, rather than the present pathetic condition, which horrifies him. And, as a final touch, he observes that the merciless process of scholarly editing has already begun!

The Italian journey gave Montaigne another opportunity to observe at first hand a great and tragic deterioration: I mean of course the ruins of ancient Rome. Having been brought up since childhood to think of Rome as the greatest city that the world had ever known, he was awe-struck to find little left but rubble. The most powerful expression of his emotion is found in the *Journal de voyage:*

> Il disoit [the *Journal,* partly dictated to a secretary, is often written in the third person] qu'on ne voioit rien de Rome que le Ciel sous lequel elle avoit esté assise et le plant de son gite; que cette science qu'il en avoit estoit une science abstraite et contemplative, de laquelle il n'y avoit rien qui tumbat sous les sens; que ceus qui disoint qu'on y voyoit au moins les ruines de Rome, en disoint trop: car les ruines d'une si espouventable machine rapporteroint plus d'honneur et de reverence à sa memoire; ce n'estoit rien que son sepulcre. Le monde ennemi de sa longue domination, avoit premierement brisé et fracassé toutes les pieces de ce corps admirable, et parce qu'encore tout mort, ranversé et desfiguré, il lui faisoit horreur, il en avoit enseveli la ruine mesme.[17]

There is also, in the essay *De la vanité,* a brief reference to the vanished grandeur of Rome:

> J'ay veu ailleurs des maisons ruinées, et des statues, et du ciel, et de la terre: ce sont tousjours des hommes. Tout cela est vray; et si pourtant ne sçauroy revoir si souvent le tombeau de cette ville, si grande et si puissante, que je ne l'admire et revere.[18]

Another sixteenth-century visitor to Rome has voiced similar feelings of awe at the transitoriness of human grandeur: Joachim Du Bellay, in his *Antiquités de Rome.* It should be remembered that, prior to 1800, very little excavation had been done; most of the ancient city lay buried under centuries of accumulated earth, with a capital or a fragment of a column protruding here and there, and untended vegetation growing over everything; for an impression of what travelers in Montaigne's day saw, the reader should look at the engravings of Piranesi—though nearly two centuries later, they give a good indication of the appearance of ancient Rome before the advent of modern archaeology. Then, too, the attention of the 1956 traveler is likely to be directed to that aspect of Rome which was just beginning to be built at the time of Montaigne's visit: the baroque city, with its Piazza Navona and Piazza San Pietro—or else to the intensely alive modern capital of Italy—

17. *Journal de voyage,* I, 214.   18. III, 9, 285.

so that now, rather than being struck by mutability and decadence, we feel that this is indeed the Eternal City. Yet this change over the centuries in the impression produced by Rome is an example of what Montaigne meant when he referred to the world as a "branloire perenne." Like the Pyramids, which he mentions for their deceptive air of stability, Rome itself is forever changing.

The author of the *Essais* confesses freely that his love of travel comes chiefly from his love of movement and change:

> Parmy les conditions humaines, cette cy est assez commune: de nous plaire plus des choses estrangeres que des nostres et d'aymer le remuement et le changement . . . J'en tiens ma part. . . . Cette humeur des choses nouvelles et inconnues ayde bien à nourrir en moy le desir de voyager.[19]

In fact, as we read over in the essay on vanity the reasons he gives for traveling, we eventually realize that he does not care specifically where he goes, so long as he goes somewhere. To be sure, as a humanist and classical scholar he was anxious to see Rome; as an invalid he wanted to try the cure in certain spas; but his basic desire is for travel itself:

> Je respons ordinairement à ceux qui me demandent raison de mes voyages: que je sçay bien ce que je fuis, mais non pas ce que je cerche.[20]

This is a state of mind recognized and disapproved by Pascal in *Le Divertissement:* the hunter is more eager for the chase itself than for the hare. The attitude is further reflected in Montaigne's manner of travel: he makes no long-range plans for seeing certain sights, but each day yields to the impulse of the moment. What is even more significant, his life as a whole follows the same pattern:

> Mon dessein est divisible par tout: il n'est pas fondé en grandes esperances; chaque journée en fait le bout. Et le voyage de ma vie se conduict de mesme.[21]

In travel or in life, the great thing is to be forever changing, forever moving.

He might very well have continued, and said: "My book is written the same way." We have already seen the passage where he defines the term *"essais,"* explaining that his book is a record of things which he has tried out on himself. Some of these experiments are successful, and are repeated until they become a permanent part of his way of life. Thus, implicit in this idea of "self try-outs" is the concept of change and evolution. The word "essais" also means literary experiments; and we have seen how success emboldened the author, encouraging him still further in the direction of self-portraiture and longer chapters. So there is literary evolution as well. We read again the famous sentence,

19. III, 9, 219.   20. III, 9, 252.   21. III, 9, 260.

Je n'ay pas plus faict mon livre que mon livre m'a faict, livre consubstantiel à
son autheur . . .[22]

and we realize that both book and man, by interacting on each other, are in
a constant state of metamorphosis.

Indeed, with respect to this baroque category of movement and metamorphosis, we must consider Montaigne's life and work as a whole. Innu-
merable passages can be adduced to show his vision of a world in flux, and
a host of others to illustrate his propensity for describing phenomena and
ideas in terms of transformation; but most significant of all is the fact that
the *Essais* themselves evolve, and their author with them. Of course the
work of any artist reveals a succession of different periods; any well-trained
critic, for example, can distinguish between an early, middle, or late Titian
or Rembrandt. Even a single work may exist in different states: consider
Flaubert's *Tentation de St. Antoine*—or *Jean Santeuil* as an earlier version
of *A la recherche du temps perdu*. Balzac's methods of revision are well
known: he treated his page proof the way most writers treat their type-
written rough drafts. But the *Essais* are something different: though they
represent twenty years of the author's life, temperament, thought, and style,
they are a single work. And contrary to other writers, Montaigne never repudiated anything once written. The 1588 edition, though it contained hundreds of additions and a whole new Book III, eliminated nothing from the
1580 text. This is the more remarkable because, in the sixteen or seventeen
years which had elapsed since he first began to write, Montaigne's opinions
on many important subjects, and indeed his whole conception of the form
of the essay, had totally changed. The retention of early passages, expressing
ideas which he no longer believed, and of whole essays constructed in a
manner which the mature writer had outgrown, can only mean one thing:
the book is the record of an evolution, moral and literary. More important
than Montaigne's thought or style at any particular moment is their metamorphosis through the years. He has been quite frank, as a matter of fact,
in telling us that he is not sure that he improves as he grows older; but
whether he improves or deteriorates, the transformation fascinates him.

This is why the chronology of the text is of fundamental importance in
Montaigne's studies. It is valuable to know not only what he said but when
he said it. All good editions of the *Essais* have adopted systems of marking
passages with letters—a, b, and c, or some similar method—so that we can
tell whether they first appeared in 1580, 1588, or 1595. And even this degree
of accuracy in dating is insufficient for a full appreciation of the evolution:
Villey precedes each essay with a critical preface in which he endeavors to

22. II, 18, 452.

determine the exact year of its composition. Half of his great and definitive work on Montaigne is, as the title indicates, devoted to this problem: *Les Sources et l'évolution des Essais de Montaigne.* It would be inappropriate and superfluous to attempt here to retrace the different stages of the development; but perhaps I may be permitted to remind the reader of a few of the significant changes in the *Essais* between 1572 and Montaigne's death.

The essays composed during the early years of Montaigne's retirement are extremely short, averaging some half a dozen pages in length. They have little originality, being put together, mosaic-fashion, from paraphrases of classical authors. Toward 1578 the chapters grow longer, largely because the author, gaining in assurance, comes to talk more and more extensively about himself, his private opinions, his tastes, and his personality. As time goes on, this personal method prevails completely, so that the essays of Book III, primarily based on the writer's own experience, become almost garrulous, and in any case average some thirty-five pages in length. Then we can detect at least three different philosophical periods: the first, stoical, corresponds roughly to the years 1572–75; the second, skeptical, expressed chiefly by the *Apologie de Raymond Sebond,* seems to have reached its climax in 1576; and the last, experimental and naturalistic, begins toward 1578, but does not come to full maturity until Book III, the "b" and "c" passages, and the closing years of the writer's life. Probably the most striking change in Montaigne's thought concerns his attitude toward pain and death: in early essays, such as *Que le goust des biens et des maux depend en bonne partie de l'opinion que nous en avons* or *Que philosopher c'est apprendre à mourir,* he adopts a lofty philosophical attitude of stern intellectual preparation and conscious striving against misfortune; whereas, in old age, in *De la phisionomie,* he finds a greater wisdom in the peasants' ignorant acceptance of life and death. Significant also are his changing views of the role of experience in life: as a stoic, he attempts to dwell above experience, in the realms of philosophical reason; as a skeptic, he despairs completely of reason's or the senses' ability to arrive at truth; in the final stage of his intellectual development, he continues to be suspicious of reason, but now accepts completely the experimental method, and ascribes great importance to those impressions of his senses which he had earlier tried to minimize. All these contradictory ideas remain in the *Essais* for us to read—and not only in different parts of the book, but often side by side in the same chapter, whenever the author, rereading himself, has decided to insert amplifications which will show how he has changed. If Montaigne had been haunted by classical obsessions of consistency and clarity, he would have made sure, by extensive excisions and emendations, that his 1588 edition at least (the last published during his lifetime) was coherent and unified. We may count ourselves fortunate that, being a baroque spirit, he has left us a book which, however difficult and confusing it may be, remains, because of its movement and metamorphosis, a living and growing organism.

9. ORGANIC UNITY AND THE ACCEPTANCE OF LIFE

As a final baroque category, illustrated abundantly by the *Essais,* I should like to present organic unity and the acceptance of life. I wish to suggest that the baroque, contrary to popular belief, and despite its enjoyment of surprise and contrast and movement, ultimately succeeds in resolving its complexities into a unity. This conception of the baroque is related to Wölfflin's fourth category: multiplicity vs. unity. The great Swiss critic makes of this opposition an important criterion for distinguishing Renaissance and baroque art. Of the latter, he says (I quote from the recent French translation of *Kunstgeschichtliche Grundbegriffe*):

> Le propre du baroque est de ne plus compter avec une pluralité d'éléments qui doivent s'accorder harmonieusement, mais avec une unité absolue où chaque partie a perdu son droit particulier à l'existence.[1]

For examples of this principle, Wölfflin contrasts a Dürer and a Rembrandt "Death of the Virgin," a Titian and a Velazquez "Venus," and two Roman palaces, the Cancelleria and the Odescalchi. In each case, he feels, the Renaissance work divides itself up into independent, equally important parts, while in the baroque work all the details, however interesting, are subordinated to a major motif, and collaborate to form a massive action. I think that the reader who examines Caravaggio's "Calling of St. Matthew," Callot's "Siege of the Ile de Ré," or a complicated church façade like Borromini's San Carlo alle Quattro Fontane, will find this to be true. It applies with particular force to what we have just said about the various stages of evolution of the *Essais.* Each stage has lost its individual right to existence. When we first read Montaigne's vivid and contemptuous description of the carefree souls who rush about their business without thought of death, this vignette may seem like a picturesque, independent detail. Similarly, the account of the Périgord peasants who, during the plague, calmly abandon their vineyards and resignedly await death, may appear to be another isolated bit of philosophic decoration. The important thing here, however, is the evolution of a human being's attitude toward the prospect of dying: at the age of thirty-nine, Montaigne admires Seneca; at the age of fifty-two, he admires his peasants. The two episodes take on full meaning only in relation to each other, and as a part of the whole chronological panorama of the writer's

---

1. Heinrich Wölfflin, *Principes fondamentaux de l'histoire de l'art,* tr. Claire et Marcel Raymond, Paris, Plon, 1952.

thought. The major motif is the aging of Montaigne; in a larger sense, as we shall see, it is the aging of all men. In like manner, the recital of strange customs—the shaving of the whole left side, while the right is allowed to grow hair, or the lending of wives to guests—may at first seem to be independent picturesque details (corresponding to Wölfflin's Renaissance multiplicity); we soon realize that they constitute part of a general picture of the absurdity of custom; but this picture, in turn, is only one stage of Montaigne's evolving attitude toward custom:

La diversité des usages d'une nation à autre ne me touche que par le plaisir de la varieté. Chaque usage a sa raison. Soyent des assiettes d'estain, de bois, de terre, bouilly ou rosty, beurre ou huyle de nois ou d'olive, chaut ou froit, tout m'est un . . .[2]

"The pleasure of variety": significant words for the understanding of the baroque. But what is more important, the evolution from condemning usages as absurd (once he had said that it would be impossible to think up any idea, however crazy, which was not the basis of some custom) to delight in their diversity and wisdom constitutes an intellectual history. Montaigne is growing older, and perhaps (though this is uncertain) wiser; the individual bits of picturesque opinion in the *Essais* take on full meaning—whether moral or literary—from the total picture of metamorphosis.

I have spoken much of the baroque love of complexity and evolution. Certainly Montaigne reveals this, not only by the infinite diversity and protean transformation of the thought in the *Essais,* but also by specific statements such as the following:

Jamais deux hommes ne jugerent pareillement de mesme chose, et est impossible de voir deux opinions semblables exactement, non seulement en divers hommes, mais en mesme homme à diverses heures.[3]

Et nous, et nostre jugement, et toutes choses mortelles, vont coulant et roulant sans cesse.[4]

However, through twenty years of self-observation, he came to see that, transcending all the momentary changes in his opinions and tastes, there existed the organic reality of his personality:

Regardez un peu comment s'en porte nostre experience: il n'est personne, s'il s'escoute, qui ne descouvre en soy une forme sienne, une forme maistresse, qui luicte contre l'institution, et contre la tempeste des passions qui luy sont contraires.[5]

So all the trivial details of his life—whether or not at different times he likes fish, melon, horseradish, or open fires, Seneca or Plutarch—take their place

2. III, 9, 270.   3. III, 13, 383.   4. II, 12, 367.   5. III, 2, 35.

in this depiction of his "forme maistresse," which is of course a dynamic and not a static thing. These likes and dislikes as to gastronomy, personal comfort, and moral philosophy may, individually, be quite insignificant; collectively, they contribute to the major motif: the evolution, according to a certain pattern, of Michel de Montaigne.

It is curious to see that, with excessive modesty, he disclaims his own literary ability to express the "forme maistresse." But we his readers can give him credit for achieving the program which he suggested to artists:

Je laisse aux artistes, et ne sçay s'ils en viennent à bout en chose si meslée, si menue et fortuite, de renger en bandes cette infinie diversité de visages, et arrester nostre inconstance et la mettre par ordre.[6]

This conception of literature, so magnificently realized by Montaigne himself, is a far cry from the coherent clarity of classicism—the single-minded passion of Phèdre or the steadfast misanthropy of Alceste—and André Gide is well advised to term it an "invite à Proust." He might have added Dostoevsky.

As quotation no. 3 (above p. 54) shows, Montaigne recognizes, and throughout his life is fascinated by, two kinds of diversity: the mutability of each individual, and the infinite variety of human beings. The first kind achieves baroque unity when he discovers the existence of the "forme maistresse": the picturesque details of his temperament continue to abound, but their full moral and literary significance derives from the pattern they form. The second kind of diversity swarms through the pages of the *Apologie;* but there, in one of the early or "a" passages, we find the unifying principle expressed:

Les ames des Empereurs et des savatiers sont jettées à mesme moule.[7]

Essential humanity transcends individual differences. Twelve years later, in the essay *De l'experience,* which is rich in examples of diversity, and from which quotation no. 3 comes, the principle of unity is even more explicitly stated:

. . . emperiere et populaire, c'est tousjours une vie que tous accidens humains regardent.[8]

Such statements provide the key for understanding in proper perspective Montaigne's insistence on the "branloire perenne," the infinite diversity of human judgments and customs, the whole mutability of life. Fascinating and disconcerting as complex phenomena may be in detail, their true function (with respect to Montaigne's thought and art) is to portray man as an organic reality. In describing man, Montaigne does not proceed as classical

6. III, 13, 396.   7. II, 12, 197.   8. III, 13, 392.

writers do, eliminating what is too concrete or too contradictory in order to present us with a clear abstraction; no, for him the vulgar and variable, physical and fantastic are essential elements of a living picture.

Hostile critics of Montaigne have reproached him for talking too much about himself, for cluttering up the pages of his book with too individual a picture of his tastes and habits (the horseradish and melon passages, the fact that he gets muddy when he walks, the indiscreet revelations about his bowel movements and sex life). As I have just remarked, these trifles take on a deeper interest when one realizes that the general evolution, not the curious intimate detail per se, is the true subject. But then again the question arises: of what importance is a single individual, however well described as a living and changing being? Here Montaigne's answer (already hinted by his remark that a common man's life is as morally instructive as Caesar's) is that to know one man well is to know all men.

Je propose une vie basse et sans lustre, c'est tout un. On attache aussi bien toute la philosophie morale à une vie populaire et privée que à une forme de plus riche estoffe: chaque homme porte la forme entiere de l'humaine condition.

Les autheurs se communiquent au peuple par quelque marque particuliere et estrangere; moy le premier par mon estre universel, comme Michel de Montaigne, non comme grammarien ou poëte ou jurisconsulte. Si le monde se plaint de quoy je parle trop de moy, je me plains de quoy il ne pense seulement pas à soy.[9]

It is interesting to observe that this passage appears on the same page as the description of the world as a "branloire perenne." Immediately after pointing out the variability of the world, the writer affirms the value of self-portraiture. The knowledge we gain from the *Essais* is not of humanity, that intellectualized abstraction, but of man. The advantages of the baroque method, with its insistence on concreteness, complexity, and evolution, are apparent. Life is neither logical nor stable. It is only through an intimate acquaintance with one flesh-and-blood man, through all the unpredictable stages of his life, that we can know man. The "forme maistresse" of the individual, and the "humaine condition" represented in microcosm by the individual—these are the twin concepts which give organic unity to the *Essais*. As Wölfflin says of baroque art, it is not a question of a plurality of elements made to harmonize together; we have a unity in which each part has lost its independence. The intimate details of the author's life emerge to create the "forme maistresse"; Montaigne himself is not autonomous, but bears witness to "l'humaine condition." In the words of another baroque writer,

9. III, 2, 27.

No man is an Iland, intire of it selfe; every man is a peece of the Continent, a part of the maine . . .[10]

The second aspect of my baroque category is implicit in the first. Closely connected with organic unity is the acceptance of life. Time and time again we have had occasion to observe that Montaigne repudiates no part of his life, and no part of his book. In old age he may have lost all enthusiasm for stoical attitudes, but he feels no shame at having once tried to be a stoic: the lofty philosophical declarations are still all there, in Book I. The skeptical crisis of 1576 continues to occupy some two hundred and fifty pages, even when the author has long since ceased to care about epistemological questions and has devoted himself wholeheartedly to a down-to-earth search for personal comfort. Repentance of past actions or thoughts, he feels, is a disavowal of the will, and correction of the *Essais* would be unfair to the early purchasers; besides, as we have just seen, the pictures of previous stages of his life are all precious. The pictures may represent states of sin or error, but they are vital contributions to the panorama of the "forme maistresse."

And Montaigne not only accepts himself: he also accepts the world around him. In the essay *De la coustume* and in the *Apologie,* the long list of strange customs, of examples of human weakness or folly, may originally have betrayed a state of anxiety or indignation. In his stoical or skeptical periods, he probably often felt despair: ever changing man could never arrive at goodness or truth. If we agree with the view that mannerism is characterized by *angoisse* and a tormented striving for the superhuman (as seen in the paintings of El Greco), the Montaigne of the early essays and the *Apologie* may be regarded as mannerist. Later, however, the human scene gives him entertainment rather than distress; and in the essay *De l'experience,* differing customs delight him because of their variety. To enjoy variety is to accept life. The late Michelangelo (as in the "Slaves" or the "Last Judgment"), Tintoretto, and El Greco express their rejection of life by elongating and contorting the human form; as against these mannerists, the baroque artists— Rubens or Callot or Caravaggio—are naturalists, and (even when representing ugly people or scenes of horror) accept life. Montaigne's final philosophy has often been called naturalistic: I should like to call it baroque.

Hence the emphasis in Book III on adaptability. Montaigne's ideal, in later years, is Socrates, who is equally at home with all sorts and conditions of men: on the battlefield with soldiers, at a drinking party with his friends, or discussing the immortality of the soul with students. The essayist recommends to us the "several-storeyed soul," capable of both intellectual tension and relaxation, able to live happily at every level of society, appreciative of the diversity of life:

10. John Donne, *Devotions,* XVII.

Je louerois un'ame à divers estages, qui sçache et se tendre et se desmonter, qui soit bien par tout où sa fortune la porte, qui puisse deviser avec son voisin de son bastiment, de sa chasse et de sa querelle, entretenir avec plaisir un charpentier et un jardinier; j'envie ceux qui sçavent s'apriviser au moindre de leur suitte et dresser de l'entretien en leur propre train.[11]

Similarly Montaigne, who in his travels takes pleasure in the varying way of life and psychology of different nationalities, feels that, in the last analysis, his interest in such peculiarities yields to his sympathy for his fellow man:

Non parce que Socrates l'a dict, mais parce qu'en verité c'est mon humeur, et à l'avanture non sans quelque excez, j'estime tous les hommes mes compatriotes, et embrasse un Polonois comme un François, postposant cette lyaison nationnale à l'universelle et commune.[12]

At one time he had felt that man's virtue was measured largely in terms of the struggle against nature: the greater the effort, the greater the virtue. But, reviewing the essay *De l'institution des enfans* between 1588 and 1592, he adds the indulgent metaphor which we have already studied: Virtue is not located on top of a rugged and inaccessible mountain but in a fertile, flowering plain which can be reached through grassy and shady slopes. And there is the positive declaration in *Sur des vers de Virgile:*

La vertu est qualité plaisante et gaie.[13]

Perhaps the best way of summing up these different baroque attitudes (the several-storeyed soul is the best; Poles and Frenchmen, however different their beliefs and customs, are to be equally loved; virtue, even if it is the result of widely varying codes of conduct, manifests itself through happiness) is the famous passage from St. John: "In my Father's house are many mansions." This is of course basic Christian doctrine, but it is more likely to be stressed by baroque spirits like Montaigne and St. François de Sales than by austere mannerists of the preceding age like El Greco, or Jansenist rigorists of a succeeding one like Pascal.

As I have indicated, I think it is dangerous to pick out one stage of Montaigne's evolution as representative of his quintessential message. And yet, if one were to select a single passage, it would be the closing pages of *De l'experience.* In a sense they constitute a general thanksgiving for his creation, preservation, and all the blessings of this life; he accepts with gratitude his whole being, body and soul, such as it is, with its weakness, complexity, and mutability:

Pour moy donc, j'ayme la vie et la cultive telle qu'il a pleu à Dieu nous l'octroyer. Je ne vay pas desirant qu'elle eust à dire la necessité de boire et de manger . . .

11. III, 13, 49.   12. III, 9, 253.   13. III, 5, 81.

J'accepte de bon coeur, et reconaissant, ce que nature a faict pour moy, et m'en
agrée et m'en loue. . . .

C'est une absolue perfection, et comme divine, de sçavoir jouyr loyalement
de son estre. . . .

Les plus belles vies sont, à mon gré, celles qui se rangent au modelle commun
et humain, avec ordre, mais sans miracle et sans extravagance . . .[14]

People whose conception of Christianity has a puritanical or Jansenistic cast
will find it difficult to accept the above declarations as truly Christian. They
will point with disapproval to Montaigne's use of the word "nature" in the
second of these statements; to which I can only reply by calling attention
to the reference to "Dieu" in the first. The fact is that the baroque mind,
having a strongly incarnational view of nature, can never escape looking at
the world as the creation of God. The baroque mind, even when most
fascinated by the complexity and mutability of phenomena, is never Mani-
chaean. The mature Montaigne rejects the idea of a dichotomy between
God and nature. There are rigorists who expect all Christians to be saints,
and who will, therefore, be shocked by the essayist's depreciation, in the last
paragraph of the above quotation, of the miraculous and extravagant. Against
them I am forced to appeal to the authority of a great baroque writer who
happens also to be an officially recognized saint: St. François de Sales. The
whole purpose of the *Introduction à la vie dévote* is precisely to show that
the most beautiful lives can adapt themselves to the common human model,
with order, but without miracles and without extravagance. Its author is
most emphatic in warning us as to the danger of ecstasies and visions. I
have heard art critics insist that Rubens was essentially pagan rather than
religious, and that he expressed the seventeenth-century worldliness of Antwerp; I would rather say that he, and his city, were simultaneously worldly
and Christian. The baroque age would have seen in this no contradiction.
Baroque art, just because it is incarnational, is inconceivable outside of a
Christian framework; and that is why romantic art, which possesses some
features in common with it, is fundamentally different from the baroque.
The romantic knows no God above himself, and accepts no system of values
but the intensity of his own sensations. Montaigne, for all his individualistic
self-portraiture, is very different from the arrogant Rousseau who declares
that nature broke the mold in which he was cast; on the contrary, the author
of the *Essais* believes that his book is valuable because it reflects the "humaine
condition"; and, never having rejected the religion of his fathers, he further
believes that man's fate is important, because God once made man.

The baroque is a Christian style, even when its exemplars are not especially devout people; indeed, it is the last of the Christian styles, for since

14. III, 13, 448–50.

its time no artistic or literary school has derived its authority, whether implicitly or explicitly, from a Christian framework. French classicism often appears to collaborate with the church, but its ultimate courts of appeal are the ancients, reason, and the rule of pleasing.

10. THE STRUCTURAL ANALYSIS OF AN ESSAY: *De la vanité* (III, 9)

At this point, a shift of perspective will be valuable. Let us turn from the baroque style to the individual baroque work of art considered as an organic whole. So far, we have noted Montaigne's general observations about his style, and have studied eight baroque categories as illustrated by examples drawn from various parts of the *Essais*. I should now like to examine the structure of a specific essay.

One of the greatest pleasures in reading Montaigne is the way in which we follow the author's mind as it moves from subject to subject. We have the impression of actually watching the birth and development of his ideas; and so in an essay of Montaigne we have not the cold and static end product of his thought but the living and growing thought itself. This is particularly true in the chapters of Book III, where the author's style and thought reach their full flowering. By analyzing the plan of a single essay, we can see in detail how subject flows into subject, and image into image. I propose to do here what Mr. R. A. Sayce has done for *Des coches* in his article on "Baroque Elements in Montaigne"; similarly, but now in the case of a rather longer essay, *De la vanité,* I hope to show that the apparent disorder is not the result of a lack of composition but is in reality the manifestation of organic form. There is in *De la vanité* much of the *ondoyant et divers;* this essay paints not "l'estre" but "le passage"; yet, despite this infinite variety and this lively movement, it constitutes an artistic unit. This resolving of variety and movement in artistic unity is, as we have seen, an important aspect of the baroque style.

Mr. Sayce prefaces his outline of *Des coches* with an instructive quotation from *De la vanité* concerning the method of composition of the essays:

C'est l'indiligent lecteur qui pert mon subject, non pas moy; il s'en trouvera tousjours en un coing quelque mot qui ne laisse pas d'estre bastant, quoy qu'il soit serré.[1]

Taking the hint from Montaigne's mention of hidden key words which bind the whole together, Mr. Sayce has capitalized these connecting links as they occur, and succeeds in showing how

1. III, 9, 283.

. . . Montaigne moves from one subject to another, apparently unconnected, without a break in the argument, not by the processes of logic but by the free associations aroused by a word, just as in silent thought or friendly conversation.[2]

In the essay which I wish to examine, these *mots en un coing* exist also to a certain extent, but the links are more frequently provided by associations of ideas and themes than by specific words. Therefore I shall not capitalize words, but in cases where the passage from one theme to the next is not clear (or where, especially, the connection reaches back over a considerable number of pages) I shall try to explain the association.

Let us now follow the thematic development of *De la vanité*. Needless to say, any such skeleton outline is a gross oversimplification of an author so full of nuances, concrete images, and digressions as Montaigne. However, it can help us to see the main movement of the essay and its artistic structure. The page numbers are those of the small Villey edition, and serve also for crossreference and the identification of important themes.
My own comments are in square brackets.

216. Writing about vanity is perhaps the greatest vanity of all.

I once met a gentleman who communicated his life only through his excrements. These writings are my excrements. [The passage is a good example of Montaigne's love of the concrete and shocking.]

217. It is a symptom of the corruption of this century that so many people write nowadays.

Each one of us contributes something to the corruption of the age; some contribute violent evils, while others, like me, contribute vanity.

In a time of serious evils, vain things are almost praiseworthy by comparison. [Note how three threads lead us through these complexities: the themes, respectively, of vanity, of writing, and of the corruption of the age.]

218. My vanity and writing are relatively minor misdeeds; in any roundup of serious offenders, I should logically be one of the last to be apprehended; so I shall have plenty of time to reform.

It is unreasonable to seek to eradicate small abuses at a time when we are afflicted with great evils.

Yet, in the midst of our troubled and disorderly period, a distinguished man has written a book suggesting various trivial reforms in clothing, cuisine, and courtroom procedure.

For my part, reform of my personal habits must be all or nothing: I scorn half-measures, and so usually I just let things slide. [This subject of petty

2. R. A. Sayce, "Baroque Elements in Montaigne," *French Studies, 8* (1954).

reforms is really a digression from the main flow of ideas; it is, however, associated with the themes of vanity, corruption, and writing.]

I am consoled by the fact that the decadence of the age corresponds to the decrepitude of my own old age.

219. A universal human vanity, which I share, is preferring the strange to the familiar: the enjoyment of movement and change.

The eagerness to see new and unknown things has made me want to travel.

A distaste for the management of household affairs has also made me want to travel. [By now a whole series of important new themes has been introduced: Montaigne's old age, the love of movement and change, travel, the problems of household and estate management, and finally the flight from unpleasant things. All of them keep recurring during the course of the essay.]

220. I started late in life to manage my estate; so I am no good at it. It is more boring and time-consuming than difficult. I don't expect to get rich; I merely try to forestall poverty by cutting down on expenses.

221. The only trouble with travel is that it is expensive.

Fortunately, in view of this extravagant taste, I have only one child to provide for. [The theme of estate management is associated with that of family responsibility, which will reappear at intervals.]

222. I am ready to accept any losses which may come to my estate through my absence.

Since small worries bother me a great deal, I prefer to turn my attention away from details and to consider my affairs as a whole. [The theme of flight from unpleasant things was first suggested on 219; it will develop later as one of the main reasons for travel. The dislike of boring details was first hinted on 220.]

223. I am not a true philosopher; I feel the full weight of any troubles. Routine worries in particular wear me down. [Here there is a characteristically effective concrete image: "Ces ordinaires goutieres me mangent."]

224. With respect to my estate, I do the best I can to carry on the work begun by my father. [The idea of family responsibility was first briefly suggested on 221.]

225. It is not through intellectual snobbishness that I am ignorant of the technical details of ploughing, wine making, harvesting, cuisine, and the making of clothes.

I wish I had my father's enthusiasm for these things.

226. I should be perfectly happy to allow someone else to run my affairs. I wish I could find a son-in-law who would look after me. [He had indirectly referred to his daughter on 221.]

When I am traveling, I allow someone else to take care of all financial problems; I dislike detailed accounts. [Compare 222.]

227. The study of money is a stupid and unattractive study; it leads to avarice.

This attitude toward my practical affairs is not a philosophical scorn of mundane and transitory things; it is pure childish laziness. [A repetition of 225.]

I am more fitted to live off someone else's fortune—if this could be done without sacrifice of independence. [This is a restatement of 226, but it introduces a new and important theme: Montaigne's intense desire for independence.]

228. When I am away from home, I no longer worry about my property and my household. At home, even if I delegate authority, I feel responsible for everything. [On 219, Montaigne first spoke of this as one of the advantages of travel.]

These worries detract from my qualities as a host. When a host makes it obvious that he is going to a great deal of trouble to entertain his guests, it is not very gracious hospitality.

229. All these remarks apply to me only: I realize that many people enjoy the peaceful, prosperous, and just administration of their own affairs. [As he often does, Montaigne pauses here to cast a backward glance over what he has said; the words constitute a kind of recapitulation of his attitude toward estate management—though he continues to refer to the subject. This is also really an apologetic restatement of 225 and 227: he wants to be sure that we do not accuse him of a silly scorn of practical matters.]

When I travel, I don't have to think of anyone but myself. [The theme of independence; see 227.]

The fact that a man has to conduct his life with constant reference to other people is very inconvenient.

230. I feel very much out of sympathy with the present condition of society in France: the religious wars. That is another reason why I like to travel abroad. [This idea proceeds by logical association from the previous statement; what is more interesting, for our purposes, is that the theme of the corruption of the age, present on 217 and 218 but absent since then, has

now returned. And of course we have, simultaneously, the flight theme: compare 219, 222, and 228.]

231. Inhumanity and treachery characterize present-day French life.

But ideal governments, like Plato's Republic, are ridiculous and impractical.

232. The best form of government for each country is that to which it is accustomed. [An important new theme: custom.]

233. Innovations are very dangerous to the state. Change leads to injustice and tyranny. Radical reform may destroy the whole structure of society. This is curing illness by death. The aim of the surgeon is not to kill unhealthy flesh but to cure it. [In these expressions of Montaigne's conservatism, the architectural and medical metaphors are developed at considerable length.]

233. When evil is destroyed, good does not necessarily follow: Caesar's assassins brought their country to such a terrible state that they regretted ever having taken part in public affairs. [Latent here, and extending back to 230, is the theme of the horror of civil war, which also underlies 216–18. The theme of Roman history, as we shall see, also plays an important part in this chapter.]

234. The citizens of Capua, though dissatisfied with their magistrates, were unable to find better officials to replace them.

States are perhaps better able to survive mortal illnesses than we imagine. [A recall of the medical metaphor.]

235. In judging our own state of affairs, we often make the mistake of looking above us rather than beneath us; very few people would care to trade misfortunes with others. [This of course relates to the general theme of the troubles of the times, but also to the idea, expressed on 217, of the relativity of evils.]

236. The study of Roman history can supply us with examples of every possible thing that can happen to a country. [This is associated with Montaigne's concern about contemporary France, 216–18 and 230–1; with the problems of changes in the structure of the state, 233–4; and continues the theme of Roman history, 233–4.]

Everything that shakes does not fall. The social structure, like that of an old building, often holds together by its very antiquity. [A recall of the architectural metaphor.]

237. Most countries collapse through foreign violence. At present, all foreign countries seem equally threatened by change and ruin. [Compare the idea of the relativity of evils, 217.]

Thus universal illness means individual health for France. [As it does for Montaigne, 217.]

238. The evils which we are suffering may partly be in the very nature of things—fatally ordained by heaven—and so not entirely our own fault.

I am afraid that my bad memory may cause me to repeat myself in these essays. [This is another of those self-conscious backward glances, where Montaigne momentarily arrests the flow of his thought to consider what he has written. Besides introducing the theme of memory, it brings back that of writing, which has been in abeyance since 218.]

239. It can be dangerous to prepare speeches in advance. My memory fails me when I rely on it too heavily.

240. The too careful preparation of a literary work makes for artificiality. [This is a justification of the improvised, conversational tone of the *Essais*. It explains Montaigne's reliance on association of ideas as a means of composition.]

Reader, please allow this third section of my self-portraiture to run on freely. I add to the essays, but do not correct them. My book is a unit. But with each new edition, I insert some added bits of patchwork.

241. I am not sure that I am progressing in wisdom. I am no more confident concerning my recent ideas than my earlier ones. My movement is like that of a staggering drunkard, or of reeds blown about by the wind. [The two metaphors describing Montaigne's style are themselves typical of that style. The idea of the improbability and vanity of any reform in his character was suggested on 218; the vain enjoyment of movement on 219.]

242. Public favor has given me self-confidence; but I would rather annoy my readers than bore them. [This is connected with several topics which I discussed in the earlier sections of this study of Montaigne's style: his self-conscious awareness of being a writer, his sense of the evolution of his style, and his resort to shock technique.]

243. I would rather write an entirely new set of essays than correct these, even for spelling and punctuation. [Compare 240, his refusal to make corrections. I have already discussed elsewhere Montaigne's disinclination to repudiate any previous stage of his thought or literary work.]

243. In my part of the country, I am in a particularly dangerous situation. I live surrounded by people with whose beliefs and way of life I am totally unfamiliar; and because our government regards them as outlaws, they have little reason to feel themselves bound by our laws. [This is, presumably, an allusion to Protestants. The theme of the danger of innovation, 233, re-

appears; and this is part of the recurring theme of the corruption of the age and the horrors of social disorder.]

My house has always been open to all; and under the present circumstances, its preservation from attack and destruction has been due more to luck than to law.

244. I want to owe my safety to law and authority, not to the grace and favor of other people. [See 226–7, Montaigne's desire not to be under obligations to others; also 232–3, his attachment to law and custom.]

245. Gratitude is a heavy burden; personally, I feel more bound by my own conscience than by any lawyer; I would rather break the walls of a legal prison than break my own word of honor. I am more severe in condemning myself than a judge would be.

246. I so dislike being under obligations to other people, that I sometimes feel that their ingratitude or offenses actually liberate me.

Family relationships should not make us blind to faults. [Here the theme of independence is blended with that of family ties, last alluded to on 221 and 226.]

247. I am satisfied if princes do me no harm. I do not want to owe anything except to God.

All my hope is in myself. I want to be self-sufficient.

248. Giving implies domination; receiving implies submission.

249. I have been able to maintain my independence better than most men.

250. It is an intolerable feeling to me that I am under obligations to someone for not having been murdered during our religious wars.

I have gone to bed a thousand times at home, expecting to be betrayed and done to death that very night.

Habit [l'accoustumance] is a great gift of nature, which hardens us so that we do not feel pain and other misfortunes. [This concept is related to Montaigne's praise of custom, 232.]

In civil war, every man has to get used to defending his house like a fortress.

251. I sometimes react against fear and laziness, and become resolute. [Montaigne had mentioned his negative weaknesses on 217, and had said that these minor shortcomings almost seemed like virtues by comparison with the active crimes committed all around him; now he asserts that the corruption of the age sometimes actually succeeds in transforming his weakness into strength.]

251–2. Perhaps, just as roses and violets develop a sweeter perfume when they grow next to garlic and onions, the neighborhood of so many evil people has had the effect of making me become better. [We have already commented on this St. François de Sales garden-and-metamorphosis image. This too, like 251, is connected with the 217 relativity-of-evil theme; but the static concept of relativity has yielded to the more dynamic idea of transformation.]

252. In my travels, I know what I am fleeing, but not what I am seeking. [The flight theme, last seen on 230, reappears, now in the form of a generalized maxim.]

252–3. No matter how angry I get against France, I always love Paris. The more I see other beautiful cities, the more I love Paris. I am French only through this great city. May God spare her our civil wars. [This great passage, perhaps the most lyrical and moving of the whole essay, has as its point of departure a reaction against some of the things the author has just said. He has seemed to be disgusted with France in her present state, and wants to affirm, by contrast, his love for Paris. The essay, in general, is composed on the principle of the free association of ideas; but ideas may frequently suggest their contraries. The movement is not always a smooth flow; the current may have sharp divergent twists. It should be further observed, with respect to the general structure of the essay, that this praise of Paris, occurring approximately at the mid-point, is balanced by a fine praise of Rome at the end. Considered in this way, the essay *De la vanité* divides itself into two halves, each of which rises to a poetic climax in expressing the love of one of the two great cities of Christendom.]

253. Like Socrates, I consider all men to be my compatriots, and love a Pole as much as a Frenchman. [This idea is suggested in part by the author's disgust with the condition of his country, but is also connected with his avowed enthusiasm for the strange and unfamiliar, 219. A little further on, he expresses his delight in the variety of customs in different countries, and this implies enjoyment of different nationalities. Finally, one of his reasons for loving Rome, as we shall see, is that there universal humanity transcends nationality.]

254. But I don't agree with the opinion of Socrates in his old age, that a sentence of exile is worse than a sentence of death. [The name Socrates is of course the mot en un coing which constitutes the link here; it provides Montaigne with the opportunity of presenting a contradictory idea, which he then rejects; and also of showing how a man's ideas may evolve from maturity to old age.]

Furthermore, travel is intellectually profitable.

255. It is hard for me to get started; but once on my way, I can go as far as any one wants. [Since 252, intermittently, the travel theme has returned. The problem of movement refers us back to 219, though there Montaigne is more aware of his eagerness for change than of the difficulty of overcoming inertia.]

255–6. I do not agree with those who criticize me for traveling when I am old and married. By now, my family have learned how to run the household. [We have the recurrence of three earlier themes: old age, 219; family responsibility, 221 and 226; estate management, 219–29.]

256. The most useful and honorable occupation for a woman is housekeeping.

I do not believe that a marriage suffers from absences; on the contrary.

257. From Rome I am able to run and enjoy my estate just as if I were home. [Cf. the advantages of absence from household problems, 219 and 228. Rome, mentioned in terms of ancient history, 233–6, is now envisaged, as it will be later, as a place to live.]

A man should be able to enjoy things and people even when they are not immediately present. [This, by application of the principle, soon to be stated, that joy should be extended and sadness limited as much as possible, is a kind of corollary in reverse of Montaigne's constant theme of fleeing from unpleasantness.]

258. One should not allow oneself to be tied down by one's wife.

259. In true friendship, I give myself to my friend more than I pull him toward me. [The idea is suggested to Montaigne partly because he believes that all human relationships should be based on free giving, and partly because he wishes to show that friendship is more ideal than marriage.]

Old age does not make travel unsuitable; on the contrary, it is youth rather which should circumscribe its activities because of criticism. [This reminds us of the statement, 229, that it is inconvenient to have to conduct one's life with reference to other people.]

260. I improvise my travel plans as I go along; I conduct my life's journey in the same way. [He has already recommended this method for literary composition, 240. Thus the themes of travel and of writing are related. In addition to these two explicit statements the composition of the whole essay is implicit testimony as to the method.]

I am not afraid of dying far from home. [The old-age theme, which we have seen on 218 and repeatedly since then, now leads to the theme of death, hinted at when Montaigne told us of his fears of being murdered in his own home, 250.]

261. When I die, I should prefer to be in a quiet, retired place, similar to the quiet and retirement of my life.

262. I do not wish to make my family and friends unhappy by the spectacle of my death.

Wherever possible, one should spread joy and limit sadness.

I study my illnesses calmly and objectively.

263. Having written this book about my way of life, I often feel obliged to live up to it.

264. The frankness of my book often disarms criticism.

Not only has this self-portraiture been morally profitable; I also hope that as a result some congenial person, reading about me, may seek my friendship. [Montaigne's relationship to his audience has been previously discussed, 240 and 242; the theme now leads to that of friendship, first mentioned in passing on 259.]

265. Friendship is the most necessary thing in life.

It is not a bad thing to die alone and far away. [A return to 260–1.]

One's family and friends become hardened to the sufferings of one's old age. [Here a reverse twist is given to 262.]

Decrepitude is a lonely state. [This important theme of decrepitude first appeared on 218; on 262 and 265 he again refers to his illnesses; the idea of loneliness is implicit on 264.]

266. I am not afraid of being ill or dying in an uncomfortable place. I have everything I need with me, and I am prepared for death. [The persistence of this theme suggests that, in reality, Montaigne did dread a lonely death. The disregard of comfort is flatly contradicted two pages further on.]

I write my book for few men and for only a few years of posterity. The French language evolves so rapidly that in fifty years nobody will be able to understand the *Essais*. [For his awareness of an audience, cf. in many places, e.g. 219, 233, 241, 254.]

267. I want to leave a record of my opinions, tastes, and feelings so that after I die people will not be able to misrepresent me. I would gladly come back from the other world to disavow anyone giving a false picture of me, even if flattering. [Gide would call this theme "authenticité."]

268. During my travels, when I arrive at an inn, I usually wonder whether I could be ill or die there in comfort.

Some forms of death are easier than others. It may be even possible to make death delightful.

270. If the weather is bad on the right, I go to the left. If I have neglected to see something behind me, I go back. I follow no definite line, straight or curved. [A reiteration of 260.]

I enjoy the diversity of customs from one country to another. [The theme of custom made its first appearance on 232, in connection with the idea of political conservatism. On 250 it assumed the slightly different form of "l'accoustumance." Here it is related to the theme of the pleasure of variety; compare 219, where Montaigne asserts his eagerness to see new and unknown things. Underlying all this is the idea of the enjoyment of travel, also first introduced on 219.]

270. It irritates me to see my compatriots so addicted to their own ways that they are upset by foreign customs.

271. Far from seeking my compatriots in foreign countries, I try to avoid them, and to seek out foreigners instead. [Note the connection with 253, where he tells us that he loves a Pole as much as a Frenchman.]

Casual travel acquaintances are not satisfactory; a good traveling companion is invaluable, but must be selected before one leaves home. I have deeply felt this lack, because I never fully enjoy pleasure unless I can share it. [This recalls the themes of loneliness and need for friendship, 264 and 265.]

272. But it is better to be lonely than to be bored. [The loneliness theme, however, suggests its opposite, independence—see 227 and 229.]

273. People tell me that I should be satisfied to remain at home; this is probably true, but they might just as well say, Be wise. [Here we have a cluster of familiar themes: Montaigne's estate, family responsibility, travel, independence, flight, and vanity.]

274. The love of travel does reveal anxiety and indecision. [Compare 219.]

I can't help it, for I love variety.

275. In traveling, I can be myself and do what I like.

This amusement may be vanity, but there is vanity in everything, including good advice. [Though the theme of vanity has been implicit all along, giving as it does the title to the essay, the actual word has not been used since the early part of the chapter.]

I am against lofty philosophical precepts which men have neither the capacity nor the desire to follow. [The connecting link here is vanity.]

276. There is much difference between the moral precepts which men approve and the actual lives which they lead. [The theme of diversity, which appears in another guise on 270.]

277. Philosophers patronize brothels as much as other people.

Moral commandments should bear some relationship to man's capacity to obey them.

If our laws were strictly enforced, the best man in the world would have to be hanged ten times over. Many people who obey laws scrupulously are far from good.

278. Human wisdom is never able to carry out the duties it sets for itself; if it could, it would then prescribe still more difficult duties. Such is the inconsistency of man's state. [Vanity; also, movement and metamorphosis.]

This inconsistency between words and deeds is not permissible for me, since I am the subject of my book. [For the idea of sincere self-portraiture, compare 263, 264, and 267. Here the concept is expressed in a characteristic image: "Il faut que j'aille de la plume comme des pieds."]

My way of life differs only slightly from that of people around me, yet it makes me unsociable; therefore I should not complain if the world criticizes me. [It is obvious that Montaigne has been greatly criticized for his love of travel. Many important passages, such as 259, 266, and 273, have as their point of departure self-justification. His preoccupation, as a writer, with the reaction of his audience, proceeds from the same sensitivity: 240, 242, 264, 266. Connected with this is his strong feeling that it is inconvenient to have to conduct one's life with constant reference to other people, 229. And yet, in another way, he has a deep desire to be loved: 264, 265, 271.]

279. A flexible moral sense is necessary in public life. It is difficult to escape with clean pants ("brayes nettes") if one is called upon to serve in government. [Here Montaigne's deprecation of moral rigorism, 275–8. comes into contact with his sense of the corruption of the age: 217–18 and 230–8. As a result, he reacts momentarily in the direction of rigorism, adopting a tone which is very different from 275–8 and indeed from the general tenor of his philosophy.]

280. Temperamentally, not only because of my moral sense but also because of my independence and idleness, I am unsuited to public life. [For independence, compare, among other passages, 229 and 275.]

If a man conducts his private affairs well, it is not a sign that he will conduct public affairs well. Skill is not necessarily transferable from one profession to another. [The theme of the contrast between private and public life is related to that of estate management, 219–29.]

. . . tel . . . faict des Essais qui ne sauroit faire des effects. [The baroque fondness for plays on words is evident here. The theme of writing returns, associated, as on 216 through 218, with vanity. Implicit also is the problem of the relation between Montaigne's book and his life, 263 and 267.]

281. In times like these, the least evil men seem good; virtue is relative. [The same concept of moral relativity is present on 217 and 237.]

282. We have some virtuous men, but according to our own relative standards.

We may wish we had other magistrates, but we have to obey the ones we have. [This proceeds logically from the 279 remarks on public life; it is also related to Montaigne's basic conservatism, 232. In that passage, having repudiated theoretically ideal forms of government, he argues that each country should retain the system it has.]

In an age like ours—or that of the Roman triumvirate—the best thing is to try to avoid the storm, and keep out of trouble. [The theme of the corruption of the age now concludes its last appearance in the essay. For Roman history, compare 233–6. The theme of flight from unpleasant things returns: see 219, 222, 228, 230, and 252.]

Perhaps I have been digressing, but I know what I am doing. My ideas follow one another, but sometimes at a distance; they are connected, though often indirectly. [This explicit statement as to the composition of the *Essais* is of course the basis for my present undertaking. My whole purpose here is to relate the themes which are separated from each other or indirectly connected. For another discussion of literary style and structure, see 240–3.]

283. The titles of my chapters sometimes do not cover the subject matter. [This would be particularly true of *Des coches,* but it also applies somewhat to the present essay; however, it is my contention that the theme of vanity is latent throughout, even if some critics, such as Grace Norton, think that the title should be *Des voyages.*]

J'ayme l'allure poetique, à sauts et à gambades. [It seems essential to leave this sentence in French, since it exemplifies so well the phenomenon it describes. It is, I feel, support for my contention that Montaigne must be considered as an artist and poet; and that baroque art is characterized by picturesque imagery and lively movement.]

Lively digressions and variations have their beauty; the careless reader may lose my subject, but I don't; there is always a sufficient word in some corner to provide the necessary link. [This is the passage which forms the basis of Mr. Sayce's analysis of the baroque structure of *Des coches*.]

284. I'd rather not be read at all than to be read sleepily or carelessly. Perhaps I may succeed in arresting the reader's attention by my complication. [The link here is provided by the preceding disparaging reference to the careless reader. The author-reader relationship has been previously discussed: 240, 242, 264, 266.]

284. Some readers may decide that I am deep because I am obscure; actually, obscurity is a trait which I dislike, and would avoid if I could.

My earlier essays were so short as to interrupt attentive reading; so I have begun to write longer ones. [Aside from the theme of the self-conscious writer, aware of his audience, we have that of metamorphosis.]

285. Reason often spoils the fun; I stress vanity and foolishness if they give me pleasure. I follow my natural inclinations without close rational supervision. [This is related indirectly to Montaigne's method of travel, 270, which is based on whim and improvisation rather than on rational planning; and to the general principle of spreading joy and limiting sadness, 262.]

I cannot help being awe-struck by the ruins of Rome. I have been taught about Rome since childhood. [Here the two different Roman themes come together: ancient history and travel. And, as we have seen elsewhere, Montaigne's emotion at seeing the vanished grandeur of Rome is related to the theme of change and metamorphosis.]

I have always been careful to show respect for the dead.

286. The history of the Roman republic—and the site of the places where the early Romans lived—interests me passionately.

287. Rome is the one international and universal city, and deserves the love of all men for that reason. [On 253 the other great city, Paris, is also praised with sincere emotion; and the same page expresses Montaigne's creed that humanity transcends nationality.]

It may be vanity to take delight in Rome; but our moods are not too vain if they give us pleasure. [A reiteration of the first theme of 285.]

288. I do not worry about what will happen when I am no longer alive; the present keeps my mind occupied. [It is undoubtedly the spectacle of ancient ruins which, by impressing Montaigne with the transitoriness of human life, has brought him back to thoughts of his own death. Compare

260–2, and 265–8. The theme of vanity thus leads, by natural associations, to that of death. When the author says that the present keeps him from brooding too much about death, it is a recurrence of the flight from unpleasantness theme: 219, 222, 228, 230, 252, 273. Montaigne has, of course, devoted a whole essay to this subject: *De la diversion,* III, 4.]

Consequently, it has never seemed to me a misfortune for a man to be without children. [His casual attitude toward descendants and family responsibilities in general begins to be discussed on 221. The concept of fortune seems to be rather a loose one in his mind, almost interchangeable with God —see 247—and nature—see 250.]

289. Fortune has spared me violent and extraordinary blows—as well as exceptional favors.

Most of fortune's favors to me have been vain. The one I like best is an authentic certificate of Roman citizenship, granted to me when I was in Rome. [A fusion of the themes of fortune, vanity, travel, and Rome.]

290. [Text of the papal bull granting him Roman citizenship.]

291. Being the citizen of no city, I am pleased to be so of the noblest one that ever was or ever shall be. [Montaigne realizes full well that this souvenir, brought back from his travels, is a vanity; yet somehow it gives him, symbolically, a satisfactory sense of having triumphed over diversity and attained universality. And since in a way the essay *De la vanité* has done just this, it seems fitting that the Latin document should occupy this climactic position.]

291. Nature has been wise in diverting our attention from our own vanity toward external things. [Here again is the rather blurred nature, fortune, and God theme. In the *Journal de voyage,* Montaigne tells us that when he visited Rome the papal censors seized his copy of the *Essais* and objected, among other things, to his abuse of the word "fortune." The themes of vanity and diversion or flight from unpleasantness are of course evident.]

We go sailing along merrily, but it is painful to reverse course; the sea becomes rough when it is pushed back toward itself. [It is interesting to note how the image of a ship changing course is suddenly changed to that of the sea agitated by a change of wind.]

292. A similarly upsetting commandment is that of the Delphic god: Know thyself.

The world is always trying to distract you from paying attention to yourself; yet the world is absorbed in self-contemplation.

Whatever you look at, inside or out, is always vanity; but the lesser the extent of what you are looking at, the lesser the vanity. [This passage, perhaps more than any other in the *Essais,* twists and turns, proceeding from contradiction to contradiction. Essentially, Montaigne is arriving at the conclusion expressed in Ecclesiastes 1:2, "Vanity of vanities, saith the Preacher, vanity of vanities, all is vanity." The theme of vanity, with which this essay began, has seemed to disappear for long stretches; actually, however, it has always been latent, and now it returns, climactically, with the full force of the author's orchestra. And now the coda, which for complete appreciation must be given in French as well as English]:

Tu es le scrutateur sans connoissance, le magistrat sans jurisdiction et apres tout le badin de la farce. [You, Montaigne says to man, are the examiner without knowledge, the magistrate without authority, and in the last analysis the fool in the comedy.]

This last sentence is a kind of recapitulation of the whole essay: it restates the theme of vanity, the fundamental one which provides the title and with which all the others are connected. It exemplifies many of the baroque categories which I have discussed. Consider, for example, moral purpose: the references to the examiner, the magistrate, and the fool all constitute statements as to the significance of human life; and while they all establish man's vanity, they are far from declaring that our experience and the universe are without meaning. It should be affirmed once more that the baroque position is very different from the romantic one: romanticism, whose effects we in the twentieth century still powerfully feel, tends to find reality only in feeling; and whenever the vanity of our experience is demonstrated, we are inevitably led to the conclusion that we live in a totally absurd universe. Such, for instance, is the message of that latter-day form of romanticism, existentialism. But Montaigne's use of the terms "examiner," "magistrate," and "fool" imply that, however vain human behavior may be, there is a higher authority (which romanticism and existentialism would deny) and therefore a meaning to life. His conclusion to the essay *De la vanité* is thus not very different from that of the *Apologie:* by purely human means we may be unable to arrive at ultimate reality, but that is not the same as saying that ultimate reality does not exist. The *Apologie* concludes with the statement that "Dieu seul est"; the manifold instances of man's moral and intellectual weakness simply show that we live in a fallen world. The idea is implicit throughout *De la vanité:* the constant judgment that man's opinions, feelings, and activities are vain is based on the idea that something exists which is not vain. And so, though this essay does not say it in so many words, once again we have the message: "Dieu seul est."

But this final sentence exhibits other baroque characteristics also. It contains a series of concrete and picturesque images, even though the thought may be abstract. (Compare what was said about incarnation as a category.) These images are, in turn, an attempt to make us visualize the idea through different perspectives. It is multiple-aspect imagery, a baroque characteristic which I placed in the category of theatricality and illusion. Man may think that he is a magistrate with authority, or a well-informed examiner (for "examiner," in modern terms, substitute the word "scholar" or "scientist"), but this is an illusion. The final image, "le badin de la farce," is again taken from the world of the theatre. The theatre, whether comedy or tragedy, is related to a system of moral and religious values: if comedy, there is an appeal to a generally accepted code of behavior, which it is ridiculous to infringe; if tragedy, the catharsis is closely related to a concept of atonement in which the spectator as well as the hero must participate.

Finally, we come to the category of organic unity, which I have been trying to illustrate throughout this analysis of the plan of *De la vanité*. The essay seems to swarm with a fantastic variety of themes: vanity, the art of writing, the corruption of late sixteenth-century France, estate management, flight from unpleasantness, travel, the diversity of custom, Roman history, the glories of Paris and Rome—to name but a few. And yet these themes are related in the same way that the opinions, feelings, and actions, however diverse and contradictory, of a single individual are connected. When we see a man over a certain length of time, we may be amazed at the diversity of the things he thinks, feels, and does; however, we are forced to admit that all this constitutes a single personality. Now any essay of Montaigne is consubstantial with its author; and so, despite all complexity and disorder, there is an organic unity. We follow the movement of Montaigne's mind through many curious associations of ideas, and through many apparently irrelevant digressions—but in the end there is a unified work of art. The work of art is all the more living and real because it is not abstract, geometric, and static. Like the creations of God, it is ondoyant et divers—in other words, incarnate.

CHAPTER 2. A Religious Handbook: *L'Introduction à la vie dévote*

ALTHOUGH an exuberant delight in surprising forms, in movement and variety for their own sakes, is everywhere evident in baroque art, many of the most important works of the period are also animated by a strong moral, political, or religious purpose. The fountains of Rome—Bernini's "Triton" or his "Rivers," for example—are pure flights of imaginative joy; Saint-Amant's *Le Melon* was obviously written for fun, and so was Corneille's *Illusion comique*. On the other hand, the piazza in front of St. Peter's, while giving the beholder delight because of the rhythmic interplay of mass and movement, has been conceived primarily to impress him with the power of the papacy; we enjoy the sweep of the colonnades, the contrast of fountains and obelisk, the gradual ascent of broad steps to Maderna's magnificent façade as a wonderful collective design, and yet we cannot escape the message which the ensemble is intended to convey: This is the religious center of the world. Rubens' Medici series is alive with color and movement, with pageant and theatricality; yet the artist's purpose is to glorify Henri IV, Marie de Médicis, and Louis XIII. Similarly, while the modern reader may enjoy d'Aubigné's *Les Tragiques* principally for its epic energy and violent imagery, the poem is above all religious propaganda. The poet is trying to convert his readers. Now this is true also of St. François de Sales' *Introduction à la vie dévote*. The saint wrote his book with a definite practical purpose: to teach the average person how to lead a devout life. Many readers undoubtedly still study this work for purposes of religious instruction; yet much of its appeal is literary. An analysis of the nature of this appeal will, I think, tell us much about the baroque style. I shall be concerned here mostly with St. François' imagery, and it is certainly possible to enjoy this book for purely artistic reasons, yet one should not lose sight of the fact that the *Introduction* is not an example of art for art's sake. The message is paramount.

Recently in America we have seen a flood of "how-to" books—how to cook French dishes, how to stop worrying, how to win friends and influence people. On a much higher level, the *Introduction* is a how-to book also. Its superiority is due not only to the far higher aim which it proposes but also to those elements of style which may be called baroque. It is not only that to teach people how to love God is a loftier purpose than to show them how to achieve success through flattery: in the language of St. François we can experience the same kind of delight as in the fountains of Rome. It is not, by the way, a coincidence that one of the most purely baroque examples of church architecture in France is the façade of the Chapel of the Visitation in Nevers, founded by the saint. The broken pediments, undulating rhythms, and fanciful exuberance of this little church front, which would seem perfectly in place in Rome or in Lecce, are as surprising to the traveler in a French provincial town as is the style of St. François to the uninitiated student of seventeenth-century literature.

We can convince ourselves of the how-to nature of the *Introduction* by examining a few chapter headings. The subtitle of Part I, for example, reads: "Contenant les advis et exercices requis pour conduire l'ame, dés son premier desir de la vie devote, jusques à une entiere resolution de l'embrasser." Each individual chapter in this first part presents one technique designed to help in the development of the spiritual life. Chapter 3 shows that piety is compatible with worldly occupations; chapter 4 demonstrates the need for a "conducteur" or spiritual adviser; chapters 9 through 18 consist of systematic meditations on various subjects such as judgment, hell, and heaven; chapter 19 explains how to make one's confession; and the concluding chapters contain advice on how to cleanse the heart of sinful desires. Part II is composed in a similar manner; its title is: "Contenant les divers advis pour l'eslevation de l'ame à Dieu par l'oraison et aux sacremens." The first few chapters in this section advise as to the proper method of prayer: chapter 9 tells what to do in periods of spiritual dryness; chapter 14 explains how to hear Mass; chapters 20 and 21 contain instructions about making one's Communion. Part III is about the exercise of the virtues, and discusses such topics as patience, chastity, proper dress, permissible and forbidden pleasures, conjugal behavior, etc. Each one of the fifteen chapters in Part IV is devoted to techniques for resisting temptation; the fifth and last part contains similar detailed exercises and advice for renewing and strengthening the spiritual life.

If we consider the first two parts of the *Introduction,* we shall see that there is an underlying theme which animates and links all these brief chapters of practical advice: it is the concept of spiritual growth. This is true, to a less extent, of the last three parts, but it is in Part I and Part II that the sense of development and evolution is most apparent. Like Montaigne, St. François is painting not "l'estre" but "le passage." Montaigne's essays record their author's gradual intellectual growth; Rotrou's *Saint Genest* portrays the stages of a religious conversion; Bernini's "Apollo and Daphne" shows us the girl changing into an olive tree. In all these examples, we have the great baroque theme of metamorphosis. In Part I, St. François leads the soul from its first desire for a devout life to a full determination to embrace it; in Part II, he gradually elevates the soul toward a communion with God. All the little how-to chapters are so many steps in a constant ascent, so many stages in the development of the spiritual life. And though Parts III and IV tend to be made up of independent topics less related to the general movement of ascent, Part V, implicitly at least, returns to the theme of spiritual growth, since its aim is to "renouveller l'ame et la confirmer en la devotion."

It is significant that St. François does not conceive of himself as having reached a static condition of spiritual perfection. In the preface to his work, he assures the reader that he is not "devot," but hopes to become so:

Au demeurant, mon cher lecteur, il est vray que j'escris de la vie devote sans estre devot, mais non pas certes sans le desir de le devenir: et c'est encore cette affection qui me donne courage à t'en instruire.[1]

In Christian terms, this is of course an entirely proper attitude of humility; it corresponds to the petition in the Book of Common Prayer for "continual growth in Thy love and service." But in its emphasis upon *becoming* rather than on *being* it is also a baroque attitude. Montaigne in his essays does not claim to be wise, but does hope to attain wisdom. Indeed, one of his principal reasons for writing essays is the desire for intellectual and moral growth: the book contributes to the author's own development. A very good way of learning, St. François comments in a passage just after the one which we have quoted, is to teach.

This interest in transformation may be seen in some of the saint's characteristic metaphors. Most of his images, in fact, are noteworthy for their concreteness and their sense of change or movement. For example, in the chapter on Communion he tries to illustrate the meaning of transubstantiation:

Non, le Sauveur ne peut estre consideré en une action, ny plus amoureuse, ny plus tendre que celle-cy, en laquelle il s'aneantit par maniere de dire, et se reduit en viande, afin de penetrer nos ames, et s'unir intimement au cœur et au corps de ses fidelles.[2]

On the words "amoureuse," "tendre," "s'unir intimement," and their relationship to baroque religious sensibility I shall have more to say in a moment; but here I should like to call attention to the expression "se reduit en viande." Not only does it have that rather shocking physical intensity—"reduces himself to meat"—which we often find in the imagery of d'Aubigné, but above all it constitutes a vivid picture of metamorphosis. The theme is presented

1. Preface.
2. II, 21. (References are to parts and chapters of the *Introduction* respectively.)

again two paragraphs further on, where St. François is recommending frequent Communions:

> . . . les lievres deviennent blancs parmy nos montagnes en hyver, parce qu'ils ne voyent ny mangent que la neige; et a force d'adorer et manger la beauté, la bonté, et la pureté meme en ce divin sacrement, vous deviendrez toute belle, toute bonne et toute pure.[3]

In attempting to explain spiritual mysteries, St. François often draws illustrations from familiar nature around him—in this case from the mountains near his home in Annecy. Scientifically, one may feel inclined to question whether he is correct in assuming that the hares turn white because they see and eat so much snow. In fact the saint, like Montaigne, has a fondness for curious natural phenomena which sometimes leads him to be too credulous. Nevertheless, the image is pleasant and striking; it serves its purpose of expressing in visual imagery a spiritual change.

Not all the transformations in the *Introduction à la vie dévote* are favorable; many of the most striking metaphors describe deterioration. The writer finds a parallel between the bruising of fruit and the loss of chastity:

> Et de vray tandis que les fruicts sont bien entiers, ils peuvent estre conservez, les uns sur la paille, les autres dedans le sable, et les autres en leur propre fueillage; mais estant une fois entamez, il est presque impossible de les garder que par le miel et le sucre en confiture. Ainsi la chasteté qui n'est point encore blessée ny violée peut estre gardée en plusieurs sortes; mais estant une fois entamée, rien ne la peut consever qu'une excellente devotion, laquelle, comme j'ay souvent dit, est le vray miel et sucre des esprits.[4]

Once more the illustration is from country life in Savoy. To St. François, as to Montaigne, all natural phenomena are in a constant state of change; fruits, if left to themselves, do not remain in the same state but rot. God alone, as Montaigne observes in the conclusion to the *Apologie,* is eternal and unchanging. It is only through "la vie dévote," St. François is saying, that we can escape this world of becoming and attain a state of being.

In his chapter on how to preserve chastity, the author repeats his image of the corruption of fruit and adds two other homely illustrations.

> Les corps humains ressemblent a des verres, qui ne peuvent estre portez les uns avec les autres en se touchant sans courir fortune a se rompre, et aux fruicts lesquels quoy qu'entiers et bien assaisonnez reçoivent de la tare, s'entretouchans les uns les autres. L'eau mesme, pour fraische qu'elle soit dedans un vase, estant touchée de quelque animal terrestre, ne peut longuement conserver sa fraicheur Ne permettez jamais, Philothee, qu'aucun vous touche incivilement, ny par maniere de folastrerie, ny par maniere de faveur.[5]

3. Ibid.   4. III, 12.   5. III, 13.

This passage contains three transformation metaphors in rapid succession: glasses that touch each other get broken; fruits that touch each other decay; water contaminated by animal contact loses its freshness; and all these examples serve to show how the touching of human bodies can lead to a progressive corruption of the soul. One illustration would have been enough to communicate the idea. In a sense, the two extra ones may appear to be gratuitous ornamentation; and if you think of the baroque in terms of needless decoration, you may feel inclined to criticize the writer on this score. Actually, each added image permits us to look at the idea from a slightly different angle; and this technique of presenting different aspects in rapid succession is another baroque device which I shall want to discuss later.

Let us look at a few more images which express deterioration or spreading corruption. St. François de Sales is acutely aware of the dangerous power of wicked words. He cautions his disciple and reader not to say anything "deshonneste," even unintentionally, for

La parole deshonneste tombant dans un cœur foible s'estend et se dilate comme une goutte d'huile sur le drap, et quelquesfois elle saisit tellement le cœur, qu'elle le remplit de mille pensees et tentations lubriques.[6]

A drop of oil which spreads on a cloth—it is a striking image, and all the more so because it is drawn from everyday household experience: a word can expand in the heart and arouse lust; the nature of evil is to dilate itself. Or consider the sting of the asp: it starts as a slight prick, an almost pleasant itching sensation, but soon spreads through the body and kills the victim:

L'aspic faict sa picqueure presque imperceptible, et son venin d'abord rend une demangeaison delectable, au moyen de quoy le cœur et les entrailles se dilatent et reçoivent le poison, contre lequel par apres il n'y a plus de remede.[7]

What, you may ask, does this illustrate? Slander. Our usual first reaction upon hearing cruel gossip about others is pleasure; but in listening to it we ourselves are contaminated, and our soul receives deadly poison.

The most virtuous of human emotions is subject to such corruption; St. François, who is far from austere, has every sympathy for married love. But he cautions husbands and wives to beware of the destructive power of jealousy; though they should constantly strive to increase their love for each other, there is always the danger that love may deteriorate into jealousy. Here again we have an image from the orchard:

. . . il arrive souvent que comme le ver s'engendre de la pomme la plus delicate et la plus meure, aussi la jalousie naist en l'amour le plus ardent et

6. III, 27.   7. III, 29.

pressant des mariez, duquel neantmoins il gaste et corrompt la substance: car petit a petit il engendre les noises, dissensions et divorces.[8]

Both in the botanical and in the psychological worlds, change is constantly occurring; and as an artist St. François makes this happen in the world of literary expression also. The saint's garden overlooking the Lake of Annecy and the background of Savoy mountains supply him with endless analogies for his book. Take mushrooms, for example, which to this day are a gastronomic treasure of the region, but can be a source of danger. The author appeals to the authority of Pliny, but is also thinking of the forests of his own province:

Les champignons, selon Pline, estant spongieux et poreux comme ils sont, attirent aysement toute l'infection qui leur est autour: si que estant pres des serpens, ils en reçoivent le venin . . .[9]

You may wonder what moral phenomenon corresponds to this. The rest of the paragraph goes on to declare:

. . . les bals, les danses, et telles assemblees tenebreuses, attirent ordinairement les vices et pechez qui regnent en un lieu; les querelles, les envies, les mocqueries, les folles amours.

As in some other passages, one may question the writer's scientific explanation, but it is impossible to escape his vision of the natural world as a place of constant movement and transformation. The botanical theories may be wrong, and the psychology appear unduly affected by puritanical ideas, but the poetry, expressing a world in a state of flux, remains valid. And it should be added that St. François is less puritanical than he sometimes seems: in fact, for a mystic, he is not austere at all. Those whose religious life is strong may, on occasion, gamble or dance; the saint cites the example of St. Charles Borromeo, who sometimes gambled with the Swiss, and of St. Elizabeth of Hungary, who consented both to gamble and to dance. Such amusements may be dangerous to those of little faith, but only reinforce the piety of true believers; and we have the inevitable comparison from nature:

Ce sont les grands feux qui s'enflamment au vent; mais les petits s'esteignent si on ne les y porte a couvert.[10]

In Part IV, the author warns us against the dangers of sadness and anxiety to the religious life. Thus sadness may destroy all our spiritual riches:

. . . elle est comme un dur hyver qui fauche toute la beauté de la terre et engourdit tous les animaux; car elle oste toute suavité de l'ame et la rend presque percluse et impuissante en toutes ses facultez.[11]

8. III, 38.   9. III, 33.   10, III, 34.   11. IV, 12.

To mow down, to benumb, to remove sweetness—all these are verbs of transformation; *accidia* in the spiritual world, like winter in the natural world, brings about a deathlike change. And excessive anxiety about the state of the soul can also worsen our condition; we struggle against evil, but get more and more deeply entangled in it:

Les oyseaux demeurent pris dans les filets et lacs, parce que s'y treuvant engagez ils se debattent et remuent dereglement pour en sortir; ce que faisant ils s'enveloppent tousjours tant plus.[12]

In the *Introduction à la vie dévote,* good and evil are not thought of as static conditions but as evolutionary forces. So the essential thing, if the religious life is to grow within us, is to engrave the name of Christ on our hearts; it will gradually expand and become manifest in all our actions. To illustrate this concept, St. François takes us once more to an orchard in Savoy. I confess that I do not know enough about arboriculture to judge whether the process he describes is scientifically accurate, but poetically the idea is picturesque and pleasing:

Ceux qui traictent des choses rustiques et champestres asseurent que si on escrit quelque mot sur une amande bien entiere, et qu'on la remette dans son noyau, le pliant et serrant bien proprement, et le plantant ainsi, tout le fruict de l'arbre qui en viendra se trouvera escrit et gravé du mesme mot.[13]

This brings us to a basic point in St. François' book: the *Introduction* concerns the growth of love in the soul rather than any strictly intellectual development. In chapter after chapter, the author is indicating specific techniques for making holy love increase until it dominates the whole life. He presents no philosophical arguments to prove the existence of God; he seldom expounds or explains dogma. His basic assumption is that the reader has the will to believe, though perhaps a tenuous and imperfect one. Starting from this basis, the aim of the book is to bring us, step by step, to the spiritual state where we really love God with all our hearts, with all our souls, and with all our minds.

The commandment to love God is of course fundamental to Christianity in all ages, and I do not wish to imply that it has a special connection with the baroque style. However, the artistic means employed to express the sense of this commandment do vary from century to century. The language and imagery of St. François are characteristic of baroque sensibility. Bernini in his "Ecstasy of St. Teresa" [14] reveals this way of feeling. The expression on the saint's face as she is pierced by the golden arrow of the angel—lips slightly parted, eyes closed—suggests the swooning of physical passion.

12. IV, 11.   13. III, 23.   14. In Santa Maria della Vittoria, Rome.

Crashaw, the English baroque poet, in a poem inscribed in a young woman's prayer book, proclaims that her greatest bliss will be to have her God become her lover.[15] The very last line of d'Aubigné's *Les Tragiques* depicts the soul swooning ecstatically on the lap of God. Whether in painting, sculpture, or literature, the artists of the late sixteenth and early seventeenth century tend to portray the love of God in strongly human, almost erotic terms.

So it is with St. François de Sales. He has visualized an imaginary feminine reader, and he bears her in mind on every page of the *Introduction à la vie dévote*. He is speaking to her as he might to one of his own penitents in the confessional. To this conception in large part the book owes it atmosphere of informality, of tenderness, of intimacy. The penitent's name is Philothée—again and again she is "ma chere Philothée." And Philothée is, of course, the lover of God—we need no profound knowledge of Greek or of etymology to understand this. I have already mentioned the fact that St. François makes no claims of saintliness for himself; instead he hopes that, in writing about "la vie dévote," he himself will be introduced into a richer spiritual life. In teaching Philothée, he will teach himself. As the penitent falls more and more deeply in love with God, so will the father confessor. Referring to "la devotion," St. François speaks of

. . . l'esperance que j'ay qu'en la gravant dans l'esprit des autres, le mien a l'adventure en deviendra sainctement amoureux.[16]

The word "amoureux" is, I feel, important. *Aimer* is to love, but *être amoureux* is to be in love. In choosing to say "amoureux," the author aligns himself with those baroque artists who have portrayed mystical love in terms of human passion.

In fact, Philothée is told that she should worship God in just the same way as she might be in love with a man:

Enfin comme ceux qui sont amoureux d'un amour humain et naturel ont presque tousjours leurs pensées tournées du cote de la chose aymée, leur cœur plein d'affection envers elle, leur bouche remplie de ses louanges, et qu'en son absence ils ne perdent point d'occasion de tesmoigner leurs passions par lettres: et ne treuvent point d'arbre sur l'escorce duquel ils n'escrivent le nom de ce qu'ils ayment; ainsi ceux qui ayment Dieu ne peuvent cesser de penser en luy, respirer pour luy, aspirer a luy, et parler de luy, et voudroient, s'il estoit possible, graver sur la poitrine de toutes les personnes du monde le sainct et sacré nom de Jesus.[17]

As is so often the case with St. François de Sales, the image has been expanded into a series of little scenes where actions are taking place: the woman in love is writing letters to her beloved, and carving his name on

---

15. Cf. "Prayer," in "Carmen Deo Nostro."   16. Preface.   17. II, 13.

the bark of a tree. The baroque metaphor is noteworthy not only for its abundance of concrete details but also for its flashes of movement. Here, in order to illustrate the nature of religion, the writer has created a little drama of romantic love. The person who is really in love is constantly speaking of the beloved; and in another passage, the father confessor urges his penitent to talk about God as much as possible.

Si doncques vous estes bien amoureuse de Dieu, Philothee, vous parlerez souvent de Dieu es devis familiers que vous ferez avec vos domestiques, amis et voisins.[18]

St. François' emphasis upon the passionate, almost erotic aspect of man's relationship to God might lead one to believe that he is an advocate of frenzied mystical ecstasies. As a matter of fact, such is very far from being the case, and the above quotation may serve as a corrective to this impression. True, he does want Philothée to be "amoureuse de Dieu," yet this love is not to take the form of a trance, it is to be intermingled with the daily affairs of life, and to be expressed in her ordinary conversations with servants, friends, and neighbors. The author of the *Introduction à la vie dévote,* though a mystic, has his feet very much on the ground. The very style of the work indicates this: it deals with spiritual life, but the images are drawn from the details of the normal practical life of the average person in Savoy.

The saint is quite firm in warning Philothée against ecstasies. God may sometimes reward the devoutly loving soul with a vision, but we should not seek for such states:

Il y a certaines choses que plusieurs estiment vertus, et qui ne les sont aucunement, desquelles il faut que je vous dise un mot: ce sont les extases, ou ravissement, les insensibilitez, unions deïfiques, elevations, transformations, et autres telles perfections, desquelles certains livres traitent . . .[19]

No, for the beginner in the devout life St. François does not recommend religious raptures. Certain books may discuss them, but not the *Introduction.* It is better, he feels, to exercise simple virtues in daily life, such as patience, chastity, and the love of our neighbor. We should be happy to serve God in the humblest capacity:

. . . trop heureux serons-nous de le servir en sa cuisine, en sa paneterie, d'estre des laquais, des porte-fais, garçons de chambre . . .[20]

This attitude is not so different as it might seem from that of St. Teresa. Although the great Spanish saint had many famous visions, she was above all a very practical woman. She had an extraordinary talent for organization. She spent her life founding, building, and administering convents. Her

18. III, 26.   19. III, 2.   20. Ibid.

contemporaries were impressed by her prodigious energy for getting things done; if she were living in the twentieth century, she would be famous for her efficiency and executive genius. As St. François remarks, God sometimes grants visions to those who are advanced in the devout life; it is such a vision that Bernini has portrayed in the chapel of Santa Maria della Vittoria. And similarly, when the author of the *Introduction* attempts to describe the love of God he uses the imagery of passion, but this does not mean that he is encouraging his followers to have ecstasies; basically, he wants them to love God passionately and yet to lead a normal life. Philothée may eventually become a mystic, but at the moment she is still under instruction; and her father confessor, warning her against dangerous desires, includes in his cautionary list not only gay parties where dancing and gambling take place, not only positions which confer prestige but also visions and ecstasies:

> Mais je vous dis de plus, ma Philothée, ne desirez point les choses qui sont dangereuses a l'ame, comme sont les bals, les jeux, et tels autres passe-temps; ny les honneurs et les charges, ny les visions et les extases.[21]

For the heart of the saint's thought is that religion is compatible with daily life. From the literary point of view this is reflected, as we have seen and shall continue to see, in the peculiar quality of his imagery, which manages simultaneously to make spiritual concepts clear and to make the activities of ordinary life poetic. This curious blend of religious fervor and naturalistic acceptance of the physical world is perhaps one of the essential characteristics of the baroque. People educated in the austerities of the New England Protestant tradition find it difficult to believe, when they find themselves in the midst of the palatial splendors of a great Roman church like the Gesù or Sant'Andrea della Valle, that the building can be the sincere expression of religious feeling. Such architecture seems to them above all worldly, and they long either for Chartres cathedral or the white wooden colonial church. The fact is, however, that the baroque mind is capable of enjoying simultaneously this world and the next—an attitude that the immediately preceding, or mannerist, generation, as exemplified by the spiritual angoisse of an El Greco, would have found it as difficult to appreciate as the American Puritan. Perhaps that is why the contemporary American, despite all his enthusiasm for Tintoretto or El Greco, does not as yet love Bernini or Rubens.

For St. François de Sales, it is evident that there need be no divorce between the religious and the worldly life. This is a point which he repeatedly stresses throughout the *Introduction à la vie dévote*. No matter

21. III, 37.

what your occupation may be, it is possible for you to practice the worship of God. In the very first pages of his preface, in an exceptionally elaborate metaphor noteworthy for its picturesque contrasts and multiple-sense imagery, he insists that amid the rush of temporal affairs we are still able to devote ourselves to the knowledge and love of God:

Et je leur montre, que comme les meres-perles vivent emmy la mer, sans prendre aucune goutte d'eau marine, et que vers les isles Chelidoines il y a des fontaines d'eau bien douce au milieu de la mer, et que les pyraustes volent dedans les flammes sans brusler leurs aisles: ainsi peut une ame vigoureuse et constante vivre au monde, sans recevoir aucune humeur mondaine, treuver des sources d'une douce pieté au milieu des ondes ameres de ce siecle, et voler entre les flammes des convoitises terrestres, sans brusler les aisles des sacrez desirs de la vie devote.[22]

The idea expressed here—the happy reconciliation of two antithetical things, the temporal and the spiritual—is deeply baroque. So also is the form in which the idea is expressed, through different vivid pictures, full of movement and concrete impressions which act upon various senses: pearls, islands in the Aegean, fountains of fresh water in the sea, legendary birds which fly into the flames without being burnt.

Jacob's ladder is also an important illustration: it links the human and the divine. Through prayer, through the sacraments, and through the practice of charity men are able to ascend it; and, at the same time, angels come down the ladder to love, inspire, and help men. Indeed, it is hard to tell, looking at the ladder, whether we see men with angelic hearts, or angels with human bodies:

Ils ont des aisles pour voler et s'eslancent en Dieu par la saincte oraison; mais ils ont des pieds aussi pour cheminer avec les hommes par une saincte et amiable conversation . . .[23]

Wings and feet are both necessary, and the saint accepts them both. It is a complete error, a heresy, to suppose that religion need be banished from any walk of life:

C'est une erreur, ains une heresie, de vouloir bannir la vie devote de la compagnie des soldats, de la boutique des artisans, de la cour des princes, du menage des gens mariez.[24]

The contemplative life, he assures Philothée, may indeed be incompatible with these occupations; but religious worship as practiced in a monastery is not the only form of devotion which is acceptable to God. Here we see

22. Preface.   23. I, 2.   24. I, 3.

that St. François is very far from the spirit of Port-Royal; he rejects the all-or-nothing attitude of a Pascal, and earnestly believes that we may love God while still doing the work of this world.

Part of Philothée's training, in fact, consists of learning how to pass easily back and forth between prayer and the conscientious fulfillment of her household or wifely duties. She is not asked to renounce her husband or her home in order to become a nun. Similarly, the lawyer and the merchant who aspire to the devout life must be able to turn rapidly from their prayers to their work. This spiritual flexibility is an essential of St. François' conception of the devout life.

> Il faut mesme que vous vous accoustumiez a scavoir passer de l'oraison a toutes sortes d'occasion que vostre vocation et profession requiert justement et legitimement de vous, quoy qu'elles semblent bien esloignées des affections que nous avons receues en l'oraison. Je veux dire, un advocat doit sçavoir passer de l'oraison a la plaidoyerie, le marchant au trafic, la femme mariée au devoir de son mariage et au tracas de son mesnage, avec tant de douceur et tranquillité, que pour cela son esprit n'en soit point troublé . . .[25]

The *Introduction à la vie dévote* is obviously not directed toward those who live in monasteries and convents. For those of us who are the true audience of this book, the neglect of our responsibilities toward the world and an excessive abandonment to prayer constitute a form of self-indulgence.

That St. François does not wish us to turn our backs on the activities of everyday life is evident not only from direct statements like the above but also from the nature of his imagery. In his attempt to make us love the devout life, he draws the majority of his metaphors and illustrations from familiar human experience, and from the natural world. This is no mere concession to the weakness of worldly readers; the saint deeply believes that this world is created by God, and that there are significant parallels between the phenomena of life on earth and the nature of God Himself. We can see in the saint's metaphors an affectionate enthusiasm for all created things: like God, he loves the world.

To begin with, he loves children. Perhaps his most effective picture of the proper attitude toward God and earthly pleasures is the following little scene. I call it a scene because, like so many of the author's more successful metaphors, it combines visual appeal and movement:

> Faictes comme les petits enfans, qui de l'une des mains se tiennent a leur pere, et de l'autre cueillent des fraises, ou des meures le long des hayes. Car de mesme amassant et maniant les biens de ce monde de l'une de vos mains; tenez tousjours

25. II, 8.

de l'autre la main de Pere celeste, vous retournant de temps en temps a luy, pour voir s'il agreable vostre mesnage ou vos occupations.[26]

As a matter of fact, sight is not the only sense to which he appeals here. Touch is evoked, since the child is holding his father's hand; and the strawberries and blackberries suggest smell and taste. The feeling of movement is vividly present: walking along the hedgerow, picking berries, and above all the admirable detail of the child who occasionally turns to look up at the expression in his father's face. Behind it all is the antithesis between God and the world; yet this antithesis is happily reconciled. It is the conscious and simultaneous fusion of these various elements which makes the baroque style.

Here is another scenic metaphor where St. François makes use of children and the countryside:

Si-tost que vous sentes en vous quelques tentations, faictes comme les petits enfans quand ils voyent le loup ou l'ours en la campagne. Car tout aussi-tost ils courent entre les bras de leur pere ou de leur mere, ou pour le moins les appellent a leur aide et secours.[27]

The ideas behind this passage are of course familiar ones: "Except ye be converted, and become as little children, ye shall not enter into the kingdom of heaven," and "Lead us not into temptation, but deliver us from evil." But the artist has blended the two together, and created with delicate humor and tenderness a visual scene.

It is characteristic of the art of St. François that the simplicity of these scenes often veils mystical concepts of some complexity. For instance,

Un enfant pleurera tendrement s'il voit donner un coup de lancette a sa mere qu'on saigne; mais si a mesme temps sa mere pour laquelle il pleuroit luy demande une pomme, ou un cornet de dragee qu'il tient en sa main, il ne le voudra nullement lascher.[28]

What is the meaning of this little vignette? We weep when we see the lance piercing the heart of Christ crucified, but when He asks us to give Him the apple which we clutch in our hand—our heart—we are reluctant to yield it. Similarly,

Les petits enfans s'affectionnent et s'eschauffent apres les papillons, nul ne le treuve mauvais, parce qu'ils sont enfans . . .[29]

but it is a silly and regrettable thing when grown men spend their time running after trivial, worldly pleasures. In all these passages, while the saint

26. III, 10.　　27. IV, 7.　　28. IV, 13.　　29. I, 23.

shows much indulgent sympathy for human frailty, he never loses sight of the eternal verities. In one metaphor, concerning the attitudes of parents toward their children, he is more severe:

Il y a des enfans vertueux, que leurs peres et meres ne peuvent presque voir pour quelque imperfection corporelle. Il y en a des vicieux qui sont les favoris pour quelque grace corporelle.[30]

We ourselves are like these parents, he insists, when we prefer the rich to the poor, or well-dressed people to those who are poorly dressed.

One of the most curious metaphors in the *Introduction à la vie dévote* is concerned with pregnancy. Like the picture of the child who weeps when he sees the surgeon bleed his mother, it seeks to bring a theological mystery within the scope of normal human experience. This metaphor comes from a chapter entitled "Consideration de l'amour que Jesus-Christ nous porte":

Ouy, sans doute, comme une femme enceinte prepare le berceau, les linges et bandelettes, et mesme une nourrice, pour l'enfant qu'elle pretend faire, encore qu'il ne soit pas au monde: ainsi Nostre-Seigneur ayant sa bonté grosse et enceinte de vous, pretendant de vous enfanter au salut, et vous rendre sa fille, prepara sur l'arbre de la croix tout ce qu'il falloit pour vous: vostre berceau spiri-tuel, vos linges et bandelettes, vostre nourrice, et tout ce qui estoit convenable pour vostre bonheur.[31]

The doctrine that Christ, as he suffered on the Cross, was individually think-ing of each one of us is a traditional Christian belief. Pascal has devoted the most moving lines of his *Mystère de Jésus* to this subject. It must be ad-mitted that St. François de Sales, with his rather farfetched analogy of the pregnant woman preparing for childbirth, is less successful. But often the failures of a literary style can be as instructive for the critic as the successes. The fact that this metaphor is not very good may teach us something about the saint's imagery. We feel here that he has tried too hard to find an ingenious and surprising comparison between religious truth and every-day life. Like all baroque artists, he enjoys expressing intangible ideas in concrete form. Here Christ's love is pregnant with Philothée; He is about to give birth to her spiritual life; He is preparing the cradle and the swaddling clothes. Artistically, this just does not work: partly because the images are too detailed and physical, partly because there are too many of them. St François is rarely content with a single image; he generally builds an elaborate succession of images into a scene. Finally, an art which is concerned with correspondences should make sure that the correspondences are really appropriate.

30. III, 36.   31. V, 13.

St. François' interest in normal human experience is by no means limited to the bearing and raising of children. Since Philothée, the imaginary reader, is a woman, it has seemed fitting to begin a discussion of the daily-life images there; but the saint's powers of sympathetic observation range over many other aspects of Philothée's life. There are many metaphors concerned with housekeeping, and others with the care of the sick. Finally, the author goes beyond the woman's sphere and draws illustrations from masculine occupations. Like Montaigne, he takes delight in the infinite variety of human activity. Each little scene reveals the artist's eye for detail. Let us look at a few of the household pictures.

The author knows that Philothée, like most women, spends time in front of her mirror. And here the mirror becomes a symbol of the fact that we can reach God the Father only through the Son. You may wonder by what curious process St. François achieves this analogy:

> . . . tout ainsi que la glace d'un mirouer ne sçauroit arrester nostre veue, si elle n'estoit enduite d'estain ou de plomb par derriere, aussi la divinité ne pourroit estre bien contemplee par nous en ce bas monde, si elle ne fust jointe a la sacree humanité du Sauveur . . .[32]

The symbol may possibly be more complex than the writer intended. The metal behind the glass enables us to see the reflection in the mirror; the humanity of Christ enables us to see God. However, what we actually see in the mirror is ourselves. Does St. François mean that through Christ's mediation we arrive at self-knowledge?

Other household images are simpler. There is, for example, the one based on sugar and salt:

> Le sucre est plus excellent que le sel: mais le sel a un usage plus frequent et plus general.[33]

This illustrates one of the saint's favorite themes: we have more occasion to practice simple everyday virtues than extraordinary ones. Munificence and magnanimity may seem more impressive than moderation and humility; but the latter are more useful in the average life.

There is also the picture of the person carrying home a precious liquid in a pitcher:

> Un homme qui aurait receu dans un vaisseau de belle porcelaine quelque liqueur de grand prix, pour l'apporter dans sa maison, il iroit doucement, ne regardant point a costé, mais tantost devant soy, de peur de heurter a quelque pierre, faire quelque mauvais pas, tantost a son vase, pour voir s'il panche point . . .[34]

32. II, 1. 33. III, 1. 34. II, 8.

In just this way, Philothée, when she has finished her prayers, should avoid distractions, occasionally looking straight ahead to see whether duty requires her to talk to others, but occasionally looking at her own heart so as to make sure not to spill the liqueur of holy prayer. Again we have multiple-sense imagery (the beautiful porcelain vase, the liqueur, the possibility of stumbling on a stone or of spilling the liquid) combined with movement.

Or let Philothée consider the coals in her fireplace:

Avez-vous jamais vu, Philothée, un grand brazier de feu couvert de cendres; quand on vient dix ou douze heures apres pour y chercher du feu, on n'en treuve qu'un peu au milieu du foyer, et encore on a peine de le treuver. Il y estoit neantmoins, puisqu'on l'y treuve: et avec iceluy on peut rallumer tous les autres charbons desja esteints.[35]

Charity, St. François tells her, is like these live coals buried under the ashes of the hearth. If we have any charity still alive in the depths of our soul, we can revive the spiritual flame within us and conquer the most violent temptations.

In fact, Philothée need only look around at the furniture of her house to find analogies with the devout life. If she is a widow, for example, there is a lesson to be learned from her lamps:

Les lampes, desquelles l'huyle est aromatique, jettent une plus suave odeur quand on esteint leurs flammes: ainsi les vefves, desquelles l'amour a esté pur en leur mariage, respandent un plus grand parfum de vertu et chasteté quand leur lumiere, c'est a dire leur mary, est esteinte par la mort . . .[36]

This is a particularly baroque metaphor. First of all, there is the appeal to two different senses: sight and smell, the light of the lamp and the perfume of the oil. Then there is the contrast between two transformations: the light goes out, and in the darkness the perfume grows stronger.

Since the care of the sick is a part of every woman's life, the *Introduction* utilizes this kind of experience too. Perhaps Philothée has had to look after hypochondriacs who are always taking medicine for trifling ailments. They are like people who worry too much about their own reputation:

. . . ceux qui sont si douillets et sensibles pour leur reputation ressemblent a ceux qui pour toutes sortes de petites incommoditez prennent des medecines: car ceux-cy, pensant conserver leur santé, la gastent tout-a-faict; et ceux-la, voulant maintenir si delicatement leur reputation, le perdent entierement.[37]

For human beings find even very slight pains hard to bear; since this is true, how infinitely more intolerable will be the torments of hell:

35. III, 3.   36. III, 40.   37. III, 7.

Helas! si une puce en nostre oreille, si la chaleur d'une petite fievre nous rend une courte nuict si longue et ennuyeuse, combien sera espouvantable la nuict de l'eternité avec tant de tourmens . . .[38]

This meditation on hell, which is probably somewhat inspired by the *Spiritual Exercises* of St. Ignatius Loyola, is one of the few places where St. François seriously tries to frighten Philothée. If Mr. Seymour is correct in his view that the founding of the Jesuit order is a mannerist rather than a baroque enterprise, and Mr. Pevsner in his judgment that the Gesù in Rome is mannerist, not baroque,[39] this particular passage should perhaps also be linked with the earlier of the two styles. In any event, it is characterized by angoisse rather than by the saint's customary happy resolution of difficulties. Usually the *Introduction* takes a more hopeful view of apparently tragic situations:

Quand un homme est pasme et qu'il ne rend aucun tesmoignage de vie, on luy met la main sur le cœur, et pour peu que l'on y sente de mouvement, on juge qu'il est en vie, et que par le moyen de quelque eau precieuse et de quelque epitheme, on peut luy faire reprendre force et sentiment; ainsi arrive-t-il quelquefois que par la violence des tentations il semble que nostre ame est tombee en quelque defaillance totale de ses forces, et que comme estant pasmee elle n'a plus ny vie spirituelle, ny mouvement; mais si nous voulons connoistre ce que c'en est, mettons la main sur le cœur.[40]

Philothée, even in the most alarming cases of illness or accident around her, is encouraged to hope, and to find in this hope an intimation of the mercy of God.

The variety of St. François' metaphors is the measure of his sympathetic interest in all human activity. Those we have seen thus far have centered chiefly around the housewife. But the author's range is greater than this: there are in the *Introduction* vignettes of many different occupations, reminiscent in their liveliness and detail of the work of the contemporary engravers, Jacques Callot and Abraham Bosse. And so we go beyond Philothée's home into the world of the artisan, the mariner, the courtier, and the hunter. The saint has observed embroiderers of gold cloth at work. Their technique has suggested to him an analogy with the spiritual life: the greatest saints, he declares, have made a speciality of some particular kind of good work —St. Louis nursed the sick in charity hospitals, St. Francis dedicated himself to poverty, St. Dominic was a great preacher, St. Gregory looked after pilgrims, and so on:

38. I, 15.
39. Cf. Nikolaus Pevsner, "The Architecture of Mannerism," in *The Mint*, ed. Geoffrey Grigson, London, Routledge, 1946.
40. IV, 5.

En quoy ils imitent les brodeurs, qui sur divers fonds couchent en belle varieté les soyes, l'or et l'argent, pour en faire toutes sortes de fleurs: car ainsi ces ames pieuses, qui entreprennent quelque particulier exercice de devotion, se servent d'iceluy comme d'un fonds pour leur broderie spirituelle, sur lequel elles practiquent la varieté de toutes les autres vertus . . .[41]

This picture is, in a way, an apt description of St. François' own life and work. His specialty is introducing worldly people to the devout life; against this background he has been able to practice the variety of all the other virtues. Still more appropriately, the metaphor describes his literary style: the cloth stands for the pedagogic purpose of his writing, and the rich variety of silk and gold and silver represents his imagery, which we are studying here. Let us look at some more examples of his "embroidery."

The art of the navigator interested St. François because he saw in its basic problem a parallel to that of the Christian: how to find one's way. And so we have two metaphors, one connected with star sights and the other with the compass. The first occurs in a chapter devoted to the distracting influence of small daily duties:

Et quand les affaires sont de si grande importance, qu'ils requierent toute votre attention pour estre bien-faicts, de temps en temps vous regarderez a Dieu, comme font ceux qui naviguent en mer, lesquels, pour arriver a la terre qu'ils desirent, regardent plus en haut au ciel que non pas en bas ou ils voguent . . .[42]

Notice that the saint as usual does not tell us to neglect our temporal affairs, but when our necessary business presses on us so much that we feel "at sea," we should look up at the heavens; by celestial navigation we shall be able to keep to our course. The second nautical metaphor is found in a chapter which deals with the mutability of the world—that aspect which fascinated Montaigne also and made him declare, "le monde n'est qu'une branloire perenne." [43] St. François, like the Montaigne of the *Apologie,* felt that without divine revelation we can arrive at no stable conclusions about the universe, and that we can know only phenomena which are in perpetual mutation.[44]

Et quoyque toutes choses se tournent et varient diversement autour de nous, il nous faut demeurer constamment immobiles a tousjours regarder, tendre et pretendre a nostre Dieu. Que le navire prenne telle route qu'on voudra, qu'il cingle au ponant ou levant, au midi ou septentrion, et quelque vent que ce soit qui le porte; jamais pourtant son eguille marine ne regardera que sa belle estoile et le pole.[45]

41. III, 1.   42. III, 10.   43. *Essais,* III, 2, 27.
44. Cf. *Essais,* II, 12, 367.   45. IV, 13.

It is interesting to note that another great baroque prose-writer, Sir Thomas Browne, whose style has many points of affinity with that of St. François de Sales (animal images, expression of the picturesque variety of the world, illustration of an idea from different points of view in rapid succession, the blending of concreteness and movement), has been struck by this same compass symbol. It is to him, amid the amazing flux of natural phenomena, an evidence of the miraculous:

> I could never content my contemplation with those general pieces of wonder, the Flux and Reflux of the Sea, the increase of the Nile, the conversion of the Needle to the North . . .[46]

There is little doubt that St. François thought of it in the same way: his mind is lost in wonder at the picturesque variety and mutability of created things, but in this one amazing property of the compass needle he sees a parallel with the soul which forever tends toward God. Of course, both as a literary artist and as a religious thinker, the saint is forever ready to feel pleasurable astonishment at natural phenomena for their own sake and to see in them evidences and symbols of the miraculous power of God.

Details of the behavior of courtiers or pilgrims can be equally instructive. The following vignette, though applicable to the saint's own day, really anticipates the reign of Louis XIV, as described by Saint-Simon:

> Combien de courtisans y a-t'il qui vont cent fois l'annee en la chambre du prince sans esperance de luy parler, mais seulement pour estre veuz de luy, et rendre leur devoir . . .[47]

We may wonder in what way this little picture corresponds to our religious life. The explanation follows: Just as courtiers pay their respects regularly to the king, so we should say our prayers regularly to God, and we should continue to do so even if we feel no immediate spiritual benefit. (The chapter in question discusses methods of dealing with our periods of spiritual dryness.) The pilgrim metaphor is also concerned with prayer, although of a different kind:

> Le pelerin qui prend un peu de vin pour rejouir son cœur et rafraischir sa bouche, bien qu'il s'arreste un peu, pour cela ne rompt pourtant pas son voyage, ains prend de la force, pour le plus vistement et aysement parachever, ne s'arrestant que pour mieux aller.[48]

St. François is here recommending that, in our journey through life, we should occasionally pause to refresh ourselves by "oraisons jaculatoires," or ardent, lyrical prayers of yearning toward God.

46. *Religio medici*, 15.   47. II, 9.   48. II, 13.

Then there are images taken from sports and games: for example, from archery and card playing. The writer's fondness for discovering hidden analogies between daily activities and spiritual truths may be appreciated from the fact that the taut bow suggests two very different symbolical interpretations. The first case occurs in a discussion of slander. The saint points out that politely apologetic prefaces to unkind remarks actually have the effect of making the backbiting words sink in deeper. ("Far be it from me to criticize him, but . . ." "She is a very nice person, but . . .") This bit of psychological observation is very much in the manner of Montaigne, as is also the image:

Ne voyez-vous pas l'artifice? celuy qui veut tirer a l'arc tire tant qu'il peut la fleche a soy, mais c'est pour la darder plus puissamment.[49]

The other archery metaphor is an episode from the life of St. John the Evangelist. A hunter had found him playing with a partridge perched on his fist, and had expressed astonishment that so great a man should amuse himself with so trivial a thing. (We are reminded of Montaigne, criticized for playing with his cat: "Who knows whether she is playing with me, or I with her!") St. John's reply to the hunter was:

. . . pourquoy ne portes-tu ton arc tousjours tendu? De peur, respondit le chasseur, que, demeurant tousjours courbe, il ne perde la force de s'estendre quand il en sera mestier. Ne t'estonne pas doncques, repliqua l'apostre, si je me demets quelque peu de la rigueur et attention de mon esprit pour prendre un peu de recreation, afin de m'employer par apres plus vivement a la contemplation.[50]

St. François is pointing out in this chapter that recreation is not only permissible but actually necessary for spiritual health. It is characteristic of the saint that in both cases he gives the image of the taut bow an unfavorable interpretation. Like the Montaigne of the last essays, he feels that goodness is more related to relaxation than to strain. In fact, the card-playing metaphor is employed to refute the customary accusation, made by worldly people, that the religious life requires a gloomy tension of the spirit:

Nous avons veu des gentilhommes et des dames passer la nuict entiere, ains plusieurs nuicts de suite a jouer aux eschecs et aux cartes: y a-t-il une attention plus chagrine, plus melancholique et plus sombre que celle-la? les mondains neantmoins ne disoient mot, les amis ne se mettoient point en peine, et pour la meditation d'une heure, ou pour nous voir lever un peu plus matin qu'a l'ordinaire pour nous preparer a la communion, chascun court au medecin pour nous faire guerir de l'humeur hypocondriaque et de la jaunisse.[51]

49. III, 29.   50. III, 31.   51. IV, 1.

This little sketch of the grim faces of the gamblers at their all-night session is reminiscent of the art of Callot. The structure of the passage as a whole has affinities with the style of Montaigne. First we have the picture of the card players, then the rhetorical question and its gently ironic answer. Then there is the contrasting picture of the devout, calmly rising early to go to Communion. There are further shifts of tone and pace in the concluding phrase; with renewed irony, the writer pictures the worldly rushing to the doctor to find out what unattractive disease afflicts the devout. The writer's attention darts from one scene to another; his mood varies from one phrase to the next; the rhythm is now fast, now slow to fit the changes in mood; but, despite all these variations, there is a unity of theme. It should be observed that this is one of the few passages of the *Introduction* which reveal disgust rather than sympathetic interest at the ordinary occupations of men.

I think that the reader must have been struck, in our discussion of St. François' imagery, with the saint's enjoyment of the picturesque diversity of human affairs. And yet, in another way, his whole book tends toward the unity of God. Both stylistically and ideologically, unity and diversity (and the contrast between them) are the underlying theme of the *Introduction,* as of the *Essais*. The saint loves God and loves the infinite variety of His creation. So it is that his sympathy goes beyond human life; in the whole of French literature, probably only Colette and La Fontaine have as great a curiosity about and affection for animals. It must be admitted that animals play a considerable part in the imagery and illustrative examples of Montaigne's *Essais*. We have not only Montaigne's cat, of whom mention has just been made, but also the lengthy fantastic catalogue of feats of animal intelligence in the *Apologie;* nevertheless, Montaigne is interested in animals primarily for intellectual reasons, rather than for love. When he tells of a magpie who learned how to imitate the music of trumpets, or discusses the possible religious feeling of elephants, his aim is to humble man's conviction of superiority; and in general he is interested by animals because they contribute to the astonishing diversity of the world. With this latter sentiment, of course, St. François would be in complete agreement—it is, in fact, a baroque attitude; but it is also evident that he loves animals for their own sake. Neither Montaigne's nor St. François' attitude has been possible for French intellectuals since Descartes: fundamentally, animals remain machines even in the twentieth century, except for those who, like Colette, are more intuitive than intellectual. The imagination of Colette is of course more pagan than Christian; but while modern French Catholic writers may take it for granted that animals have no souls, the seventeenth-century baroque saint has not yet arrived at so dogmatic a solution of this question.

When I speak of St. François' love of animals, I should, as a matter of fact, broaden the term so as to include birds and insects; and finally, without attempting to define the saint's belief as to which of God's creatures have souls, I should point out that, like his namesake from Assisi, he deeply loves flowers and fruits and trees.

It seems to me that the saint's interest in nature, as reflected in his imagery, may be divided into three main categories—at least if we are to judge by the mere frequency of references. The first of these would be concerned with the normal fauna and flora of Savoy, such as would be likely to be encountered by his friends and neighbors in the countryside around Annecy. Among these we should include deer, owls, chestnut trees, violets, butterflies, nightingales, wolves, mules, cherries, apricots, chickens, goats, etc. A second category, not really distinct from the first except that the examples are so numerous as to constitute a very special interest on the writer's part, is devoted to bees and honey. This interest is, after all, natural on the part of one living in the Alps. And finally, there are those exotic beasts which have never been seen in Savoy, but which delight the saint because they are strange and picturesque and demonstrate the infinite variety of creation: elephants, parrots, crocodiles, and so forth.

Let us begin with nature in the saint's own countryside. The reader may very plausibly object that there are no ostriches on the shores of the Lake of Annecy. The other birds in my first example, however, have nothing exotic about them, and the metaphor as a whole beautifully expresses the writer's half-humorous wonder at the marvelous diversity of nature:

Les autruches ne volent jamais, les poules volent pesamment, toutesfois basse-ment et rarement; mais les aigles, les colombes, les arondelles volent souvent, vistement et hautement . . .

Returning to the fundamental aim of the book, we may be pardoned for asking what is the purpose of this curious illustration. It is obvious that ostriches, hens, eagles, pigeons, and swallows amuse St. François; but what is he driving at? The explanation follows:

. . . les pecheurs ne volent point en Dieu, ains font toutes leurs courses en la terre, et pour la terre. Les gens de bien qui n'ont pas encore atteint la devotion volent en Dieu par leurs bonnes actions, mais rarement, lentement et pesamment; les personnes devotes volent en Dieu frequemment, promptement et hautement.[52]

In other words, most of us, for whom the book is written, are ostriches—or at best hens.

It is presumably through the report of travelers that St. François knew that

52. I, I.

ostriches do not fly, whereas personal observation had taught him that it is difficult for chickens to do so; and similarly, his own life in Savoy had given him opportunities to learn the habits of deer: when they have grown too fat, they withdraw from their enemies into the depths of the forests:

> Les cerfs ayant pris trop de venaison s'escartent et retirent dedans leurs buissons, cognoissant que leur graisse les charge, en sorte qu'ils ne sont pas habiles a courir, si d'avanture ils estoient attaquez . . .

This is an illustration of what happens to man when he weighs himself down with the love of useless and dangerous things:

> . . . le cœur de l'homme se chargeant de ces affections inutiles, superflues et dangereuses, ne peut sans doute promptement, aysement et facilement courir apres son Dieu, qui est le vray poinct de la devotion.[53]

The same illustration is repeated in another place, but this time with the object of proving that excessive mortification can be as dangerous as excessive indulgence of the flesh—an idea which conforms very much to the saint's ideal of the golden mean:

> Les cerfs courent mal en deux temps, quand ils sont trop chargez de venaison, et quand ils sont trop maigres. Nous sommes grandement exposez aux tentations quand nostre corps est trop nourry et quand il est trop abattu . . .[54]

Birds and deer are combined in a metaphor illustrating the desirability of spiritual retreats:

> Comme les oyseaux ont des nids sur les arbres pour faire leur retraite, quand ils en ont besoin, et les cerfs ont leurs buissons et leurs forts, dans lesquels ils se recellent et mettent a couvert, prenant la fraischeur de l'ombre en esté; ainsi, Philothée, nos cœurs doivent prendre et choisir quelque place chaque jour . . . pour y faire leur retraicte a toutes sortes d'occasions . . .[55]

It is the inclusion of the sensuous detail—the coolness of shade in summer—that constitutes the specifically baroque touch here.

In a passage evidently inspired by the Sanctus of the Mass, the saint urges us to join with angels and archangels and all the company of heaven in praising God. There is a parallel for this in the way in which nightingales learn how to sing:

> Ma Philothée, joignons nos cœurs à ces celestes esprits, et ames bienheureuses: car comme les petits rossignols apprennent à chanter avec les grands, ainsi par le sainct commerce que nous ferons avec les Saincts, nous sçaurons bien mieux prier et chanter les louanges divines . . .[56]

53. I, 23.   54. III, 23.   55. II, 12.   56. II, 16.

I do not know whether it is really true that adult nightingales teach the young ones how to sing; in painting this pleasant picture the writer may have been carried away by his love of nature. Similarly, in the following example, which deals with the harmful effect of goats' tongues on almond trees, St. François probably shows himself to be too ready to believe in curious natural phenomena:

Car comme les boucs, touchant de la langue les amandiers doux, les font devenir amers, ainsi ces ames puantes et cœurs infects ne parlent gueres a personne, ny de mesme sexe, ny de divers sexe, qu'elles ne le fassent aucunement dechoir de la pudicité: elles ont le venin aux yeux et en l'haleine comme les basilics.[57]

As is generally the case, the above passage may be regarded as baroque in several different ways. There is an amusing element of grotesque realism in the picture of the licking goats, and of course the phenomenon has been selected as one more example of the surprising diversity of the world. The parallel established here—with the conversation of immoral people—is in itself somewhat surprising. As a matter of fact, many of the saint's analogies have this quality of unexpectedness. Baroque writers enjoy finding far-fetched symbolic correspondences between things. Then there is the great interest in transformations, which we have already discussed at some length; the passage is essentially a comparison of two metamorphoses. At the end, after the word "pudicité," an entirely new set of images is brought in—the poisonous eyes and breath of basilisks. With this new illustration, the writer is looking at his subject from a new angle. But St. François' multiple-aspect imagery is an important topic in itself, which will require further analysis in another place.

Despite the unusual breadth of his sympathies, there are indeed certain animals which the saint does not like very much. Among these are not only goats, as we have just seen, but also mules:

Helas! les mulets laissent-ils d'estre lourdes et puantes bestes, pour estre chargez de meubles precieux et parfumez du prince?[58]

What is the religious connection here? This is a lesson in humility. The good works which we perform come to us by the grace of God; they do not belong to us any more than the prince's treasures belong to the mule. Considered in ourselves, we are merely ponderous and smelly beasts. Sir Thomas Browne, the English Protestant baroque writer, is perhaps more catholic than St. François in his acceptance of all animals:

57. III, 13.   58. III, 5.

I hold there is a general beauty in the works of God, and therefore no deformity in any kind of species of creature whatsoever: I cannot tell by what Logick we call a Toad, a Bear, or an Elephant ugly . . .[59]

Yet St. François, as I have remarked, does go much further than most French writers in his liking for animals; and in a moment we shall see how great is his interest in the exotic beasts.

Trees and plants also have an important place in the imagery of the *Introduction*. Thus, the just man is compared to a tree growing by a stream:

Le juste est comme l'arbre qui est plante sur le cours des eaux, qui porte son fruict en son temps, parce que la charité arrousant une ame, produit en elle les œuvres vertueuses chacune en sa saison.[60]

But elsewhere, a walnut tree suggests a very different comparison: it prevents crops from growing and is therefore like a love affair, which hinders the development of our spiritual life:

Le noyer nuit grandement aux vignes et aux champs, esquels il est planté, parce qu'estant si grand il attire tout le suc de la terre, qui ne peut par apres suffire a nourrir le reste des plantes: ses feuillages sont si touffus, qu'ils font un ombrage grand et espais, et enfin il attire les passans a soy, qui pour abattre son fruict, gastent et foulent tout autour. Ces amourettes font les mesmes nuisances a l'ame: car elles l'occupent tellement, et tirent si puissamment ses mouvements, qu'elle ne peut pas apres suffire a aucune bonne œuvre . . .[61]

The writer goes on to explain that the foliage of the tree corresponds to the flirtatious conversations of a love affair, the trampling of the earth around the tree to temptations and jealousies. The metaphor is developed in remarkable detail, so that it becomes in effect a dramatic scene in a landscape. Considered as a whole, this kind of imagery in the *Introduction* constitutes a kind of landscape painting—or a compendium of agricultural knowledge. The leaves of trees do not seem to have much value in themselves, but they protect young fruit; similarly, a good reputation serves to protect our budding virtues.[62] Some fruits, like the quince, are so sour that they are not good unless made into jam; others, like cherries and apricots, are so perishable that they too should be preserved as rapidly as possible. This is an illustration of the principle that religion is equally necessary for men and women; it sweetens the sourness of the former and preserves the fragile virtue of the latter! [63] Winter strikes down the beauty of the countryside and benumbs all the animals; worldly sadness does the same thing to our

59. *Religio medici*, 16.   60. III, 1.   61. III, 18.
62. III, 7.   63. III, 38.

spiritual life.[64] A devout widow is like a March violet, spreading forth the perfume of her piety: she is always hidden under the wide leaves of her humility; her color expresses the subduing of the passions; she grows in cool, remote spots, where she can preserve the freshness of her heart from the heat of worldly desires.[65]

Among the nature metaphors of the *Introduction,* one group is so important as to deserve special study: those referring to bees and honey. With a few exceptions, which we shall note, bees and honey have a favorable symbolic meaning for St. François de Sales. Generally speaking, he invites us to observe bees and to imitate them. As early as the second chapter of the book they are proposed as models of conduct:

Regardez les abeilles sur le thin, elles y treuvent un suc fort amer; mais en le suçant, elles le convertissent en miel . . .[66]

The pious, St. François assures us, act in a corresponding manner: their spiritual exercises and mortifications of the flesh may be bitter at first, but are all transformed into sweetness and softness. The metamorphosis theme merges in the next sentence into the antithesis and illusion vs. reality themes:

. . . les feux, les flammes, les roues et les espées sembloient des fleurs et des parfumes aux martyrs, parce qu'ils estoient devots.

The honey made from Alpine wild thyme is, as a matter of fact, famous to this day. A little further on, our attention is directed to another good quality of bees: they do not harm the flowers where they gather their honey. However, religion is still better, for it not only does not have a bad effect on our other activities but actually is an ornament to them. Passing from bees to honey, the writer states that precious stones thrown into honey become more brilliant, each according to its own color; even so, "la devotion" heightens the sparkle of every good human action.[67] In rapid succession, two different images express the same concept from slightly different points of view.

The good bees have enemies; the apiculturists of Annecy know that spiders are a pest, though not a mortally dangerous one. St. François explains this to us in an effort to make us comprehend the nature of venial sins:

Les araignes ne tuent pas les abeilles, mais elles gastent et corrompent leur miel, et embarrassent leurs rayons des toiles qu'elles y font, en sorte que les abeilles ne peuvent plus faire leur mesnage, et cela s'entend quand elles y font du sejour: ainsi le peché veniel ne tue pas nostre ame, mais il gaste pourtant la devotion . . .[68]

64. IV, 12.   65. III, 40.   66. I, 2.
67. I, 3.   68. I, 22.

Developing the image further, he warns us that, if we do not clean out these venial sins,

> . . . bien-tost nous verrons nostre miel perdu, et la ruche de nostre conscience empestrée et defaicte.

The bee even becomes a symbol of the priest giving the Host to the communicant:

> O Philothée! imaginez-vous que comme l'abeille, ayant recueilly sur les fleurs la rosee du ciel et le suc plus exquis de la terre, et l'ayant reduit en miel, le porte dans sa ruche; ainsi le prestre, ayant pris sur l'autel le Sauveur du monde, vray Fils de Dieu, qui comme une rosée est descendu du ciel, et vray Fils de la Vierge qui comme fleur est sorti de la terre de nostre humanite, il le met en viande de suavité dedans vostre bouche, et dedans vostre corps.[69]

This metaphor deserves comment. The dogmas of Incarnation and Transubstantiation are of particular interest to the baroque artist. A dominant concern of the baroque style in literature is to give concrete expression to intangible concepts. The writer is a creator, and within his own limited field is attempting to do what St. John describes in the first chapter of his Gospel: "The word became flesh, and dwelt among us." But he is also deeply interested in metamorphoses, and the greatest of these is the miraculous transformation of the bread and wine into the body and blood of Christ. Here St. François expresses these ideas in images drawn from the daily life of the peasants of Savoy—bees, flowers, dew, honey, beehives—and his picture appeals simultaneously to the senses of sight, smell, and taste. The richness, complexity, and movement of the metaphor are altogether extraordinary; they suggest the painting of Rubens, or the sculpture of Bernini.

Bees are commended also because of their horror of what is corrupt:

> Les abeilles non-seulement ne veulent pas toucher les charognes, mais fuyent et hayssent extremement toutes sortes de puanteurs qui en proviennent.[70]

We should follow their example, and through an instinctive feeling of horror avoid what is unchaste and sinful. Bees are also contrasted with other insects which are either useless or harmful, such as drones or wasps:

> Les bourdons font bien plus de bruit et sont bien plus empressez que les abeilles; mais ils ne font sinon la cire, et non point de miel: ainsi ceux qui s'empressent d'un soucy cuisant et d'une solicitude bruyante ne font jamais ny beaucoup ny bien.[71]

(Though St. François does not refer to it in this passage, in contrasting the officious drones with the constructive bees he probably has in mind the contrast between Martha and Mary in St. Luke 10.)

69. II, 21.   70. III, 13.   71. III, 10.

The difference between a swarm of bees and a swarm of wasps is symbolically representative of the difference between kindly social intercourse and malicious gossip. Conversation should be

> . . . comme essaims d'abeilles, assemblees pour faire le miel de quelque doux et vertueux entretien, et non pas comme un tas de guespes, qui se joignent pour succer quelque pourriture.[72]

This concept of the art of conversation is not so far removed from that expressed by Montaigne in his *Art de conferer,* and the imagery, lively and homely, is similar to much of that in the *Essais.*

Bees can at times be unpleasant, and St. François, whose view of the world is after all remarkably practical—despite his intense piety he is scarcely less so than Montaigne—does not attempt to conceal this fact. But even in the sting of the bee he finds moral instruction:

> Car tout ainsi que les picqueures des abeilles sont plus cuisantes que celles des mouches, ainsi le mal que l'on reçoit des gens de bien, et les contradictions qu'ils font, sont bien plus insupportables que les autres . . .[73]

The bee, even with its sting, remains a symbol of good. However, sometimes bees can be corrupted, and their honey, which ordinarily in the *Introduction* stands for all good qualities, may be dangerous. This is the case of the honey of Heraclea, in Asia Minor:

> Certes, les abeilles qui amassent le miel d'Heraclée ne cherchent que la miel, mais avec le miel elles succent insensiblement les qualitez veneneuses de l'aconit sur lequel elles font leur cueillette.[74]

"Aconit" is translated into English as "dog's bane" or "wolf's bane"; and whatever the properties of this mysterious herb may be, for St. François it possesses strange powers of corruption, corresponding, in the moral world, to the destructive influence of evil friendships. The selection I have given constitutes only a fraction of the multitudinous bee images in the *Introduction.* We learn also that bees cannot stand noise, and that in this respect they resemble the Holy Ghost, which is never present in a house where there is much loud altercation; [75] bees in foggy weather remain in their hives, just as the thoughts of good souls never dwell upon murky subjects; [76] when spring weather is fine, bees make much honey, whereas if it is bad they produce their young; we should follow their example and be spiritually productive whether we find ourselves in a period of unhappiness or melancholy.[77] The saint never tires of finding analogies of the spiritual life in the bee.

72. III, 27.   73. III, 3.   74. III, 22.
75. III, 38.   76. III, 28.   77. IV, 14.

Before we leave the topic of nature imagery, we should mention the important place occupied by exotic animals. The *Introduction* reflects not only the civilized world of the gardens and farms of France but also reveals its author's awareness of strange foreign beasts. God's creation is even more varied and wonderful than may appear in the countryside of Savoy. There the most unusual creatures are perhaps the peacock and the wild boar. St. François mentions them both in passing: the strutting peacock is an example of the human male showing off to seduce a woman; [78] the boar, sharpening their tusks against their teeth, teach us to develop our virtues in competition against each other.[79] But in speaking of exotic creatures I really mean those not normally seen in Europe. For example, the lioness:

La lyonne qui a este accostee du leopard va vistement se laver pour oster la puanteur que cette accointance luy a laissee, afin que le lyon venant n'en soit point offensé et irrité.[80]

Whenever I present to you some of the more curious specimens of the saint's imagery, it is a little like a guessing game: what can be the meaning of this picture of the lioness who has mated with a leopard and is trying to wash away his scent? This time the analogy is even more bizarre than usual, and by its very strangeness should convince us, if we still remain skeptical, of the writer's baroque sensibility. The chapter is entitled "De la saincte confession," and St. François is illustrating the nature of this sacrament.

Throughout the sixteenth and early seventeenth centuries, voyages of exploration to America were an exciting novelty; it is not surprising that they should be reflected in literary works, such as Rabelais' *Quart livre* or Montaigne's essay *Des cannibales*. St. François too mentions the conquistadores:

Car comme ceux qui viennent du Perou, outre l'or et l'argent qu'ils en tirent, apportent encore des singes et perroquets, parce qu'ils ne leur coustent gueres, et ne chargent pas aussi beaucoup leur navire . . .[81]

This means that those whose essential aim is to lead a virtuous life may accept rewards of rank and honor so long as these trivial distinctions do not cost them distracting amounts of trouble and time.

The elephant, in whose strange appearance Sir Thomas Browne refused to see deformity, and in whom Montaigne professed to see evidences of the religious instinct, has also attracted the attention of St. François. I do not know whether it is true that the sight of a baby lamb quiets an enraged elephant,

78. III, 20.   79. III, 1.   80. II, 19.   81. III, 4.

but the saint, in a chapter devoted to the general theme that a quiet answer turns away wrath, illustrates the idea with these two very different images:

> Rien ne matte tant l'elephant courroucé que la vue d'un agnelet, et rien ne rompt si aysement la force des canonades que la laine.[82]

He also has something to say about the sex life of the elephant, in a passage similar to his remarks on the lioness; the chapter in question discusses "l'honnesteté du lict nuptial":

> Il ne change jamais de femelle et ayme tendrement celle qu'il a choisie, avec laquelle il ne parie que de trois ans en trois ans, et cela pour cinq jours seulement, et si secretement que jamais il n'est vu en ceste acte; mais il est bien vu pourtant le sixieme jour, auquel avant toute chose il va droit a quelque riviere, en laquelle il se lave entierement tout le corps, sans vouloir aucunement retourner au troupeau, qu'il ne soit auparavant purifié.[83]

Once again the metaphor has become a vignette, full of concrete detail and dramatic interest. The baroque quality, however, does not reside in this alone but in the fact that so curious an image has been chosen to illustrate conjugal fidelity.

The crocodile is also present in the variegated world of the *Introduction à la vie dévote*. He is there to prove that virtuous persons need not fear slander:

> Les crocodiles n'endommagent que ceux qui les craignent ny certes la medisance sinon ceux qui s'en mettent en peine.[84]

The writers of the great classic generation hardly allow us to suspect that any world exists beyond the streets of Paris and the park of Versailles—or if it exists, it is a desert; St. François knows that beyond Annecy and Savoy there is Africa, full of picturesque marvels which testify to the glory of God. The saint's readiness to feel wonder at the infinite variety of creation leads him to a naïve belief in fabulous monsters. For into this category I put the salamander, despite the testimony of the autobiography of Benvenuto Cellini:

> On dit que la salamandre esteint le feu dans lequel elle se couche, et le peché ruine l'amitié en laquelle il se loge . . .[85]

In teaching us how to remain poor in spirit though surrounded by riches, he calls upon the example of that mythical bird, the halcyon:

> Les halcyons font leurs nids comme une paume, et ne laissent en iceux qu'une petite ouverture d'en haut; ils les mettent sur le bord de la mer, et au demeurant les font si fermes et impenetrables, que les ondes les surprenant, jamais l'eau n'y

82. III, 8.   83. III, 39.   84. III, 7.   85. III, 22.

peut entrer, ains tenant tousjours le dessus ils demeurent emmy la mer, sur la mer, et maistres de la mer.[86]

The description is as painstakingly detailed as that of a bird's nest in Savoy. The halcyon has never existed, but Philothée is asked to keep her heart like its nest, open only to heaven!

There remains to be discussed one other feature of St. François' style: multiple-aspect imagery. By this term I mean to characterize the writer's tendency to illustrate a single concept by a rapid succession of different metaphors. Each metaphor, constituting a separate picture, gives concrete expression to an aspect of the idea. The series as a whole gives us the impression of a man moving around an object to view it from different angles. In baroque city planning, architectural ensembles are generally arranged with the intention of encouraging the spectator to move and to obtain a succession of oblique views. There is no single symmetrical best view, but a series of picturesque aspects. Thus, if Bernini's plans for the Piazza San Pietro had been fully carried out, there would be an additional colonnade extending most of the way between the ends of the two existing ones, and leaving only enough space for two narrow oblique entrances to the square. We should thus be forced to approach the whole ensemble from an angle instead of from straight ahead. This would prevent us from feeling that there is a single best view (actually, the straight-ahead aspect, with the obelisk bisecting the façade of St. Peter's, is the least satisfactory), and would encourage us to roam at will through the area, pausing from time to time to admire a new and picturesque composition of columns, fountains, obelisk, dome, and façade. This is also the way in which we should look at the Piazza Navona. Here things are, from the baroque point of view, better arranged: Bernini's "Fountain of the Rivers" is not directly in front of Borromini's concave façade of Sant'Agnese. We instinctively feel that no one aspect of the piazza is enough, we shift our position, and we delight in the succession of multiple aspects. Our pleasure is made up of a kaleidoscopic series of pictures; it is a pleasure composed of movement and variety. We have seen how St. François is interested in movement and transformation (the whole *Introduction* emphasized growth, change, and metamorphosis; its ultimate aim is to bring about a conversion of the reader's soul). The rich profusion of nature imagery, particularly that dealing with animals, reveals the writer's joy at the diversity of the world. So it is that his characteristic technique of multiple-aspect imagery combines movement and variety. Our sensations as we read many passages of the *Introduction* are similar to those we feel in wandering through the Piazza San Pietro or the Piazza Navona; only

86. III, 14.

here we are looking at concepts visually represented from a rapid succession of angles.

For example, in the second chapter of the Part I there is a veritable cascade of images expressing the relationship of piety to charity:

> Si la charité est un laict, la devotion en est la creme; si elle est une plante, la devotion en est la fleur; si elle est une pierre precieuse, la devotion en est l'esclat; si elle est un bausme precieux, la devotion en est l'odeur, et l'odeur de suavité qui conforte les hommes et resjouit les anges.[87]

A writer of another period, if resorting to metaphor, might feel that a single image was enough for the adequate expression of his idea; but the baroque temperament of St. François leads him to accumulate four: cream, flower, sparkle, perfume. Though there is a single idea here, the author feels that we understand it more fully if we look at it from a variety of aspects. Aside from that, of course, he loves the rapid flashing of these images for their own sake; and it should be noted that they appeal to different senses: taste, sight, smell. This is multiple-sense imagery as well as multiple-aspect imagery.

The best form of prayer, St. François assures us, consists in meditation upon the life and Passion of Our Lord. And here the saint attempts to express in metaphors the nature of Christ:

> Il est la lumiere du monde; c'est doncques en luy, par luy, et pour luy, que nous devons estre eclairez et illuminez . . .

(The attentive reader will have recognized here an important passage from the Canon of the Mass.)

> . . . c'est l'arbre du desir, a l'ombre duquel nous nous devons rafraischir; c'est la vive fontaine de Jacob, pour le lavement de toutes nous souilleures.

After these three images of the light, the tree, and the fountain, the writer quickly moves on to another picture: As children learn to talk by listening to their mothers, so we, through contemplating Christ, learn to become like Him. There follows the image, already discussed, of the metal behind the glass of the mirror (corresponding to Christ's humanity): an illustration of how, in this world, we can contemplate God's divinity. Finally, the Saviour is bread from heaven:

> . . . car comme le pain doit estre mangé avec toutes sortes de viandes, aussi le Sauveur doit estre medité, consideré et recherché en toutes nos oraisons et actions.[88]

The last image is not only connected with the consecrated Host of the Mass but is also illustrative of the saint's favorite idea that religion should be

87. I, 2.   88. II, 1.

associated with all the details of our daily life. And while, as we have seen, the writer often likes unusual imagery, such as elephants or celestial navigation, in the above rapid series the pictures are familiar ones: after the light, the tree, and the fountain come the children, the mirror, and the bread.

Because God is present everywhere, it is easy to lose our awareness of Him. Two pictures illustrate this:

. . . les oyseaux, ou qu'ils volent, rencontrent toujours l'air, ainsi, ou que nous allions, ou que nous soyons, nous treuvons Dieu present; chascun sçait cette verité, mais chascun n'est pas attentif a l'apprehender. Les aveugles ne voyant pas un prince qui leur est present ne laissent pas de se tenir en respect, s'ils sont advertis de sa presence; mais la verité est que parce qu'ils ne le voyent pas, ils oublient aysement qu'il soit present, et s'en estant oubliez, ils perdent encore plus aisement le respect et la reverence.[89]

After contemplating the idea by means of the metaphor of the birds in the air, we move on immediately and the concept manifests itself in another form: the blind men in the presence of the prince.

Honors, though pleasant at first, soon become dangerous to the soul. Here we have three illustrations, all taken from nature:

Quand le paon fait sa roue pour se voir, en levant ses belles plumes, il se herisse tout le reste, et monstre de part et d'autre ce qu'il a d'infame; les fleurs, qui sont belles plantees en terre, flestrissent estant maniées. Et comme ceux qui odorent la mandragore de loin, et en passant, reçoivent beaucoup de suavité: mais ceux qui la sentent de pres et longuement en deviennent assoupis et malades: ainsi les honneurs . . .[90]

This example of multiple-aspect imagery may also be regarded as baroque because all three of the illustrations are concerned with a contrast between first and later impressions. At first we see the beautiful plumage of the strutting peacock; then inevitably we notice his behind. The flowers growing in the ground are pretty, but soon after being picked they wilt. The smell of the mandrake is pleasant at first, but before long makes us drowsy and ill. The contrast, in each case, is partly the illusion-reality antithesis, and partly a metamorphosis. Each metaphor has in itself movement and variety; the rapid succession has even more. The reference to the peacock's behind provides that note of coarsely realistic humor which the baroque, in its exuberant naturalism, often likes to introduce: Callot's vast engraving of the "Siege of the Ile de Ré," with its swarming array of delicate ships, presents in the center foreground a small dog misbehaving itself.

In a discussion of humility, the saint similarly uses a series of little con-

89. II, 2.   90. III, 4.

trasting vignettes to explain the difference between honorable and degrading ills. He asks us to consider a devout hermit, in rags and cold; everyone honors his tattered clothing, but would despise and mock a poor workman, gentleman, or lady in the same costume. We proceed at once to the second group of examples: a monk accepts with pious submission his superior's reprimand, and a child that of his father; however, if a knight or a lady, even for the love of God, were to submit to severe criticism, everyone would consider it cowardice and pusillanimity. Finally we have the third illustration: one person has a sore on his arm, and the other on his face; the former suffers physical pain only, whereas the latter undergoes scorn and degradation as well.[91] Earlier I mentioned the image of the bees of Heraclea, who suck both poison and honey from aconite blossoms; in reality, this image is one of a series illustrating the fact that in every friendship we absorb evil along with the good. Immediately after describing the bees of Heraclea, St. François tells us to be careful to avoid receiving counterfeit coins in the midst of genuine ones, and he concludes with a picture of prospectors panning gold from the gravel of the Tagus river.[92]

As we strive toward the devout life, worldly people are bound to criticize us; they will observe all our doings very carefully and pick on our slightest faults to magnify them, while minimizing the sins of the irreligious. St. François urges us not to be troubled by such criticism, and he provides three images, one right after the other, to reassure us:

. . . les araignées gastent toujours l'ouvrage des abeilles. Laissons cest aveugle, Philothée; qu'il crie tant qu'il voudra comme un chat-huant pour inquieter les oyseaux du jour: soyons fermes en nos desseins, invariables en nos resolutions; la perseverance fera bien voir si c'est a certes et tout de bon que nous sommes sacrifiez a Dieu et rangez a la vie devote. Les cometes et les planetes sont presque esgalement lumineuses en apparence, mais les cometes disparaissent en peu de temps, n'estant que de certains feux passagers; et les planetes ont une clarté perpetuelle. Ainsi l'hypocrisie et la vraie vertu . . .[93]

If the taunts of the worldly are undermining our confidence, we have the choice of looking at the situation in three ways—they are spiders and we are bees; they are owls and we are daytime birds; they are comets and we are planets. It is a cascade of antitheses.

No less rich in multiple-aspect imagery are the two consecutive chapters in Part IV which deal, respectively, with our moments of direct experience of God and with our periods of spiritual dryness: the "consolations spirituelles et sensibles" and the "seicheresses et sterilitez spirituelles." Fittingly, the writer begins chapter 13 with one of his favorite themes, the

91. III, 6.   92. III, 22.   93. IV, 1.

perpetual flux of the world as God has created it: day changes into night, spring into summer, summer into autumn, autumn into winter, winter into spring; weather varies from foggy to rainy to dry to windy:

   . . . varieté qui donne une grande beaute a cest univers.[94]

Man's life flows on earth like the waters,

   flottant et ondoyant en une perpetuelle diversite de mouvemens . . .

an image which might be taken from Montaigne. Amid this mutability of the world God alone is constant and permanent, and we should keep our attention directed toward Him; there follows the image, which we have already studied, of the compass aboard the storm-tossed ship, which always points to the north. But the chapter is full of warnings not to confuse pleasurable religious emotion with a true state of "devotion":

   . . . on treuve que comme les pluyes passageres d'un esté bien chaud qui tombent a grosses gouttes sur la terre, ne la penetrent point, et ne servent qu'à la pro- duction des champignons: ainsi ces larmes et tendretez tombant sur un cœur vicieux et ne penetrant point, luy sont tout-à-fait inutiles: [95]

Shortly thereafter comes the picture of the child who weeps when he sees his mother lanced, but is unwilling to give up his toy for her sake (sym- bolizing, as we have seen, the attitude of those who weep greatly over Christ crucified but are unwilling to give Him their hearts). Yet the sensuous experience of religious emotions can be spiritually useful; though we should not confuse it with "la devotion" itself, it can increase in us the desire for true religion. After such feelings, we shall be less eager for worldly pleasures:

Les mammelles et le laict, c'est-à-dire les faveurs du divin Espoux, sont meilleures à l'ame que le vin le plus precieux des plaisirs de la terre; qui en a gouste tient tout le reste des autres consolations pour du fiel et de l'absinthe. Et comme ceux qui ont l'herbe scytique en la bouche en reçoivent une si extreme douceur qu'ils ne sentent ny faim ny soif, ainsi ceux à qui Dieu a donne ceste manne celeste des suavitez et consolations interieures ne peuvent desirer ny recevoir les conso- lations du monde, pour au moins y prendre goust et y amuser leurs affections. Ce sont des petits avant-gousts des suavitez immortelles que Dieu donne aux ames qui le cherchent; ce sont des grains sucrez qu'il donne a ses petits enfans pour les amorcer; ce sont des eaux cordiales qu'il leur presente pour les comforter; ce sont aussi quelquesfois des arrhes des recompenses eternelles. On dict qu'Ale- xandre le Grand, cinglant en haute mer, descouvrit premierement l'Arabie heureuse par l'assentiment qu'il eut de suaves odeurs que le vent luy donnoit; et sur cela se donna du courage et à tous ses compaignons . . .[96]

94. IV, 13.   95. Ibid.   96. Ibid.

Having accumulated the images which are favorable to our indulging our religious emotions, the saint now passes on to a series of other images designed to guard us against excessive confidence as to our spiritual state. Sugar in the mouth does not mean that the mouth is sweet; spiritual sweetness is good, and God who gives it to us is good, but that does not mean that we are good. We are like little children, who in order to be encouraged to drink our milk have to have sugar put in it. From time to time, God gives us a little candy, as a mother does to her child; however, the truly intelligent child will value his mother's kindness more highly than the sweetness of the candy.[97]

There are also states of spiritual dryness, when we no longer feel the sweetness of religion. The writer develops further the above imagery:

Comme une mere refuse le sucre à son enfant qui est sujet aux vers; ainsi Dieu nous oste les consolations quand nous y prenons quelque vaine complaisance . . .[98]

The Israelite who did not rise early enough to gather manna found that the sun had melted it all. We are lying upon a bed of sensual pleasure when the divine Bridegroom knocks at the door, we argue with Him when he tries to persuade us to perform our spiritual exercises; so He goes away and leaves us to ourselves. If we delight in the flour of Egypt, we shall have no manna from heaven. Then a bee image:

Les abeilles haïssent toutes les odeurs artificielles; et les suavitez du Sainct-Esprit sont incompatibles avec les delices artificieuses du monde.[99]

Shortly after this, a drunken-pigeon image:

. . . les colombes ja saoules, dict l'ancien proverbe, treuvent ameres les cerises.[100]

So we, satiated with the pleasures of this world, find no joy in spiritual delights. The grace of God is compared to rain, which has an opposite effect on plants according to whether or not they still have the greenness of life in them:

. . . la pluye vivifie les plantes qui ont de la verdeur; mais a celles qui ne l'ont point, elle leur oste encore la vie qu'elles n'ont point; car elles en pourrissent tout-à-faict.[101]

The conclusion of these two chapters on spiritual pleasure and dryness is that we must continue to serve God no matter what the state of our inner feelings This idea is expressed by four metaphors in succession. During a fine spring the bees produce more honey and fewer pupae, whereas in bad weather they do just the opposite. (So we, in the fine spring seasons of

97. Ibid.   98. IV, 14.   99. Ibid.
100. Ibid.   101. Ibid.

spiritual consolation, suck the honey of religious delights; and in darker
seasons we should accumulate good works.) We should not think that, in
those periods of our life when we serve God without pleasure and without
feeling, our worship is less pleasing to Him:

> . . . au contraire, nos actions sont comme les roses, lesquelles bien qu'estant
fraisches elles ont plus de grace; estant neantmoins seiches, elles ont plus d'odeur
et de force.[102]

Now the third metaphor:

> Ce n'est pas si grand cas de servir un prince en la douceur d'un temps paisible
et parmy les delices de la cour; mais de le servir en l'aspreté de la guerre, parmy
les troubles et persecutions, c'est une vraye marque de constance et fidelité.

And finally we return to the child and its mother:

> . . . l'enfant baise aysement sa mere qui lui donne du sucre, mais c'est signe qu'il
l'aime grandement, s'il la baise apres qu'elle luy aura donne de l'absynthe ou du
chicotin.

Proust, in his novel, has studied what he calls "les intermittences du cœur";
and in these chapters St. François is speaking of an analogous phenomenon
in our spiritual life. As he leads us through this topic, the author of the
Introduction pauses frequently so that we may visualize its many varied
aspects. And just as, when we walk around the Piazza Navona, we obtain
a succession of picturesque views but sometimes come back to a spot where
the relation of things pleased us especially, so St. François, wandering from
metaphor to metaphor, occasionally returns to a favorite image. At the
beginning, there was the sea (its perpetual diversity of movement, the
compass guiding the ship through its vastness). After this there is a long
and varied series of images: summer rain, child and mother, breasts and
milk, the Scythic herb, sugar given to children, the liqueur, the down pay-
ment—and then we find ourselves at sea again, with Alexander the Great,
smelling the unseen coast of Arabia. Amid the kaleidoscope of images, others
which recur from time to time in these two chapters are those of sugar and
the mother and child. But our dominant impression is one of movement and
diversity.

   In discussing St. François' multiple-aspect imagery, I have generally
spoken of these metaphors as pictures, seeming to imply that they appeal
primarily to our sense of sight. But of course many of them appeal to other
senses, and to several simultaneously; in the section we have just studied,
on spiritual consolation and dryness, many of the images are concerned
with smell or taste (sugar and roses, for instance). Multiple-aspect imagery

102. Ibid.

is often multiple-sense imagery as well. And so, in concluding this study of
the style of St. François, it is fitting to speak of that famous spiritual exercise which he so frequently recommends: gathering the spiritual bouquet.
The systematic instructions as to methods of prayer, to be found in Part I,
nearly always end with the words: "Faites un petit bouquet de devotion,"
and later, in a most characteristic passage, the saint explains what he means
by this:

A tout cela j'ai adjousté qu'il fallait cueiller un petit bouquet de devotion: et
voicy ce que je veux dire. Ceux qui se sont promenez en un beau jardin n'en
sortent pas volontiers sans prendre en leur main quatre ou cinq fleurs pour les
odorer, et tenir le long de la journee: ainsi nostre esprit ayant discouru sur quelque
mystere, par la meditation, nous devons choisir un, ou deux, ou trois poincts que
nous aurons trouvez plus a nostre goust et plus propres a nostre advancement,
pour nous en ressouvenir le reste de la journee, et les odorer spirituellement. Or
cela se faict sur le lieu mesme auquel nous avons faict la meditation, en nous y
entretenant ou promenant solitairement quelque temps apres.[103]

This passage can stand as a fair specimen of the thought and style of the
Introduction à la vie dévote. The thought is characteristic, for prayer is
represented as an agreeable occupation, comparable to walking in a beautiful garden. Furthermore, piety is compatible with our other activities; it
is like a bouquet which we carry with us wherever we go. Then there is
the idea of spiritual growth: it is for our advancement in the religious life
that we are asked to reconsider at various times during the day our morn-
ing meditations. The style is also most typical of St. François: spiritual
thought assumes such concrete form that the metaphor becomes a landscape.
We walk in this garden, we gather flowers in it. Within the landscape, there
is movement. And there is the appeal to several senses: we see the flowers,
we pick them, we hold them, we smell them throughout the day. It is
perhaps not too much to suggest that St. François views all his images as
spiritual flowers; he wants the reader to gather them and to breathe their
scent throughout life. In this way the artist will have contributed to our
spiritual advancement.

103. II, 7.

JEAN DE LA CEPPÈDE is one of those poets of the late sixteenth and early seventeenth centuries who have, after long neglect, been rehabilitated in our time. Actually, as early as 1910 the Abbé Brémond made a first attempt to rescue him from oblivion, pointing out that the *Théorèmes* are pictures which possess

. . tour à tour la vie bariolée, éclatante d'un Rubens, le mordant d'une eau-forte, la candeur appliquée, paisible d'une enluminure.[1]

Although the Abbé Brémond was of course unaware of our more recent concept of a literary baroque, with its relation to painting and the other fine arts, the characteristics he discovers in La Ceppède are, in fact, some of those which I should consider baroque. His allusion to the variegated and dazzling life of Rubens' painting is significant, as is also his reference to the pungent keenness of the etcher's art: Jacques Callot is not mentioned by name, but the comparison fits him well.

A generation was to pass, however, before La Ceppède came into his own. At the time of the Second World War and after, his sonnets began to occupy an increasingly important place in anthologies. Arland in 1941, Ramuz in 1942, Dominique Aury in 1943, all include him; and Thierry Maulnier's *Poésie du XVIIᵉ siècle,* published in 1945 by La Table Ronde, gives us twenty-one of the *Théorèmes,* three translations of psalms, and a rendition of the *Vexilla regis.* In 1947 M. Jean Rousset (author, since then, of *La Littérature de l'âge baroque en France*) brought out a booklet devoted entirely to La Ceppède, which contains an excellent selection of thirty-eight of the sonnets, plus one penitential psalm. The most recent contribution to our knowledge of La Ceppède is M. François Ruchon's *Essai sur la vie et l'oeuvre de Jean de la Ceppède,* which is number 8 in the series *Travaux d'humanisme et Renaissance* (1953). Here the selection is much more complete, though we still have only 170 of the 515 *Théorèmes;* there are thirteen psalms and other miscellaneous poems, and the whole is preceded by an interesting study of the poet's life and work. To this preface, especially for biographical information, I am much indebted.

1. *Histoire littéraire du sentiment religieux en France* (Paris, Alcan, 1916–23), I (*L'Humanisme dévot*), 347.

Here a few remarks will be useful to situate La Ceppède in the world of his contemporaries. He was born in Marseille in 1548: in other words, fifteen years after Montaigne, two years before d'Aubigné, and five before Malherbe. From 1578 on he was Conseiller au Parlement d'Aix; and here his life offers an interesting parallel to that of Montaigne, who occupied a similar position in the Parlement of Bordeaux from 1557 to 1570. La Ceppède, like Montaigne, was both a magistrate and a humanist; like him, he enjoyed travel; but he seems to have been much more sensitive to the fine arts than was the author of the *Essais*. The poet was a protégé of Marie de Médicis; this provides an indirect link with Rubens, since the great Flemish painter's outstanding work in France is the great series of pictures which honors the wife of Henri IV and mother of Louis XIII. La Ceppède, all his life, was loyal to the royal cause and devoted to Henri de Navarre; as a result, he incurred the enmity of the Ligue, and narrowly escaped being murdered. Once again we are reminded of Montaigne, whose traditionalism and moderation made him favor the legal heir to the throne. We know from the essays *De la vanité* and *De la phisionomie* that Montaigne, because he would not identify himself with either extremist position—the Ligue or the Protestants—was in real physical danger from both parties, and that his house narrowly escaped being sacked on a number of occasions. And, in the first of these two essays, we can see that he is very proud of having entertained Henri de Navarre at the Château de Montaigne. Just as Montaigne sought refuge from the troubles of civil war by writing essays, so La Ceppède endeavored to find relief by composing religious poetry.

In the commentary to one of his sonnets, La Ceppède expresses an ideal of moderation very similar to that of Montaigne or of St. François de Sales (who was nineteen years his junior). The following passage, which reveals that the Christian poet was also a humanist and an *honnête homme,* would not be out of place in the *Essais* or the *Introduction à la vie dévote:*

[Les delectations], celles du corps et de l'ame ensemble, moderees si justement par la raison que leur usage n'aporte point d'amertume, ni d'exces, ni de re-pentance, et ne nous asservit, ny empesche point de bien faire . . . Il nous est bien permis de nous plaire modestement en la beauté des choses crées. Mais il n'en faut pas tellement flatter le goust, ny en avaller si avidement les douceurs que nostre affection se tourne en folie. Tant que nous usons des richesses que Dieu nous donne simplement, honorablement, et avec une liberalité mesnagere, sans en abuser, ni nous passionner indignement ou injustement pour les accroistre, nous jouissons de ceste volupté sans reproche . . . Le desir de l'honneur et la gloire jusques aux bornes de la raison est licite et genereux . . . Il n'est point interdit à l'homme d'user, et de jouyr de la grandeur de son courage . . . L'amour des femmes est naturel et peut estre innocent; mais s'il outrepasse les loix de

Dieu et de l'honnesteté, et se deborde aux exces, il devient brutal et se tourne en rage et frenezie . . . Pour donc que cette volupté detourne et debauche les meilleures functions de nos esprits, qu'elle asservit la vertu mesme . . . qu'elle est la peste capitale de nos ames, et qu'elle les divertit de la poursuite des biens eternels . . . nous supplions tres humblement la Divine bonté . . . de nous distraire tout à fait d'icelle et de nous reunir et rejoindre à luy, comme notre principe, et nous faire aboutir à luy, comme notre fin.[2]

In my analysis of Montaigne, I attempted to show that such an attitude is essentially baroque. On the one hand, the passage is strongly animated by a moral and religious purpose; on the other hand, it expresses a total acceptance of life. We recognize here two of the baroque categories. The aim of St. François de Sales, as we have seen, is to reconcile the worldly and the devout life; an early chapter of the *Introduction* argues that piety is suited to all sorts and conditions of men: the housewife, the soldier, the merchant, the magistrate—they can go about their daily occupations, and even have fun in moderation, while also worshiping God.

La Ceppède died in Avignon in 1623. It should be noted that, although the next three centuries were very unjust to him, his own contemporaries were not. Among these contemporaries, the most surprising tributes come from Malherbe. I say surprising, because the neglect of those poets now considered as baroque stems in large part from the official classical attitude, succinctly summed up by Boileau in the three words, "Enfin Malherbe vint." It is a kind of sigh of relief, and implies that the poetry written before Malherbe is of no value. Of course this sweeping condemnation really includes poets of the Renaissance, such as Ronsard and Du Bellay, as well as mannerist ones like Sponde or baroque ones like d'Aubigné and La Ceppède. Eventually, in the nineteenth century, critical common sense revolted against this tyrannical and academic dictum; the beauties of the Pléiade came to be appreciated once more. In our century, one of the pioneers in the movement to rehabilitate the mannerist and baroque poets has been Mr. Alan Boase; with ironic appropriateness, he entitled his first article on Sponde, which really revealed the significance of this poet to the public, "Then Malherbe Came."

But Malherbe himself admired La Ceppède. The following little poem of six lines has as its title, "A Messire Jean de La Ceppède"; it was written in 1621, on the occasion of the publication of the second part of the *Théorèmes*:

> Muses, vous promettez en vain
> Au front de ce grand Escrivain
> Et du laurier et du lierre.

2. Cf. *Théorèmes*, II, 1, introductory prose passage.

Ses ouvrages, trop precieux
Pour les couronnes de la terre,
L'asseurent de celle des cieux.[3]

The fullest statement of his admiration, however, is in a sonnet addressed
to Marie de Médicis, who was the patroness of both poets:

J'estime La Ceppède, et l'honore et l'admire
Comm'un des ornemens les premiers de nos jours:
Mais qu'à sa plume seule on doive ces discours,
Certes, sans le flatter, je ne l'oserois dire.
L'Esprit de ce grand Dieu, qui ses grâces inspire
A celui qui sans feinte en attend le secours,
Pour eslever nostre ame aux celestes amours
Sur un si beau sujet l'a fait si bien escrire.
Reine, l'heur de la France, & de tout l'Univers,
Qui voyez chaque jour tant d'hommages divers,
Que presente la Muse aux pieds de vostre image,
Bien que vostre bonté leur soit propice a tous,
Ou je n'y cognois rien, ou devant cet ouvrage
Vous n'en vistes jamais qui fut digne de vous.[4]

In other words, the *Théorèmes* are inspired by the Holy Ghost. When
Malherbe speaks of the many different kinds of homage which the Muse
lays at the feet of Marie, it is interesting to recall that Rubens painted his
series of biographical pictures for the queen in 1622–25. It is difficult to
date the above sonnet with precision; it appears in the 1630 edition of
Malherbe's poems, but presumably was written, at the latest, soon after
the appearance of the second part of the *Théorèmes*. The chances are, therefore, that Malherbe had not seen Rubens' Medici pictures; though perhaps
if he had he might have continued to consider La Ceppède's sonnets as the
greatest artistic offering to the queen. There is, incidentally, a parallel between Malherbe's elaborate flattery of Marie and Rubens' grandiose ideali-
zation of the events of her life. In any case, it would be somewhat exaggerated—except in a purely artistic and symbolic sense—to characterize
Malherbe's court poetry or the Galerie de Médicis as inspired by the Holy
Ghost; whereas, applied to La Ceppède, the remark is not altogether inappropriate.

For the complete text of the *Théorèmes* it is necessary to refer to the
original editions which appeared in the author's lifetime, as these poems have
never, since then, been reproduced in their entirety. There are two parts,

3. *Poésies diverses*, no. CXIV (Lavaud ed. 2, 277).
4. Cited by François Ruchon, *Essai sur la vie et l'oeuvre de Jean de La Ceppède* (Genève,
Droz, 1953), p. 13.

which were published, respectively, in 1613 and 1621 in Toulouse. The actual composition of the first part probably began in the last years of the sixteenth century, shortly after Henri IV came to the throne. At this time, La Ceppède had already written his *Imitations des Psaumes*. The title pages of the two editions are unusually full in their explanations:

Les Theoremes de Messire Iean de La Ceppede, Seigneur d'Aigalades, Chevalier, Conseiller du Roy en ses Conseils d'Estat & Priue, & premier President en sa Cour des Comptes, Aides, & Finances de Prouence, sur le sacre Mystere de nostre Redemption, Diuisez en trois Liures, & enrichis de trois Tables tres-amples au sujet des Sonnets, des Matieres & des Autheurs: Suiuis de l'Imitation de quelques Pseaumes, & autres Meslanges spirituels.

La Seconde Partie des Theoremes de M I de La Ceppede, Seigneur d'Aigallades, (etc.) Sur les Mysteres de la descente de Iesus-Christ aux Enfers, de sa Resurrection, de ses apparitions apres icelle, de son Ascension, & de la Mission du S. Esprit en forme visible. Diuisee en quatre Livres.

The first part contains three books consisting of a hundred sonnets each. Book I concerns the events on the Mount of Olives: Christ's agony, the betrayal of Judas, the arrest of Christ. Book II tells the story of the return to Jerusalem, the trial before Herod and Pilate, and the condemnation. Book III describes the bearing of the Cross, the Crucifixion, Christ's death and burial. Each book is preceded by a detailed prose argument, and between each sonnet is a prose meditation on themes suggested by the poetry. The passage which I have quoted (no. 2) on worldly delights is a fairly representative specimen of these meditations. The second part is shorter (215 sonnets, similarly interspersed with meditations) and, on the whole, of lesser poetic merit. Book I is an elaboration of two sentences from the Creed: "He descended into hell"; "The third day he rose again from the dead." Book II concerns all Christ's appearances after the Resurrection. The subject of Book III is the Ascension; of Book IV, the descent of the Holy Ghost on the day of Pentecost.

It is now my purpose to examine a few of the finer sonnets from the *Théorèmes,* and to show how, stylistically, they may be regarded as belonging to the baroque period. My first example describes Christ's ascent into the Mount of Olives:

> Mais qui vous meut, Seigneur, de sortir à cette heure?
> De passer ce torrent? de gravir sur ce mont?
> De revoir ce jardin ou l'Apôtre parjure
> Conduit mille assassins pour vous faire un affront?
> Vous fuites l'autre jour pour ne voir votre front
> Ceint du bandeau royal; maintenant on conjure

De vous assasiner, et vous êtes si prompt
D'aller pour recevoir une mortelle injure.
O doux-forçant amour, que ton pouvoir est fort!
Ni l'effroi des tourments, ni l'horreur de la mort
Ne peuvent arrêter cet amoureux courage.
Mon Roi, puisque pour moi vous courez au trépas,
Faites que votre grâce a ce coup m'encourage
Et me donne pouvoir de talonner vos pas.[5]

The succession of questions in the first quatrain are, in effect, exclamations. We have seen how Montaigne is fond of this type of rhetorical question. The reader will remember that I consider *emphasis and exaggeration* to be one of the essential baroque categories and that among the devices used for this purpose are exclamation and accumulation. Here four exclamations are heaped up—and line 9 constitutes a fifth. The whole octet is a theatrical picture: Christ leaves the city, crosses the torrent, and climbs the mountain, while a thousand assassins plot his death. *Theatricality* is indeed an ever present characteristic of the *Théorèmes;* the majority of the sonnets are, at the same time, paintings and dramas. I have already compared La Ceppède to Rubens; he might perhaps even more fittingly be likened to Caravaggio or to the great French baroque painter Georges de La Tour, especially since so many of the *Théorèmes* are night scenes of martyrdom like the former's "Death of St. Matthew" or the latter's "St. Sebastian." The Passion of Christ is a subject which appeals to baroque artists: *horror and martyrdom* are an important baroque category. The emphasis on "amour" and "amoureux," which we shall see again and again in these poems, is a particular aspect of *incarnation:* among the forms of concrete imagery frequently adopted by baroque artists, the erotic-ecstatic is one of the most characteristic. (I have studied this question at some length in my book on d'Aubigné.) We should also notice the *contrast* in the second quatrain: Christ fled to avoid the royal crown, and now rushes to receive mortal injury. This sonnet is rich in *movement*—the whole octet is full of verbs expressing intense activity: "meut," "sortir," "passer," "gravir," "faire un affront," "fuites," "aller"; and in the last tercet we have "courez" and "talonnez." This last tercet reveals the poet's *moral and religious purpose*—a purpose which, of course, animates all the *Théorèmes.* La Ceppède prays to be granted the courage to follow in the footsteps of Christ.

Ni des pôles glacés les éternelles nuits
Ni l'épaisse noirceur des nuits cimméroniques,
Ni la palpable horreur des nuits pharaoniques
Ne peuvent s'égaler à votre nuit, ô Juifs.

5. I, I, 8. (References are to part, book, and sonnet of the *Théorèmes* respectively.)

Mais, grand Christ, ce n'est pas chose étrange, depuis
Que vous avez ouvert les gouffres plutoniques
Et que vous retirez de ces tourbes iniques
Vos rayons lumineux en vous-même réduits.
Ainsi l'avez-vous dit en paroles funèbres,
Que c'est ici leur heure et l'effort des ténèbres.
O nuit profonde, noire et des nuits la greigneur.
Mais pourquoi peut hélas! cette nuit à cette heure
Brunir un si beau jour! hé! dites-le, Seigneur,
C'est afin d'accomplir mainte vieille Ecriture.[6]

This sonnet is a remarkable development of the image of darkness: darkness conceived both visually as the setting for a tragic drama and symbolically as an expression of man's spiritual state. It is the darkness (to quote the Book of Common Prayer's Canon of the Mass) of "the night in which he was betrayed." Set against all the words suggesting darkness—"nuits," "noirceur," "gouffres," "ténèbres"—stands the single image of light: "rayons lumineux." It is like the single torch dramatically illuminating the darkness of Georges de La Tour's "St. Sebastian" or his "St. Mary Magdalene." We are reminded also of the chiaroscuro of other baroque artists, such as Caravaggio or Rembrandt. It is the artistic expression of the verse from the first chapter of St. John: "And the light shineth in darkness; and the darkness comprehended it not." The extraordinary repetition of the word "nuit" should be noted: four times in the first quatrain, seven times in all. An even more striking example of the technique of emphasis through accumulation is the way in which lines 1, 2, and 3 are each introduced by the word "ni." The baroque love of strangeness (related to the category of *surprise*) reveals itself in the exotic adjectives "cimméroniques," "pharaoniques," and "plutoniques." Multiple-sense imagery is present also: along with the feeling of darkness we have that of coldness—the "pôles glacés." The whole first quatrain is hyperbolic in tone, even though exclamation points are absent—and there are three of them in the final tercet. The word "brunir," related to the general chiaroscuro scheme of the sonnet, is also expressive of *metamorphosis*.

Or sus donc, serrez fort, liez fort, ô canaille,
Celui qui vient à vous pour dénouer vos noeuds,
Tiraillez, travaillez cestui-ci qui travaille
Pour soulager les griefs de vos travaux peineux.
Resserrez, captivez dans un roc caverneux
Cil qui sa liberté pour vos libertés baille;
Combattez, abattez cestui-ci qui bataille

6. I, I, 77.

> Pour abattre, abattu, vos antiques haineux.
> O liens, ô travaux, ô mystiques etreintes,
> O combats, si les Juifs de vos fortes épreintes
> Ne font bien leur profit, profitez-les sur nous.
> Déliez nos liens, soulagez nos misères,
> Délivrez-nous des fers de l'éternel courroux
> Et combattez l'effort de nos forts adversaires.[7]

This sonnet is built of imperatives: "serrez," "liez," "tiraillez," "travaillez," "resserrez," "captivez," "combattez," "abattez," "profitez," "deliez," "soulagez," "delivrez," "combattez": thirteen in all for a space of fourteen lines. This is not only a remarkable example of heaping: since these are all verbs, the impression of movement, change, and struggle is very strong; and since they are all imperatives, we feel that energetic power of the will which so often characterizes the baroque. In the octet these imperatives all express intense physical effort and combat: we are reminded of such pictures of Rubens as the "Erection of the Cross" in Antwerp cathedral or the "Battle of the Amazons" in the Munich museum—or of Caravaggio's "Martyrdom of St. Matthew" in San Luigi dei Francesi, and Callot's engravings of the horrors of war. Then the sestet verbs are in contrast, for the most part, since they express ideas of release, relief, and deliverance; this has the effect of establishing an antithesis between the two parts of the sonnet. On the other hand, of course, the whole octet is bitterly ironical, and this adds the characteristically baroque element of paradox to those of mass and movement. Yet the sonnet does not leave us with this impression of violence and irony: in the end, all conflicts are resolved in the confident hope of Christ's ultimate victory; moral and artistic unity are re-established, and the world (felt in the last analysis to be the creation of God) accepted, as is usually the case in baroque art. A word should be said also about the curious blend of the echo technique (which is an aspect of heaping) with semipunning and etymological byplay (a form of surprise and paradox). Note, in line 6, the echoing, contrasting repetition of "liberté," and above all, in lines 7 and 8, the ingenious interweaving of all the words associated with "battre." The theme comes back in line 10 ("combats"), and in the final line ("combattez"). A verbal and imagistic link is provided whereby the agitated tensions of the octet lead to the resolution of the sestet: Christ is going to win the battle.

> O l'amour de mon âme, ô non-pareil Amant,
> Vous avec qui le crime onques n'eut acointance,
> Souffrez d'être lié pour moi si rudement!
> Portez de mes péchés la dure pénitence!

7. I, I, 91.

> J'ai commis le forfait, vous aurez la potence,
> A moi seul est l'offence, à vous le châtiment;
> Au moins que je vous fasse à cette heure assistance,
> Puisque je vous attache et suis votre tourment.
> O trop ardent amour à nul autre semblable!
> Pour le serf malheureux, pour l'inique coupable,
> Le maître, l'innocent est saisi prisonnier.
> O mon âme, à le suivre à ce coup soit hâtive,
> Que ton corps soit du sien maintenant prisonnier,
> Qu'en lui tu sois toujours heureusement captive.[8]

With the expressions "love of my soul," "matchless Lover," "O too ardent love," we find ourselves in the characteristically baroque world of erotic religious sensibility. The feeling is similar to that of certain *Holy Sonnets* of Donne—especially number 14, "Batter my heart, three-personed God," which ends with the line,

> Nor ever chaste, except you ravish me.

And we are reminded also of Crashaw's poem on St. Teresa, "The Flaming Heart," where the great Spanish mystic's devotion to Christ is expressed in imagery suggestive of passionate human love. The greatest manifestation of this kind of sensibility is, of course, Bernini's sculpture of the vision of St. Teresa: the saint swoons with ecstasy while a handsome smiling angel pierces her heart with a golden arrow. Incidentally, it is interesting to note that La Ceppède claimed relationship with this favorite baroque saint: her family name was Cepeda, and this, it seems, was the original form of the poet's name.

But to return to sonnet 94. It is constructed of antitheses: You have committed no crime—you are bound for my sake; you do penance for my sins; I have committed the crime—you will be hanged; the offense is mine alone—yours the punishment; for the wretched slave, the iniquitous guilty man—the innocent master is seized as a prisoner. In other words, the whole poem expresses a fundamental tension. Needless to say, La Ceppède here, as throughout the *Théorèmes,* is stating traditional Christian dogma; neither he nor the baroque period in general can claim to have invented the doctrine of the Atonement. And yet, to give this basic Christian belief artistic expression by means of five dramatic contrasts (implying always a final resolution)—this is characteristically baroque. So, also, is the use of three ardently exclamatory sentences. Lines 13 and 14 recall an idea which is implicit throughout the Gregorian Canon of the Mass, and which is explicitly stated in the Book of Common Prayer: ". . . that we . . . may . . . be made one body with him, that he may dwell in us, and we in him."

8. I, I, 94.

> Les erreurs, les horreurs de cette nuit m'effraient,
> Comme aurai-je le cœur d'apprendre le succès
> Du noir dessein, mon Christ, de vos Juifs qui s'égaient
> A commettre sur vous toute sorte d'excès?
> Mon Sauveur, je n'ai point à vos juges d'accès,
> J'ai perdu le sentier que vos ennemis fraient,
> Se n'ois rien que glapir ces chiens qui vous aboient,
> Comment pourrai-je donc savoir votre proces?
> Rassurez-moi, mon Prince, et donnez à mon âme
> Pour la guider partout la colonne de flamme,
> Qui guide les aïeuls de ces neveux pervers.
> Ainsi parmi les feux en dépit des ténèbres,
> Et la gloire et l'opprobre éclateront célèbres:
> Votre gloire en Horeb, votre opprobre en ces vers.[9]

This is another dramatic chiaroscuro picture in the manner of Caravaggio, Georges de La Tour, and Rembrandt. In the midst of the horrors of the night, La Ceppède calls for a column of fire like that which guided the Israelites out of Egypt. And here a further contrast is implied: whereas the Jews of Moses' day followed the light of God, those of Christ's day are enveloped in darkness ("and the light shineth in darkness, and the darkness comprehended it not"). The yelping of the dogs adds a new element of dramatic horror, and brings another sense, that of hearing, into play. The theme of martyrdom is of course present throughout the *Théorèmes,* but is here given added force with the mention of the Jews mocking Christ as they lay hands on him and buffet him. This sonnet also contains an example of a half-pun ("erreurs"-"horreurs") and ends with an echoed contrast ("gloire"-"opprobre," l. 13, repeated in l. 14). The final reference to Horeb (Mt. Sinai) gathers together all the parts of the sonnet and establishes unity: just as the word of God appeared on Horeb and in the person of Christ, says the poet, so may I here, by describing the Passion, make Him manifest amid the darkness of the world.

> Blanc est le vêtement du grand Père sans âge,
> Blanc sont les courtisans de sa blanche maison,
> Blanc est de son esprit l'étincelant pennage,
> Blanche est de son Agneau la brillante toison.
> Blanc est le crêpe saint dont, pour son cher blason,
> Aux noces de l'Agneau l'Epouse s'avantage.
> Blanc est or le manteau dont par même raison
> Cet innocent Epoux se pare en son noçage.
> Blanc était l'ornement dont le Pontife vieux
> S'affublait pour dévot offirir ses vœux aux cieux.

9. I, II, 1.

Blanc est le parement de ce nouveau grand prêtre.
Blanche est la robe due au fort victorieux.
Ce vainqueur, bien qu'il aille à la mort se soumettre,
Blanc sur la dure mort triomphe glorieux.[10]

This sonnet might indeed be called "Symphonie en blanc majeur." But on the whole a pictorial analogy is more appropriate than a musical one. It is of course part of the general tradition of Christian art to represent God in terms of radiant light, but this technique reaches its climax in the baroque period. In Caravaggio's "Fall of St. Paul," the presence of Christ is expressed by the flood of white light which bathes the horse and its thrown rider. Barocci's "Stigmatization of St. Francis" represents God as a light so dazzling that the attendant friar has to ward off the intense glare with his arm. Rembrandt's "Christ and the Pilgrims at Emmaus," and Callot's engraving "Le Bénédicité," which shows the Holy Family at their evening meal, both depict a radiant whiteness emanating from the divine persons. And in baroque poetry, as I have shown elsewhere, d'Aubigné provides examples of a parallel technique. Whenever God or heaven is mentioned in *Les Tragiques,* there are images of whiteness and the frequent recurrence of such words as "blanc," "brillant," "radieux," "lumière," "clarté," "resplendir," etc. A constant feature of baroque art is the attempt to express things invisible in terms of things visible. Here in La Ceppède's sonnet, the divinity of Christ is communicated to our senses through the overpowering impression of whiteness. This stylistic device comes under the category which I have called incarnation; and in the present case, we can see a close relationship between the artistic and theological ideas of incarnation.

I have remarked that the impression of whiteness is overpowering; and if this is so, it is because La Ceppède has used the heaping device to an extraordinary extent. Ten of the fourteen lines of the sonnet begin with the word "blanc"; in a sense it would be more appropriate to speak of the echo device—but what I should like to point out here is that the sonnet consists essentially of a list, an accumulation, of white things: the white robe of God the Father, the white angels, the white plumage of the Holy Ghost, the white fleece of the Lamb of God, the white veil of the nun, the white cloak of Christ, the white chasuble of the pope, again the white vestment of Christ considered as a high priest, the white victor's robe, the white triumphant Christ. All these different white things achieve organic unity in the very fine closing line. I do not think it farfetched to suggest that this last line, which foreshadows the Resurrection and the world to come, has affinities with that aspect of baroque painting called by Wölfflin "open form."

10. I, II, 54.

Allez, victime sainte, allez donc au trépas
Portant sur votre dos toutes nos injustices.
Sus, qu'on gorge ces loups du désiré repas,
Qu'un supplice termine un monde de supplices.
Allez et consommez tous les vieux sacrifices;
Mais qui vous accompagne? au moins avez-vous pas
Quelques consolateurs? las! comme deux complices,
Deux insignes voleurs vont talonnant vos pas.
Les Juifs vous ont pourvu de cette compagnie
Pour accroître leur gloire et votre ignominie,
Pour brunir le beau jour de vos faits glorieux.
Mais tous ces noirs efforts de leur aveugle rage,
Dissipés, se perdront comme un faible nuage
Disparaît au lever du soleil radieux.[11]

This is another martyrdom sonnet, as indicated by such words as "victime" and "supplice." The third line, with its reference to gorging wolves, is a typical example of baroque hyperbole. The scene of Christ bearing the Cross is conceived theatrically, with the two thieves providing dramatic contrast. The movement-and-metamorphosis category becomes important in lines 11–14, which are full of verbs expressing transformation: "accroître," "brunir," "dissipés," "se perdront," and "disparaît." It should be noted that the image "brunir le beau jour" has been repeated from I, I, 77 above. As is so often the case with La Ceppède, the triumphant last line resolves the conflicts of the poem and is suggestive of open form.

L'Autel des vieux parfums dans Solyme encensé
Fait or d'une voierie un temple vénérable
Ou du Verbe incarné l'Hypostase adorable
S'offre tres odorante à son Père offensé
Le vieux Pal, sur lequel jadis fut agencé
En Edom le serpent aux mordus secourable,
Elève ores celui qui piteux a pensé
Du vieux serpent d'Eden la morsure incurable.
Le pressoir de la Vigne en Calvaire est dressé,
Ou ce fameux raisin ce pressoir a pressé
Pour noyer dans son vin nos léthales vipères.
L'échelle israélite est posée en ce lieu,
Sur laquelle aujourd'hui s'appuyant l'homme-Dieu
Nous fait jouir des biens qu'il promit à nos Pères.[12]

We have here an exceptionally interesting example of La Ceppède's method of gathering material from varied biblical sources. Frequently with this poet, as with many baroque artists, the themes and images are not

11. I, II, 96.   12. I, III, 23.

original but belong to the Christian tradition; the originality and the baroque style manifest themselves in the conscious arrangement of these themes and images so that sensuous variety is fused into an organic unity.

The altar with incense comes from Exodus 30:1: "And thou shalt make an altar to burn incense upon."

The pole, mentioned in numbers 21, 8, and 9, has always been taken to prefigure the Cross: "And the Lord said unto Moses, Make thee a fiery serpent, and set it upon a pole: and it shall come to pass, that every one that is bitten, when he looketh upon it shall live. And Moses made a serpent of brass, and put it upon a pole, and it came to pass, that if a serpent had bitten any man, when he beheld the serpent of brass, he lived." This passage is recalled by Christ in his conversation with Nicodemus (St. John 3:14-15): "And as Moses lifted up the serpent in the wilderness, even so must the Son of man be lifted up: That whosoever believeth in him should not perish, but have eternal life."

Likewise the vine traditionally foreshadows the cross. The reference is to Isaiah 5:1-2: "Now will I sing to my wellbeloved a song of my beloved touching his vineyard. My wellbeloved hath a vineyard in a very fruitful hill: And he fenced it, and gathered out the stones thereof, and planted it with the choicest vine, and built a tower in the midst of it, and also made a winepress therein: and he looked that it should bring forth grapes, and it brought forth wild grapes." In St. Matthew 21, Christ tells the parable of the wicked husbandmen, who killed the servants and the son of the owner of the vineyard. Verse 33, with which the story begins, contains reminiscences of the passage from Isaiah: "Hear another parable: there was a certain householder, which planted a vineyard, and hedged it round about, and digged a winepress in it, and built a tower and let it out to husbandmen, and went into a far country."

The ladder appears in Jacob's dream, Genesis 28:12: "And he dreamed, and behold a ladder set up on the earth, and the top of it reached to heaven: and behold the angels of God ascending and descending on it." This too is often regarded as prophetically symbolic of the Cross.

La Ceppède makes no attempt to conceal his scriptural sources; on the contrary, an author's footnote supplies all the necessary references. In other words, he takes no pride in having invented anything, but rather in having transformed his materials into a work of art. He is like Montaigne's bees, which fly from flower to flower pilfering nectar, but make of it a substance all their own: honey. I have already said that I consider this metaphor a good description of Montaigne's style.

In discussing the biblical allusions, it has hardly seemed necessary to explain the very obvious one to the serpent in the Garden of Eden. The poet has been very ingenious in his development of the serpent theme: Moses' brass serpent cures the bites of serpents; the crucified Christ (likened to the life-giving serpent of Moses) cures the death-dealing bite of the serpent of Eden; and finally, line 11, the vipers are symbolic of our sins. Note how the two contrasting serpents—the good and the evil one—are linked by the similar, semipunning sound of the names: Edom and Eden.

The poem is a remarkable example of multiple-sense imagery: each of the four natural divisions appeals to a different sense. The first quatrain is concerned with smell: the incense of the Old Testament altar, and the sweet perfume of Christ's sacrifice of Himself to God. Suggested by this, of course, is the incense offered during the sacrifice of the Mass. The association between worship and incense is further indicated by the juxtaposition of two similar-sounding words: "adorable" and "odorante." It is possible also that La Ceppède had in mind another biblical passage which he does not mention: Psalm 141:2: "Let my prayer be set forth in thy sight as the incense; and let the lifting up of my hands be an evening sacrifice."

The second quatrain, dealing with snake bite, is concerned with sensations of touch. The first tercet, with its references to the vine, grapes, winepress, and wine, appeals to the sense of taste. Here again, though it is not explicitly stated, La Ceppède has in mind the Mass and the doctrine of Transubstantiation; the wine becomes the blood of Christ, and takes away the sins of the world:

> Pour noyer dans son vin nos léthales vipères.

(Another scriptural source of this passage, closely linked with the twenty-first chapter of St. Matthew which the poet mentions, is obviously St. John 15:1: "I am the true vine, and my Father is the husbandman.")

In the final tercet, Jacob's ladder is essentially a visual image. The ladder links heaven and earth. It should be pointed out that mannerist and baroque art are fond of grand pictorial scenes taking place simultaneously on heaven and earth: consider for example El Greco's "Burial of Count Orgaz," which shows, on the lower level, a realistic portrait gallery of sixteenth-century Spaniards attending the funeral, while on the upper level, the count is received before the throne of God. And just as Jacob's ladder had angels providing the link between heaven and earth, so here, in the midst of the actual historical scene, St. Stephen and St. Augustine have come down to carry the body of Count Orgaz. In poetry, d'Aubigné's *Les Tragiques* also mingles the two levels: at the end of his account of the Massacre of St. Bartholomew, the heavens open and angels descend with golden chalices to gather up the blood of the martyrs.

Since this sonnet is about the Incarnation, it is natural that it should make extensive use of concrete, or incarnational, imagery; and since it is about the Redemption, it is also natural that there should be images of transformation and metamorphosis. And so we have the dressing and curing of the wound, the drowning of the vipers in wine, and finally the curious composite image of the Jacob's ladder and cross, whereby man may become Christlike and ascend into heaven.

> Cependant le soleil fournissant sa journée
> Voit son Maître à la croix de tourments foisonné,
> Ja prêt à rendre l'âme, il blêmit étonné
> Et volontiers sa course eût ailleurs détournée.
> Il se fâche de voir sa tête environnée
> D'un brillant diadème et dit passionné:
> Dois-je avoir de rayons ma tête couronnée,
> Voyant mon Créateur d'épines couronné?
> A ces mots il arrache avec violence
> Sa flambante couronne, et dépité l'élance
> Dans les abîmes creux, soudain le jour s'enfuit.
> O comme tu sers bien, ô soleil, ce bon Maître.
> Tu fils naître un beau jour ce nuit qui le vit naître,
> Et ce jour qu'il se meurt tu fais naître une nuit.[13]

La Ceppède appears to have gone about composing this sonnet in a very different way from "L'Autel des vieux parfums dans Solyme encensé." In the previous example, he has woven together a multitude of Bible texts and Christian dogmas; here, on the other hand, there are only two main sources, but the poet has developed them at great length. His point of departure is the phenomenon recorded in the Synoptic Gospels: the three hours of darkness which preceded Christ's death upon the cross. (See, for instance, St. Matthew 28:45: "Now from the sixth hour there was darkness over all the land unto the ninth hour.") From this statement, the poet has elaborated a dramatic and somewhat *précieux* personification. The sun is the principal actor in this scene. Here I should mention the second source. It is the declaration, in the Nicene Creed, that Christ was the agent of creation: ". . . one Lord Jesus Christ . . . By whom all things were made." And so the sun, seeing his Master dying on the cross, turns pale with astonishment. Feeling ashamed that his own head should be crowned with rays of light while his Creator is crowned with thorns, he violently tears off his flaming crown and plunges into the abyss, bringing darkness to the earth. Prosopopoeia is of course not an exclusively baroque figure, and yet it is evident that baroque writers and artists enjoy detailed and elaborate personifications. Once more I refer the reader to Rubens' Medici series. In the "Presentation

13. I, III, 65.

of the Portrait," Hymen and Cupid hold the portrait aloft for Henri IV to admire; the allegorical figure of France, in full armor, stands behind the king, pressing him to accept Marie as his queen. Again, in the "Government of the Regent Queen" Apollo is driving out the writhing figures of Discord, Hatred, and Rebellion. Like the sonnet which we are examining, both these pictures are theatrically conceived. Or consider one of Bernini's most famous fountains, that of the "Rivers," in the Piazza Navona: in this spectacular composition, a huge artificial rock, pierced with grottoes, rises from the basin, supporting an ancient obelisk; at the four corners of the rock, which represent the four quarters of the globe, are gigantic statues of the gods of the rivers Danube, Ganges, Nile, and Rio de la Plata. If we turn to baroque poetry, we shall find this same tendency to make personification theatrical. In France, some of the most elaborate examples are to be found in Book III of *Les Tragiques,* "La Chambre dorée," where d'Aubigné gives us a picture gallery of the vices which corrupt justice in his time. The portrait of Drunkenness will serve as an illustration:

> Comment d'un pas douteux en la troupe bacchante,
> Estourdie au matin, sur le soir violante,
> Porte dans le senat un tizon enflambé,
> Folle au front cramoisi, nez rouge, teint plombé,
> Comment l'Yvrongnerie en la foulle eschauffée,
> N'oyant les douces voix, met en pieces Orfée,
> A l'esclat des cornets d'un vineux Evoué
> Bruit un arrest de mort d'un gosier enroué! [14]

Perhaps I should explain, in order that the full picturesqueness of the last line may not be lost, that "bruit" means "belches." But my point is that d'Aubigné has added so many vivid details that he achieves an effect far greater than that of ordinary prosopopoeia: this is a dramatic scene. The closest parallel in *Les Tragiques* to this sonnet of La Ceppède's may be found toward the end of "Les Fers." As part of the aftermath of the Massacre of St. Bartholomew, the bodies and blood of the Protestant martyrs flow down the Seine and into the sea. There Neptune, swimming around, is suddenly shocked to find his beard and skin covered with blood. He makes a violent protest to the Seine and the other rivers, ordering them to change course and to carry the bloody remains upstream. But when the heavens open and angels descend with golden chalices to gather up the blood of the martyrs, the ocean god repents of his error:

> Venez, enfans du ciel, s'escria le viellard,
> Heritiers du royaume, a qui le ciel depart

14. "La Chambre dorée," ll. 309–12.

> Son champ pour cemitiere. O saincts que je repousse!
> Pour vous, non contre vous, juste je me courrouce.[15]

And he goes about the task of giving pious burial to the martyrs. The action recalls that of the grieving sun in "Cependant le soleil fournissant sa journée."

We can also look at La Ceppède's scene in other ways: it is an example of chiaroscuro, in the Caravaggio manner. Likewise, it is a case of metamorphosis: day spectacularly turns into night. The metamorphosis theme is developed into a typically baroque paradox at the end of the sonnet: being born and dying are, in a sense, transformations, and the poet, playing upon the literal and figurative meanings of "naître," establishes an ingenious contrast:

> Tu fis naître un beau jour la nuit qui le vit naître,
> Et ce jour qu'il se meurt tu fais naître une nuit.

The following sonnet, from the second part of the *Théorèmes*, concerns the Resurrection of Christ and of man:

> Ce mystère est partout marqué par la nature;
> La lumière se meurt à l'abord de la nuit,
> Puis revit et reluit; le grain sous la culture
> De la terre se meurt, puis nombreux se produit.
> Nous voyons tous les jours des arbres choir le fruit,
> Dont le jardin parait sa plaisant clôture,
> Qui se meurt et pourrit, pour bien qu'il soit réduit,
> Puis revit et renaît après sa pourriture.
> Dans l'onde de Solin, le brandon plus ardent
> Est promptement éteint, la même eau va rendant
> La flamme à ce brandon, si dans elle il retombe.
> Le flot de ce bas monde éteint notre flambeau,
> Mais après que la mort l'a trempé dans la tombe,
> Il revit et rebrille et plus clair et plus beau.[16]

La Ceppède has here adopted the procedure, so common in St. François de Sales' *Introduction à la vie dévote*, of accumulating examples from nature in order to illustrate a religious doctrine. We find ourselves in the same garden world as the saint of Annecy: light dies as night comes, and then is born again at daybreak; the grain of wheat falls into the ground and dies, only to bring forth much fruit (cf. St. John 12:24); fruit falls from the orchard trees to rot upon the ground, but new life springs up from the seeds; and each one of these familiar natural phenomena becomes a symbol of spiritual significance. Very reminiscent also of the *Introduction* is the

15. "Les Fers," ll. 1515–18. 16. II, I, 47.

learned reference to an obscure marvel of the ancient world. St. François
speaks of the beautiful red flowers of the isles of Tylos, which are closed
all night but open with the rising sun—even so, he declares, humility hides
all our virtues and reveals them only when the sunlight of charity shines.
The honey of Heraclea in Pontus is poisonous because the bees gather it
from aconite flowers—in the same way, friendship based on false goods is
poisonous.[17] La Ceppède has discovered, in a book by Solinus entitled
De mirabilibus mundi, the mention of an extraordinary fountain: if you
dip a lighted torch in it, the flame goes out, but if, withdrawing the ex-
tinguished torch, you dip it in a second time, the flame relights itself. After
the three familiar examples we have the fourth somewhat pedantic and
fantastic one; but all four serve as analogies of the Resurrection. Here La
Ceppède is probably guilty of the same credulity about strange obscure phenomena described in ancient books as is Montaigne. But the greatest simi-
larity to Montaigne lies in the poetic sense of the flux of the world: this
sonnet as a whole, like so many passages in the *Essais,* rejoices in the fact
that "le monde n'est qu'une branloire perenne." And just as the *Essais,*
despite their awareness of the unstable, transitory nature of all things, end
with a triumphant acceptance of life, so this poem ends on a note of triumphant affirmation:

> Il revit et rebrille et plus clair et plus beau.
>
> Le cerf que le veneur relance au bois sauvage
> Voit un fleuve, s'y jette, nage et gagne le bord.
> Christ poursuivi de Juifs nage aux eaux de la mort,
> Les passe et vient surgir à l'immortel rivage.
> Le cerf hait le serpent, l'attaque, le ravage,
> Le mord et l'engloutit; Christ mortellement mord
> Le serpent qui fournit à la mort son breuvage;
> Cette mort engloutit et détruit son effort.
> Il a, pour ce qu'il est le vivant et la vie,
> Cette mort dévorée à son être asservie,
> Comme l'estomac change en lait son aliment.
> A ce victorieux la trompe prophétique
> Comme au cerf matineux a chanté son cantique
> Et nous semond fidèle au même compliment.[18]

I include this final example not because I consider it one of the best of the
Théorèmes but because it contains a number of characteristically baroque
devices. The animal imagery is of the sort enjoyed by St. François de Sales; in
addition, it is in part hunting imagery, which has, as the Norwegian scholar

17. *Introduction à la vie dévote,* III, 17.   18. II, I, 50.

Vedel once pointed out, a certain importance in poetry of this period. (Compare Sponde's great line,

> Je suis cet Acteon de ses chiens deschiré!) [19]

Very curious, and on the whole not very pleasing to modern taste, is the simile of the stomach changing its nourishment into milk. There is a far more extreme example of the same type of sensibility in "Misères," where d'Aubigné compares France of the religious wars to the body of a giant whose stomach has sucked up all the nourishment while the arms, legs, and head are wasting away.[20] The opening lines of the sonnet constitute the sort of theatrical scene which we have frequently encountered in our study of the baroque. Especially noteworthy throughout is the violent energy of the verbs and the precipitous way in which they pile up: a succession of five in the first two lines, and four more in the next couplet; then (my italics):

> Le cerf *hait* le serpent, l'*attaque,* le *ravage,*
> Le *mord* et l'*engloutit* . . .

Movement, metamorphosis, energy, violence, massive accumulation—when these characteristics appear in conscious conjunction we have a sure indication of the baroque style. In the last tercet, the visual images yield to auditory ones, and we have the blast of the prophetic trumpet and the singing of the hymn. Line 14, which is rather weak poetically, reminds us that the poem is a lesson in theology which we are to apply to ourselves; here, as in all the *Théorèmes,* the religious and moral purpose is evident.

For in the last analysis, we must always come back to the fundamental fact that the sonnets of La Ceppède are religious poetry; and since we have seen in them virtually all the main characteristics of the baroque, the question inevitably arises: Must the baroque be regarded as a Christian style? To the eight categories which we discovered in our analysis of Montaigne must we now add a ninth, Christianity? A recent archbishop of Canterbury once remarked that Christianity is the most unashamedly materialistic of religions. By this paradox he meant to stress the belief that, since God made all things, matter cannot possibly be evil; and above all, he was pointing to the dogma of the Incarnation: the Word made flesh. We find in all baroque writers and artists a deep enjoyment of the physical diversity of the world; and implicit in this enjoyment is a sense that physical things, whether beautiful, horrifying, strange, or ever changing, do have meaning. Furthermore, when they seek to express intangible concepts they resort, to an extraordinary degree, to incarnational imagery. As creators of a particular kind, they do what Christianity holds that God Himself has done.

---

19. *Sonnets d'amour,* no. V, l. 9.   20. "Misères," ll. 145–56.

Christianity is not only, in a certain sense, materialistic: it is also highly paradoxical. What is more paradoxical than this very doctrine of the Incarnation: the idea that Christ was at the same time true God and true man? Paradoxical also is the relationship of faith to works: on the one hand we are told that we are saved by faith rather than works, on the other that faith without works is dead. And the teaching of Christ is full of paradox: God obviously prefers the prodigal son to his virtuous brother, and the publican to the pharisee. One could go on and on citing examples; however, I hope I have made my point clear that I regard baroque art as essentially paradoxical, and in this respect also, then, it has close parallels with Christianity.

Each of the four Gospels devotes an altogether disproportionate amount of space—if we are to consider them as biographies—to the Passion and Crucifixion; and of course the very symbol of Christianity is an instrument of torture: the Cross. We have seen that horror and martyrdom are important aspects of baroque art also. The Christian story is essentially dramatic; theatricality is one of the great baroque categories. Christianity places great emphasis on transformation, conversion, spiritual growth, rebirth, resurrection; movement and metamorphosis are essential aspects of the baroque. Despite all these complexities and apparent contradictions, Christianity possesses an organic unity; so does baroque art. Finally, Christianity has all these different characteristics in conscious conjunction; one cannot isolate one aspect from the rest, and say: This is Christian. Neither can one choose one or two of the stylistic categories I have discussed, and say: There is antithesis, or concrete imagery, in this poem, therefore it is baroque. The characteristics must appear simultaneously.

These parallels are, to my mind, highly significant; yet I do not think that we should regard all baroque art as Christian art. There was a time when scholars identified it with the Counter Reformation. This attitude is to be encountered in the works of Weisbach, such as *Der Barock als Kunst der Gegenreformation*. It is implicit in Mâle's book on religious art from the end of the sixteenth to the eighteenth century; the subtitle is *Etude sur l'iconographie après le Concile de Trente*. True, Mâle is not concerned with the term "baroque"; we gather from his work, however, that the art of this whole period is essentially related to the Counter Reformation. This view is reflected in current French speech, in the expression *l'art jésuite*.

Personally, I feel that Wölfflin was right to concentrate on stylistic rather than on iconographic problems, and to point out that such a northern and Protestant artist as Rembrandt is baroque. To me the baroque transcends national and religious frontiers: it is a form of the sensibility, a kind of *Zeitgeist*, which appears all over Europe in the late sixteenth and part of the seventeenth centuries. Some of the most important baroque poets are Protestant: d'Aubigné, Milton, and Donne. It appears to me a mistake, which limits and distorts the whole concept, to restrict the baroque to post-Tridentine Roman Catholicism.

Now it will be observed that in this book many of the literary works which I examine are not primarily—sometimes not at all—religious in subject. La Ceppède's *Théorèmes,* St. François' *Introduction à la vie dévote,* and Rotrou's *Saint Genest* fall within the domain of Christian art; but what of the others? Montaigne is at times concerned with religious problems, as in the *Apologie* and certain essays like *Du repentir* (which, by the way, is decidedly unorthodox in tone), but humanism and self-portraiture occupy a larger place. The plays of Corneille which I study—*Mélite, Clitandre,* and *L'Illusion comique*—can scarcely be regarded as religious, nor can the shorter poems of Saint-Amant. Nevertheless, they belong to the baroque style.

I think the solution to the problem is this: Christian imagination, sensibility, and values tend to underly the whole period in question, 1570–1650. Even those writers who are not specifically Christian, or whose books are not primarily so, are deeply colored by Christianity in their modes of thought and artistic creation. The same is true, of course, of painters, sculptors, and architects: Bernini remains baroque while designing palaces, fountains, and his "Apollo and Daphne"; so does Rubens while painting the "Kermesse" or the Medici series, though these works are not religious art. The Christian and the baroque ethos are intimately connected; and it would be impossible to conceive of baroque art outside of Christian civilization. Since this period, and particularly for the last two hundred years, intellectuals and creative artists have been much less affected by the Christian ethos; and so it is that, although romanticism, for example, possesses some of the characteristics I am discussing in this book, it is in reality very different from the baroque. The baroque style is of Christian inspiration; and since its disappearance, there have been no Christian styles.

1. "LE MELON"

IN BAROQUE art, humor is often mingled with the more spectacular effects. In Bernini's lovely church of Sant'Andrea al Quirinale, cherubs tumble and swing and play whimsically with the decorative garland beneath the dome; in his "Fountain of the Rivers" in the Piazza Navona, huge sea monsters strain to drink the basin dry; and Rubens, when he depicts King Henri IV gazing ecstatically at a portrait of Marie de Médicis held by angels in a cloud, surely has his tongue in his cheek. And thus a delightful minor baroque poet who should be better known, Saint-Amant, is above all amusing. The familiar baroque effects of exaggeration and concrete sensual imagery are all the more striking when interspersed with humor. An outstanding example is his poem on "Le Melon." It begins with an ecstatic evocation of the sense of smell:

> Quelle odeur sens-je en cette chambre?
> Quel doux parfum de musc et d'ambre
> Me vient le cerveau resjouir
> Et tout le cœur espanouir?

But soon all the senses come into play in a series of whimsically exclamatory sentences:

> Baillez-le-moi, je vous en prie,
> Que j'en commette idolatrie:
> O! quelle odeur! qu'il est pesant!
> Et qu'il me charme en le baisant!
> Page, un cousteau, que je l'entame;

Having smelled the melon, felt its weight, and kissed it, he addresses a prayer to Pomona before cutting the fruit open. The prayer is granted, for the poet proceeds to swoon at the color, taste, and smell:

> O dieux! que l'esclat qu'il me lance,
> M'en confirme bien l'excellance!
> Qui vit jamais un si beau teint!
> D'un jaune sanguin il se peint;

And when he begins to eat,

> Ha! soustenez-moy, je me pame
> Ce morceau me chatouille l'ame
> Il rend une douce liqueur
> Qui me va confire le cœur;
> Mon appetit se rassassie
> De pure et nouvelle ambroisie,
> Et mes sens, par le goust seduits,
> Au nombre d'un sont tous reduits.

The gastronomic subject matter and the joking tone should not hide from us the fact that we are in the presence of an exceptionally lush example of multiple-sense imagery. The poet's senses all come together in a single ecstatic swoon. Though I may be accused of comparing great things to small, I feel that this passage calls to mind d'Aubigné's vision of heaven in "Jugement": having experienced through his five physical senses the delights of heaven, the poet swoons away. And here Saint-Amant declares that he prefers the sensations given him by the melon to the kisses of his mistress. There follows, as is so often the case in poetry of this period, a long catalogue. These are the taste sensations which, along with the kisses of his mistress, are inferior to the melon: apricots, strawberries and cream, manna from heaven, honey, pears from Tours, fresh figs, muscat grapes! All this part of the poem has been in octosyllabics; it ends with an invocation ("O vive source de lumiere!") to Apollo as the god of both fruit and poetry. Saint-Amant dedicates to him an ode in alexandrines, which constitutes approximately two-thirds of "Le Melon" as a whole.

The alexandrine part of the poem is a kind of burlesque description of a banquet on Mount Olympus. The gods are celebrating their victory over the giants. The whole tone is mock-heroic: in battle, Pan has lost his gloves and Mercury a garter. The nymphs are waiting on them at table:

> Soudain, de tous costez sur l'Olympe se virent
> Plats deçà, plats delà, que les Nymphes servirent
> Le bras nud jusqu'au coude et le sein descouvert,
> Orné de quelque fleur avec un peu de vert.

This picture of bacchanalian feasting, with a profusion of dishes and half-naked nymphs, is reminiscent of Rubens. One should note Saint-Amant's pictorial sense: the uncovered breasts are decorated with flowers and a touch of greenery! Baroque artists are always sensitive to color combinations.

Each god has brought an especially delicious dish to the banquet, and each god is ironically described with a picturesque and grotesque epithet. Jupiter, here called Jupin, is introduced as "Ce dieu qui des premiers autorisa l'inceste," and he offers a vast amount of game caught by his eagle. Juno, in her cart drawn by peacocks (the peacock, that symbol of ostentation, is always a favorite with baroque artists, as M. Rousset has pointed out),

> Prit de la main d'Iris un bouquet d'ortolans
> Qui fleurissoit de graisse, et convioit la bouche
> A luy donner des dents une prompte escarmouche,
> Durant qu'il estoit chaud, et qu'il s'en exhaloit
> Un gracieux parfum que le nez avaloit.

Concrete sensations follow each other in rapid succession here: the unctuous texture of the ortolans, the bite of the teeth, the heat of the dish, the delicious aroma. Bacchus, with his "trogne vermeille" instead of nectar, has contributed fifty bottles of "vin d'Ay"; this I take to be the wine which we now call *champagne nature*. Ceres is whimsically described as "La déesse des fours, des moulins et des plaines"; in fact these epithets may leave the reader a little puzzled at first, and it is not until half-a-dozen lines further along that she is explicitly identified by name, so that the word "Ceres" comes as a humorous half-surprise. Her offering consists not of bread but of cakes. Neptune brings oysters. Diana, who is rather unflatteringly depicted as

> La princesse des flots, qui comme sage-femme
> Assiste a ce travail ou l'on pisse des os

is also the goddess of hunting, and so her dish is roast venison with a garlic sauce. The crippled blacksmith presents the assembled company with a huge ham and six ox tongues.

You may wonder how Venus is characterized. She is

> La garce qui nasquit de l'excrement de l'onde
> Pour courir l'esguillette en tous les lieux du monde,
> Venus, la bonne cagne aux paillards appetits . . .

and her gift to this dinner party is a pie of squab and artichoke hearts. The tone of grotesque realism is maintained in the description of this pie,

> . . . plein de culs d'artichaud.
> Et de tout ce qui rend celuy de l'homme chaud.

And there are many other dishes: Pan brings a larded leg of lamb, "la vieille au cul crotté, la terrestre Cybelle" offers new mushrooms cooked in lamb gravy, morels, and truffles. The method of gathering truffles is described in a picturesque little vignette:

> . . . des truffes . . .
> Qu'un porc qu'on meine en lesse, eventant d'assez loin
> Fouille pour nostre bouche et renverse du groin.

Vertumna and Pomona present asparagus, peas, salad, and all kinds of extraordinary fruit.

Of course, this long procession of gastronomic delights is simply leading up to the grand climax: the arrival of the Melon. The composition of the whole scene is strongly baroque: the amassing of exuberant abundance, with a host of picturesque details and a constant appeal to the senses, and the final lyric outburst in praise of the melon. The melon is offered by Thalia, the Muse of comedy, in honor of her master Apollo. Just as Apollo is the god of fruit and of poetry, so Thalia blends in divine unity melons and comedy. The poem as a whole has mingled gastronomy and poetic humor; and in this climax, the melon and poetry become one. We have seen how the baroque enjoys blurring the lines between different artistic domains— or, if you prefer, seeks to show the secret correspondences between different things. The arrival of the melon on the table causes the gods to shout for joy:

> Dès qu'il fut sur la nape, un aigu cry de joye
> Donna son corps de vent aux oreilles en proye;
> Le cœur en tressaillit, et les plus friands nez
> D'une si douce odeur furent tous estonnez;
> Mais quand ce vint au goust, ce fut bien autre chose:
> Aussi d'en discourir la muse mesme n'ose;
> Elle dit seulement qu'en ce divin banquet
> Il fit cesser pour l'heure aux femmes le caquet.

The boisterous cries of pleasure, the sweet smell, and the delicious taste come together to constitute another example of multiple-sense imagery. Then silence falls; as Saint-Amant remarks, even the women keep quiet! The lyric enthusiasm gently melts into irony. But then Apollo carves out a piece of the melon and makes of it a musical instrument; it is the first lute ever invented.

> Ainsi, de cette escorce en beauté sans pareille
> Fut fabriqué là-haut ce charmeur de l'oreille,
> D'où sortit lors un son, par accens mesuré,
> Plus doux que le manger qu'on en avoit tiré.

We have here not only the usual baroque fusion of different senses but also a metamorphosis: the melon is divinely *transformed* into a musical instrument. All this is none the less significant because it is a joke; Saint-Amant looks at his story half seriously, with lyric enthusiasm, and half humorously, with mock-heroic irony. This shifting of the point of view constitutes an ambivalence; in the hands of a mannerist artist it would produce a sense of uneasiness; the baroque artist draws from it only delight.

The poem concludes with ecstatic exclamations; the fact that they are to be taken in part humorously does not detract from their lyric exuberance:

> O manger precieux! delices de la bouche!
> O doux reptile herbu, rampant sur une couche!
> O! beaucoup mieux que l'or, chef-d'oeuvre d'Apollon!
> O fleur de tous les fruits! O ravissant melon!

Note the picturesque comparison of the melon to a hairy reptile creeping on its couch of leaves. The climactic closing lines are in the burlesque vein; the poet heaps up a long list of ironically impossible events:

> Les bordels de Rouen seront francs de verolle,
> Sans vermine et sans galle on verra les pedents
>
>   .   .   .
>
> Les meilleurs cabarets deviendront soliteres

All these things and many more will happen before Saint-Amant forgets the charming taste of the melon. Sensuous imagery, amusing realistic detail, exuberant heaping of examples, sprightly movement, the blending of the lyric and ironic tones—the conscious fusion of such elements makes of this poem an especially delightful example of the baroque style.

2. "La Solitude"

It is somewhat unusual to find a seventeenth-century French poem in praise of solitude. Alceste's house in the country—in all probability a very pleasant château—is called a "désert," and Célimène seems to be voicing the general reaction of the age when she shudders at the idea of burying herself in the wilderness:

> Moi, renoncer au monde avant que de vieillir,
> Et dans votre désert aller m'ensevelir!

And, a little further on, she says:

> La solitude effraie une âme de vingt ans.
> Je ne sens pas la mienne assez grande, assez forte,
> Pour me résoudre à prendre un dessein de la sorte.[1]

However, at the age of thirty Saint-Amant feels no such terror of solitude, and does not think that unusual fortitude of soul is required to bear it. The presumed date of this poem is 1624; and that, perhaps, is a key to the attitude it expresses. When the *Misanthrope* was written, forty-two years later, a change in sensibility had occurred: classicism had triumphed over the

1. Ll. 1774-76.

baroque. Saint-Amant composed his ode on solitude in a cave on Belle-Ile, off the Breton coast. He had come to the island as a part of the suite of his patron, the Duc de Retz, and wrote the greater part of his works there. A friend of his, M. Roger, in later years expressed the growing classical attitude that a man must be mentally unbalanced to enjoy such a place, by remarking in a letter to Desforges-Maillard that the poet used to retire to this cave "quand il étoit malade à force d'avoir bu." The shocked tone of the letter is entertaining, and reveals, it seems to me, not only the writer's disapproval of Saint-Amant's debauched mode of life but also a general classical condemnation of the baroque age:

Saint-Amant étoit un débauché. La nature seule l'avoit fait poète. Le vin lui donnoit de l'enthousiasme. . . . Souvent le maréchal de Belle-Isle et lui montoient sur une vieille crédence où ils avoient une petite table chargée de bouteilles de vin. Là, chacun étant sur sa chaise, ils y faisoient des séances de vingt-quartre heures. Le duc de Retz les venoit voir de temps en temps dans cette attitude. Quelquefois la table, les pots, les verres, les chaises, les buveurs, tout dégringoloit du haut en bas.[2]

The implication is clear: the poetry of Saint-Amant is mostly drunken raving, undisciplined by reasonable rules.

"La Solitude" is a poem of two hundred lines, divided into twenty stanzas of ten lines each. The opening of the first stanza sets the tone:

> Que j'ayme la solitude!
> Que ces lieux sacrez à la nuit,
> Esloignez du monde et du bruit,
> Plaisent à mon inquietude!

The poem expresses an anxious spirit, but anxiety is felt to be a pleasant state. The paradoxical attitude is typically baroque. Later passages will discuss suitable places for suicide, ruined castles, witches, skeletons, and storms at sea, but always with a sense of enjoyment, never with a feeling of romantic melancholy. The two exclamations are merely the first of a dozen or more.

The world of the "Solitude" is actually peopled with ancient gods and goddesses: Pan, Jupiter, Neptune, Phoebus, Tritons, and nymphs. Not that the poet takes them very seriously; their function is essentially to maintain him in a pleasurable state of daydreaming:

> Que sur cette espine fleurie,
> Dont le printemps est amoureux,
> Philomèle, au chant langoureux,
> Entretient bien ma resverie![3]

2. Saint-Amant, *Œuvres complètes* (1st ed.), p. xiii.   3. Ll. 21–4.

Among baroque features, one should note the antithetical juxtaposition of the flowering thorn, the prosopopoeia of line 22 (the spring is in love), and the exclamatory form of the sentence. During the rest of the stanza, the poet finds enjoyment in considering that the cliffs of Belle-Ile would be a fine place for unhappy people to commit suicide:

> Que je prens de plaisir à voir
> Ces monts pendans en precipices,
> Qui, pour les coups du desespoir,
> Sont aux malheureux si propices,
> Quand la cruauté de leur sort
> Les force à rechercher la mort! [4]

Saint-Amant is not for a moment entertaining thoughts of committing suicide himself. There is here none of the romantic's total surrender to *mal du siècle*. The author of "La Solitude" is no René or Werther; the precipices are convenient for the *malheureux,* but he is not unhappy. He is daydreaming with detachment. With a characteristically baroque delight in theatricality, but without being, like the romantics, the victim of his own illusions, he contemplates the rocky coast of the island as a wonderful setting for a tragic scene.

The same feeling prevails when he looks at ruined castles:

> Que j'ayme à voir la decadence
> De ces vieux chasteaux ruinez,
> Contre qui les ans mutinez
> Ont deployé leur insolence!
> Les sorciers y font leur sabbat;
> Les demons follets s'y retirent,
> Qui d'un malicieux ébat
> Trompent nos sens et nous martirent;
> Là se nichent en mille troux
> Les couleuvres et les hyboux.
>
> L'orfraye, avec ses cris funebres,
> Mortels augures des destins,
> Fait rire et dancer les lutins
> Dans ces lieux remplis de tenebres.
> Sous un chevron de bois maudit
> Y branle le squelette horrible
> D'un pauvre amant qui se pendit
> Pour une bergere insensible,
> Qui d'un seul regard de pitié
> Ne daigna voir son amitié. [5]

4. Ll. 25–30.   5. Ll. 71–90.

Saint-Amant is not really deeply upset at the sight of the unhappy lover's skeleton—assuming that it exists at all, and is not just a flight of his fancy. No; once again it is just that the ruined castle seems to him a wonderful theatrical setting, so he indulges himself in the pleasure of imagining a tragedy of love. Neither is he terrified at the witches' sabbath: it is fun to pretend to believe that demons are dancing amid the ruins. The spirit is very much that of Callot's engraving of the "Temptation of St. Anthony" (1635): there the huge, bat-winged dragon breathing forth fire, the strange creature which is half live monster and half cannon, and all the myriads of other grotesque demons are intended rather to amuse than to frighten us. Or, if Saint-Amant and Callot are actually trying to make us shudder slightly, the sensation is meant to be fascinating rather than disagreeable. The baroque interest in demons derives, it seems to me, from two sources. On the one hand, men of this period take pleasure in all phenomena which contribute to the sense of the strangeness of the world: the more surprising things they can discover, the happier they are. Hence Montaigne's fondness for collecting examples of strange customs, and St. François de Sales' delight in curious animals. On the other hand, illusions are felt to be fascinating; and in order to enjoy the experience to the full, one should first allow oneself to be taken in (partly at least) and then see clearly that the whole impression was an illusion. In the Roman church of Sant' Ignazio, first put yourself in the spot where the flat ceiling appears to be a vast colonnade open to the heavens; then move to another position and watch the illusion disappear. Saint-Amant realizes perfectly well that his witches and demons "trompent nos sens," but he enjoys nursing the illusion for a little while, pretending to frighten himself. The romantic wants to be completely taken in, and wants his readers to be permanently swept off their feet also. The baroque writer, by retaining a certain detachment, preserves his sense of humor as well, without, however, losing his sense of wonder.

The poet continues, in the following stanza (X), to play with his illusions; he decides that the ruin must be haunted, and imagines that the ghost of the lover is hovering near the bones:

> Autour de ces vieux ossemens
> Son ombre, aux peines condamnée
> Lamente en longs gemissemens
> Sa malheureuse destinée.[6]

Enjoying himself thoroughly, Saint-Amant wanders into a graveyard adjoining the castle and tries to read the epitaphs on the stones, but time has almost effaced them, as it has the inscriptions carved on the trees. And here, though

6. Ll. 95–8.

he does not develop the theme, we can imagine him conjuring up the lovers'
ghosts. Going back into the ruin, he notices that the flooring of the top
storey has fallen into the cellar,

> Que la limace et le crapaut
> Souillent de venin et de bave; [7]

Here we have the baroque interest in the ugly realistic detail. Finally, he
explores a vaulted underground hall so dark that Phoebus himself, he declares, would be unable to see a thing. Here it should be observed that
stanzas VIII–XII constitute a series of night scenes: the witches' sabbath, the
suicide of the lover, the groanings of the ghost, the poet's own wanderings
through the deserted castle. Baroque artists like to depict dramatic scenes
against a night background: consider Caravaggio's "Conversion of St. Paul,"
his "Martyrdom of St. Matthew," Georges de La Tour's "St. Sebastian Wept
by St. Irene," and Rembrandt's "Christ and the Pilgrims at Emmaus."

Returning to his grotto, Saint-Amant delights in its coolness, and pretends
to feel the presence of mythological deities:

> Au creux de cette grotte fresche,
> Ou l'Amour se pourroit geler,
> Echo ne cesse de brusler
> Pour son amant froid et revesche.[8]

The poem is rich primarily in visual imagery, but as is usually the case in
the baroque period, other senses are present too: in the castle we hear the
groanings of the ghost, and now we feel the cold air of the cave. The
hyperbole ("Love himself would freeze here") is similar to that expressing
the darkness of the subterranean vault ("Phoebus himself would see nothing"). And here we have an example of metaphoric antithesis: despite the
cold, Echo is burning for her cold lover. Throughout the four lines, the
contrasting themes of heat and cold are interwoven. And in the latter part of
the stanza, multiple-sense imagery returns, for the poet, in this chilly cave
begins to play the lute to accompany the lamentations of Echo.

Stanzas XV–XVII are an enthusiastic evocation of the sea: after all, Saint-
Amant's cave is on an island. It is evident that what appeals to him most
about the ocean is its mutability, what Montaigne called "les mouvemen
espouvantables de cette mer infinie." [9] Like the author of the *Essais*, and
like nearly all baroque spirits, he enjoys flux, movement, and metamorphosis
"Le monde n'est qu'une branloire perenne." And so, sitting on the shore
he takes pleasure in the calm after the storm:

7. Ll. 107–8.   8. Ll. 121–4.   9. *Essais*, II, 12, 161.

> Que c'est un chose agreable
> D'estre sur le bord de la mer,
> Quand elle vient à se calmer
> Après quelque orage effroyable! [10]

He imagines the hairy Tritons blowing their hoarse trumpets to calm the wind and the waves. Amid the serenity of fine weather, it is a delight to re-create, in one's mind's eye, the theatricality of a raging sea, and to day-dream about the ocean's changing aspects:

> Tantost l'onde, brouillant l'arène,
> Murmure et fremit de courroux,
> Se roullant dessus les cailloux
> Qu'elle apporte et qu'elle r'entraine.
> Tantost, elle estale en ses bords,
> Que l'ire de Neptune outrage,
> Des gens noyez, des monstres morts,
> Des vaisseaux brisez du naufrage,
> Des diamans, de l'ambre gris,
> Et mille autres choses de pris.
>
> Tantost, la plus claire du monde,
> Elle semble un miroir flottant,
> Et nous represente à l'instant
> Encore d'autres cieux sous l'onde.
> Le soleil s'y fait si bien voir,
> Y contemplant son beau visage,
> Qu'on est quelque temps à sçavoir
> Si c'est luy-mesme, ou son image,
> Et d'abord il semble à nos yeux
> Qu'il s'est laissé tomber des cieux. [11]

Saint-Amant's meditations on drowned men, dead whales, and shipwrecks are of the same order as his suicides and demoniacal dances. He likes to think of such dramatic scenes precisely because he does not take them too seriously. It is all a game: the baroque mind enjoys the wonder and variety of surging water provided that it does not have to take the spectacle too seriously. It is this same type of sensibility which led the Romans, from the sixteenth century to the eighteenth, to build their marvelous series of turbu-lent fountains—from Tivoli, with the cascading handrails of its staircases and the gushing geysers of its grottoes, to the Trevi, with its grand torrential rush of water over vast illusionistic rocks dominated by Neptune and his horses. Fountains are loved for their movement and metamorphosis, and their

---

10. Ll. 141–4.   11. Ll. 151–70.

theatricality is just as conscious an illusion as Saint-Amant's daydreaming visions of a tempestuous sea succeeded by a glassy calm. Neither the Roman strolling past the Trevi fountain nor Saint-Amant walking on the beach at Belle-Ile in fine weather is in danger, but both have the fun of thinking of stormy floods of water. In "La Solitude" the pleasures of illusion are further prolonged by the sight of the sun reflected in a mirror-like sea: Which is the reality and which the illusion—the sun or its reflection? Not that there is actually any doubt, but it is entertaining to pretend that there is. In an earlier passage of this same poem, the author describes the beauties of an interior valley on the island; here again he expresses his love of water and transformation:

> Que je trouve doux le ravage
> De ces fiers torrens vagabonds,
> Qui se preciptent par bonds
> Dans ce valon vert et sauvage!
> Puis, glissant sous les arbrisseaux,
> Ainsi que des serpents sur l'herbe,
> Se changent en plaisans ruisseaux,
> Où quelque Naïade superbe
> Règne comme en son lict natal,
> Dessus un throsne de christal! [12]

I think it is evident that Saint-Amant would have been thoroughly happy gazing at the fountains of Rome. The Turtle fountain (1585) was built nine years before he was born; the Barcaccia in the Piazza di Spagna, three years after the composition of the present poem (1627); the Triton, when the poet was forty-six (1640); the "Fountain of the Rivers," in his later years (1647–52); the one he would have liked best of all, the Trevi, dates from the century after his death (1732–62) but corresponds admirably to the spirit of certain passages of "La Solitude."

Attention should be called to the way in which certain lines begin with "Tantost." This is the case with line 131 ("Tantost, sortant de ces ruines"); line 151 ("Tantost l'onde, brouillant l'arene"); line 155 ("Tantost, elle estale en ses bords"); and line 161 ("Tantost, la plus claire du monde"). This transitional adverb reveals a significant fact about the structure of the poem: "La Solitude" is a succession of different picturesque aspects. The author wanders around his island, seeking varying views of the sights he likes; indeed, many passages, particularly in the section where he is exploring the ruined castle, could equally well have been introduced by "Tantost" if he had been indifferent to repetitiousness. This is the baroque procedure which

12. Ll. 31–40.

I have discussed in the chapter on St. François de Sales: multiple-aspect imagery. It has analogies with the sentence structure of Montaigne and Sir Thomas Browne, as these two authors stroll around an idea, offering it to the reader in a succession of aspects.

There is another affinity with the *Introduction à la vie dévote* in this poem: the richness and variety of the flora and fauna, proceeding, as with St. François, from the author's delight in the diversity of natural phenomena. Looking over the text, I find the following species identified: the flowering thorn (roses?), snakes, service trees, alders, willows, osiers, reeds, gladioli, frogs, aquatic birds, roebucks, fish, grass snakes, owls, slugs, toads, ivy, walnut trees, poppies, sponges, and "monsters." All arouse the poet's sympathetic interest: it is the baroque love and acceptance of the strangeness and complexity of the world.

The concluding stanzas (XVIII–XX) are directly addressed to Bernières, one of Saint-Amant's patrons. To a certain degree, they indulge in that servile, hyperbolic flattery which is characteristic of much of the art of the period (compare Malherbe's ecstatic praises of the royal family, or Rubens' glorification of Marie de Médicis); they also serve to pull together the varied parts of the poem. "La Solitude" does not have a very logical plan, but it possesses a certain organic unity based on the temperament of the poet; like the *Essais* of Montaigne, it offers us "mes songes que voicy." Saint-Amant admits to Bernières that all this is a "fantasque tableau Fait d'une peinture vivante" (ll. 173–4). He confesses that he likes to seek the wilderness, and daydream by himself; but his most agreeable thoughts are about Bernières. The last twenty lines attempt to define the poet's style (note the reappearance of "Tantost, tantost!"), and by reasserting his love of solitude, provide a link with line 1 (compare the way the theme of vanity explicitly returns at the end of Montaigne's essay); the final note is one of flattery, expressed in a witty *pointe* ("The only trouble with solitude is that it prevents me from seeing you").

> Tu vois dans cette poësie
> Pleine de licence et d'ardeur
> Les beaux rayons de la splendeur
> Que m'esclaire la fantaisie:
> Tantost chagrin, tantost joyeux,
> Selon que la fureur m'enflame,
> Et que l'objet s'offre à mes yeux,
> Les propos me naissent en l'ame,
> Sans contraindre la liberté
> Du demon qui m'a transporté.

O que j'ayme la solitude!
C'est l'element des bons esprits,
C'est par elle que j'ay compris
L'art d'Apollon sans nulle estude.
Je l'ayme pour l'amour de toy,
Connoissant que ton humeur l'ayme;
Mais, quand je pense bien à moy,
Je la hay pour la raison mesme:
Car elle pourroit me ravir
L'heur de te voir et te servir.[13]

Stanza XIX could serve as a description not only of the style of Saint-Amant but also that of Montaigne. What are the traits mentioned? Freedom, fervor, and fancy. In just this way, Montaigne gives free rein to his mind as it moves in untrammeled enthusiasm, through association of ideas, from one picturesque subject to another. We have seen the procedure in the essay *De la vanité*.

3. "Le Contemplateur"

There are many resemblances between "La Solitude" and "Le Contemplateur." Both poems are composed of octosyllables, arranged in ten-line stanzas. Both have Belle-Ile as their setting; in both the poet contemplates the sea at length; finally, in both Saint-Amant allows his fancy to roam freely from scene to scene and subject to subject. But "Le Contemplateur" is considerably the more important poem—by its length first of all, 460 lines as against 200, but also because of its greater depth of thought and feeling. Without going quite so far as the poet's contemporary Nicolas Faret, who regarded "ce divin *Contemplateur* [comme] une sublime leçon de la plus haute philosophie chrétienne et morale," [1] I should be inclined to agree that it is Saint-Amant's masterpiece.

"Le Contemplateur" is dedicated to Philippe Cospeau, Bishop of Nantes. The first three stanzas are a hyperbolic eulogy of the sort common in the baroque era. We are reminded of the tone of Malherbe's ode "Pour le Roi allant châtier la rebellion des Rochelois," which was written at about the same time:

Prends ta foudre, Louis, et va comme un lion
Donner le dernier coup à la dernière tête
        De la rébellion.

Fais choir en sacrifice au démon de la France
Les fronts trop élevés de ces âmes d'enfer.[2]

13. Ll. 181–200.
1. Saint-Amant, *Œuvres complètes* (Livet ed.), p. xv.   2. Ll. 2–6.

(This is incidentally, the event commemorated in one of Callot's greatest engravings, the "Siege of the Ile de Ré.")

Just as Malherbe praises Louis XIII for stamping out Protestant rebellion, so Saint-Amant lauds the bishop for destroying heresy:

> Vous par qui j'espere estre exemt
> De choir en l'eternelle flamme,
> Apostre du siecle present,
> Cause du salut de mon ame,
> Divin prelat, sainct orateur,
> Juste et souverain destructeur
> Des infernales heresies; [3]

Very nearly contemporary ("Le Contemplateur," "Pour le Roi," and the "Siege of the Ile de Ré" all date from the years between 1625 and 1630) is Rubens' painting, "The Government of the Regent Queen" (shortly prior to 1625), which represents Apollo expelling Discord, Hatred, and Rebellion from the realm of Marie de Médicis. And in 1640, Pietro da Cortona did his vast ceiling fresco in the Palazzo Barberini, of the monstrous Barberini bees stinging to death the enemies of religion. All these works have two characteristics in common: flattery of a powerful patron, and glorification of a political or religious cause. I have spoken of moral purpose as an important baroque category; sometimes the moral purpose is so intense that the work of art becomes an instrument of propaganda or indeed of holy war: the enemy is infernal, and must be destroyed in battle. On the Protestant side, but still within the sphere of militant baroque art, are the warlike opening lines of *Les Tragiques*:

> Puis qu'il faut s'attaquer aux legions de Rome
> Aux monstres d'Italie, il faudra faire comme
> Hannibal, qui par feux d'aigre humeur arrosez
> Se fendit un passage aux Alpes embrasez. [4]

Actually, Saint-Amant never has the violence of d'Aubigné, and he does not maintain for very long the tone of strident propaganda. Much more characteristic is the third of the stanzas directly addressed to the bishop, in which he explains what his poem is going to be like:

> Vous, dis-je, qui, daignant cherir
> Les nobles travaux de la muse
> Avez voulu vous enquerir
> A quoy maintenant je m'amuse;
> Je vous le veux dire en ces vers;
> Ou d'un art pompeux et divers
> Je feray briller mes pensees; [5]

---

3. Ll. 1–7.   4. "Misères," ll. 1–4.   5. Ll. 21–7.

In other words, "Le Contemplateur" is a sprightly conversation with a friend. The author describes his occupations, and talks of the things which amuse him. In many ways this is an excellent definition of the *Essais* of Montaigne! The Callot engraving which I have just mentioned has, as its point of departure, the desire to honor an exalted patron and his cause; Louis XIII and Monsieur, on horseback, survey the naval battle from a hill, but the artist then goes on to depict the things which really amuse him: the bustling activities of soldiers, the picturesque loading of boats, the swirling, rhythmical array of graceful ships in battle formation. Saint-Amant, having done homage to his patron and affirmed his detestation of heresy, now turns to the delights of his imagination. The flattery and propaganda themes will recur, but essentially we have what Montaigne would call "un tableau de mes humeurs."

"Un art pompeux et divers": this is indeed an admirable description of the baroque style. Pompous and varied, Callot's "Ile de Ré," Cortona's "Triumph of the Barberini," and Rubens' "Government of the Regent Queen." Pompous and varied, the façade of San Vincenzo ed Anastasio, with its massed columns and angels blowing trumpets; pompous and varied, the exuberant Trevi fountain beside which it stands. In effect, Saint-Amant has summed up here several of the leading baroque categories: exaggeration, theatricality, and contrast.

In stanza IV we learn that we are back where we were in "La Solitude" —on Belle-Ile, where Saint-Amant is dancing attendance on the Duc de Retz:

> Loin, dans une isle qu'à bon droit
> On honora du nom de Belle,
> Ou s'esleve un fort qui tiendroit
> Contre l'Anglois et le rebelle,
> Je contente à plein mon desir
> De voir mon Duc à mon plaisir,[6]

The mention of the fortress which can hold out against the English and the Protestants calls to mind that other island off the French Atlantic coast, where Callot represents the forces of King Louis XIII engaged against the same two enemies.

And now the seaside daydreaming begins. The poet, as in "La Solitude," watches the aquatic birds; he communes with Thetis; the expanse of the ocean, by association of ideas, makes him think of the Deluge, and he meditates on Noah. A passing dove reminds him of the one that brought back the olive branch to Noah; and he reflects that the Holy Ghost is usually represented in the form of a dove (stanzas V–VIII). Delighted by the activ-

6. Ll. 31–6.

ity of his own mind, he feels that no philosophic secrets are hid from his intellectual curiosity:

> Et, dans ma recherche profonde
> Je loge en moy tout l'univers.
>
> La, songeant au flus et reflus,
> Je m'abisme dans cette idee; [7]

The whole movement of Saint-Amant's thought in this section is reminiscent of that of Montaigne, as I presented it in my discussion of *De la vanité:* theme leads to theme, not in accordance with any systematic plan but following the free play of a lively mind. As with the *Essais,* the reader feels that he watches the ideas being born. "Je loge en moy tout l'univers" has affinities with Montaigne's "Chaque homme porte la forme entiere de l'humaine condition"; and the "flus et reflus" with his "branloire perenne." Watching the ships on the horizon, the poet is led to marvel at the mysteries of the compass:

> La, mainte nef au gré du vent
> Sillonnant la plaine liquide
> Me fait repenser bien souvent
> A la boussole qui la guide;
> La miraculeuse vertu
> Dont ce cadran est revestu
> Foule ma raison subvertie,
> Et mes esprits, en ce discort,
> S'embrouillent dans la sympatie
> Du fer, de l'aymant, et du nort. [8]

This sense of wonder at natural phenomena which appear to transcend reason recalls the interest shown by Montaigne in the *Apologie* and St. François in the *Introduction* in the mysterious instincts of animals. The baroque mind delights in a feeling of occult correspondences between diverse and seemingly unrelated things—as here, the iron, the magnet, and the north. One of the greatest monuments of English baroque prose, the *Religio medici,* published in 1643, expresses in a surprisingly similar sequence of thought the author's awe:

I could never content my contemplation with those general pieces of wonder, the Flux and Reflux of the Sea, the increase of the Nile, the conversion of the Needle to the North; and have studied to match and parallel those in the more obvious and neglected pieces of Nature, which without further travel I can do in

7. Ll. 89–92.   8. Ll. 101–10.

the Cosmography of my self; we carry with us the wonders we seek without us; There is Africa and all her prodigies in us . . .[9]

The universe within the author; the flux and reflux of the sea; the sympathy of the compass for the north: these same three ideas are to be found within in a space of twenty lines in "Le Contemplateur."

For a moment (stanza XII) Saint-Amant allows himself to play with the verbal associations aroused by the French word for magnet (*aymant*). It is the baroque love of punning—and perhaps also, to a lesser extent (since after all Richelieu had re-established order), Montaigne's distress at the corruption of the times:

> O mœurs! dis-je, o monde brutal!
> Faut-il que le plus fier metal
> Plus que toy se montre sensible!
> Faut-il que, sans te reformer,
> Une pierre dure au possible
> Te fasse honte en l'art d'aymer![10]

Note also the prosopopoeia which proceeds from the pun: the poet endows the magnet with the capacity of loving. And he indulges himself in a rapid series of four exclamations. At times in baroque poetry exclamations spurt forth like jets from a Bernini fountain. And then, as we so often see in the *Essais,* association of ideas calls up a contrary, causing the author to reverse himself. How can I complain of a lack of love among men, he exclaims, when the great duke who reigns here is a proof of the opposite? The theme of flattery of the mighty returns, although this time the incense is offered to the Duc de Retz rather than the Bishop of Nantes. In stanza XIV Saint-Amant pauses to evaluate what he has written, as Montaigne occasionally does:

> Voilà comme, selon l'objet,
> Mon esprit changeant de projet
> Saute de pensée en pensée.
> La diversité plaist aux yeux,
> Et la veue en fin est lassée
> De ne regarder que les cieux.[11]

But before leaving the sea, he meditates for a while on various mythological deities—in particular Camoens' marine god, the Giant of the Cape (stanzas XVII–XIX). And then, for the sake of variety, he starts on a stroll. He too likes "le remuement et le changement" and feels an "humeur avide des choses nouvelles"; all this may be, as Montaigne says, a "temoignage d'inquietude," but at the beginning of "La Solitude" the poet has freely admitted

9. Sec. 15.   10. Ll. 125–30.   11. Ll. 135–40.

that he has an anxious temperament. Indeed, a certain kind of anxiety is characteristic of the baroque spirit; not so much an unhappy *angoisse* as a restless curiosity to see the diversity of the world.

Saint-Amant's contemplative wanderings, as in "La Solitude," bring forth a cascade of stanzas introduced by the word "Tantost": this is true of stanzas XX, XXI, XXII (here it is "quelquefois," but it is really the same thing), XXIV, XXV, XXVIII, XXIX, XXX, and XXXI. I have already discussed, in connection with the *Introduction à la vie dévote* and "La Solitude," the importance of multiple-aspect imagery in the baroque style. This can take many forms: the conscious arrangement of an architectural ensemble, as in the Piazza San Pietro or the Piazza Navona, so that a kaleidoscope succession of points of view is necessary to appreciate the whole; it can be a jumping from thought to thought, as in *De la vanité* or "Le Contemplateur," so that the reader senses an organic whole only after he has proceeded through a bewildering series of entertaining ideas; or it can be the division of a prose passage into clauses unrelated by conjunctions, separated by semicolons, and each one of which presents a different way of looking at the same concept. For examples of the latter, I suggest that the reader examine almost any page of Montaigne or St. François—or the above quotation from Sir Thomas Browne.

The poet's amusements on Belle-Ile are numerous. Sometimes he sets traps for rabbits, sometimes he shoots cormorants, sometimes he fishes from a boat in the bay. The account of angling for *dorade* is typically baroque:

> Tantost, nous allant promener
> Dans quelque chaloupe à la rade,
> Nous laissons après nous traisner
> Quelque ligne pour la dorade.
> Ce beau poisson, qui l'apperçoit,
> Pipé de l'espoir qu'il conçoit,
> Aussi tost nous suit à la trace.
> Son cours est leger et bruyant,
> Et la chose mesme qu'il chasse
> En fin l'attrappe en le fuyant.[12]

The scene is full of movement: the rowing of the boat, the trolling of the line in the water, the noisy swimming of the fish in pursuit. The theme of illusion is stressed: the dorade thinks he is chasing prey, but is really about to be caught himself. And illusion is intimately linked with paradox: the object which the fish is pursuing finally catches him by running away from him (cf. the category of surprise and contrast).

At other times Saint-Amant retires to some remote spot to read the works

12. Ll. 201–10.

of an ancient historian or moralist (the occupation of Montaigne in his
tower). If night comes upon him unaware on a lonely beach, he returns to
the duke's castle by the light of a glowworm. Meditation upon this little
luminous insect is for him another opportunity to marvel at the wonders of
God's creation. Baroque writers are always delighted to discover surprising
natural phenomena: compare Montaigne's Thracian fox, who gauges the
thickness of ice by listening to the sound of the water underneath,[13] or St
François' pelican, who can revive his young by feeding them with his
blood.[14] Unlike the classicists, these men have not lost their enthusiasm for
being amazed.

> O bon Dieu! m'escriay-je alors,
> Que ta puissance est nonpareille
> D'avoir en un si petit corps
> Fait une si grande merveille!
> O feu qui, tousjours allumé,
> Brusles sans estre consumé!
> Belle escarboucle qui chemines,
> Ton eclat me plaist beaucoup mieux
> Que celuy qu'on tire des mines,
> Afin d'ensorceler nos yeux![15]

Aside from everything else, the four exclamation points testify to the writer's
sense of wonder. This is not, properly speaking, the *merveilleux chrétien*,
since it is not a question of supernatural miracles; and yet, in a sense, Saint-
Amant feels that the extraordinary little glowworm declares the glory of
God. The baroque, as I have remarked elsewhere, is a Christian style; it is
also a style which delights in the merveilleux; in the absence of miraculous
visions, it seeks out and admires the marvelous in nature. One of these
marvels is, precisely, this fire which burns without being consumed: a
paradox which pleases the poet greatly.

As a matter of fact, Saint-Amant deliberately *tries* to have visions. We
saw how, in "La Solitude," he gave himself thrills by pretending to see the
midnight revels of witches. Here, in stanza XXIV, we have the same self-
induced but pleasurable terror:

> Tantost, saisi de quelque horreur
> D'estre seul parmy les tenebres,
> Abusé d'une vaine erreur,
> Je me feins mille objets funebres;
> Mon esprit en est suspendu,

13. *Essais*, II, 12, 175.   14. *Introduction à la vie dévote*, II, 12.
15. Ll. 221–30.

Mon coeur en demeure esperdu,
Le sein me bat, le poil me dresse,
Mon corps est privé de soutien,
Et, dans la frayeur qui m'oppresse,
Je croy voir tout, pour ne voir rien.[16]

"Je me feins," the poet says—in other words, "I pretend, I imagine all this on purpose." And yet, though he knows perfectly well that these visions are self-induced, the physical symptoms are real: the beating heart, the hair standing on end, the trembling knees; so that, in lines 241 and 242, he is grateful to be delivered from the torment of nocturnal illusions. To create an illusion, to be taken in by it, and then, recovering, to derive intellectual pleasure from the contrast between illusion and reality, is a frequent pattern of the baroque mind, and explains much of the architecture of the period. Santa Maria della Pace, when we look at the façade, seems a large and impressive church; when we go inside, we realize that it is actually rather small. A careful analysis will then show us that our initial sense of grandeur was an illusion fostered by the way in which the façade extends like a veneering over the private house on each side; we feel this to be a clever architectural trick, and, after successive stages of admiration and disappointment, finally experience delight at an ingenious idea. (The architect, Pietro da Cortona, is the painter of the Barberini bee fresco mentioned earlier.)

After the terrors of darkness come the contrasting pleasures of dinner at the Duc de Retz's table, and there the poet and his patron laugh together at the "spectre trompeur." The word DUC is printed in capital letters; one is reminded of the emphatic inscriptions which form so important a part of the decoration of Roman churches, palaces, and fountains, with the pope's name and PONT MAX in huge block letters. The theme of conversation at dinner is the exaltation of the crusade of the king and Richelieu against the enemies of France and the Roman faith—the English and the Huguenots:

Tantost, les cœurs tous rejouis,
Nous celebrons du Grand LOUYS
L'heur, la prudence et le courage,
Et disons que le Cardinal
Est à la France dans l'orage
Ce qu'au navire est le fenal.

Tantost, sur le bruit que l'Anglois
Une visite nous prepare,
Nous projettons tous les explois
De quoy la victoire se pare.[17]

16. Ll. 231–40.   17. Ll. 275–84.

We are back in the atmosphere of Callot's "Siege of the Ile de Ré" and of Malherbe's "Pour le Roi"; the enemy shall be vanquished:

> Laisse-les espérer, laisse-les entreprendre:
> Il suffit que ta cause est la cause de Dieu,
> Et qu'avecque ton bras elle a pour la défendre
>   Les soins de Richelieu: [18]

The varied recital of Saint-Amant's diversions continues ("tantost . . . tantost"). Withdrawing to his bedroom, he sometimes devotes himself to the Muses, composing poems on the sufferings of love, and sometimes accompanies himself on the lute while singing the Psalms of David. One has the impression that, like Montaigne, he is capable of enjoying the most diverse activities: love (as in *Sur des vers de Virgile*), religious and philosophical meditation (as in the *Apologie*), travel (as in *De la vanité*), the reading of ancient authors (*Essais,* I, throughout), eating and drinking (see especially the essay *De l'experience*). In his bed, before going to sleep, the poet likes to read the Bible:

> Puis, jusqu'à tant que le sommeil,
> Avec un plaisir sans pareil,
> Me vienne siller la prunelle,
> Je ly ces sacrez Testamens
> Où Dieu, d'une encre solemnelle,
> Fait luire ses hauts mandements,[19]

The curious image "siller la prunelle" is worth mentioning. The modern spelling would be *ciller,* and the word means "to seel," that is, to close the eyes of a falcon by drawing threads through its lids. This is an example of that hunting imagery occasionally to be encountered in baroque poetry. It is somewhat unusual to hear a French seventeenth-century poet declare that he reads the Bible before going to sleep.

The composition of "Le Contemplateur" has certain analogies with two famous English baroque poems: Milton's "L'Allegro" and "Il Penseroso." Like it, they are both written in octosyllables; like it, they both consist in a recital of pleasures, contemplative and intellectual for the most part, connected by the frequent use of words like "oft" and "sometimes" (cf. "tantost . . . tantost"). Many of Milton's pleasures are the same as Saint-Amant's: walks in the country, watching the stars, reading ancient philosophy or poetry in a lonely spot. It is probably "Il Penseroso" that is the closer to "Le Contemplateur"; the title itself is similar, and in the course of the poem Milton invokes the cherub Contemplation.

Sometimes, though he admits that this does not happen very often (see

18. Ll. 37–40.   19. Ll. 305–10.

stanza XXXI), Saint-Amant likes to rise before daybreak and watch the sun come up out of the sea. (In "Il Penseroso," Milton, after a night of study and contemplation, enjoys seeing "civil-suited Morn appear.") The sunrise leads the poet to thoughts of the Last Judgment:

> Ainsi, dis-je en le regardant,
> Verra-t-on, quoy que l'oubly face,
> Au point du dernier jour ardant
> Ressusciter l'humaine race;
> Ainsi, mais plus clair et plus beau,
> Verra-t-on, comme ce flambeau,
> Monter au ciel le corps du juste,
> Après qu'avecques majesté,
> Dieu, seant en son trosne auguste,
> L'aura par sa bouche arresté.[20]

As he paints this picture, he remembers Michelangelo's great fresco in the Sistine Chapel:

> L'immortelle et sçavante main
> De ce fameux peintre romain
> N'a rien tracé d'émerveillable
> Que ce penser de l'advenir,
> Plein d'une terreur agreable,
> Ne ramene en mon souvenir.[21]

It is significant, I think, that Saint-Amant should refer to Michelangelo's "Last Judgment," because this work is now considered by art historians to be the ancestor of all baroque painting. This powerfully dramatic composition, with its muscular elect rising from their graves on earth and ascending to heaven, while a stern Christ sends the writhing forms of the damned hurtling down to hell, anticipates many characteristics of the baroque discussed here: mass, movement, theatricality, contrast of darkness and light, realism, horror, merveilleux chrétien. Note the aspects which the poet singles out for approval: the painting is "émerveillable," and fills him with a "terreur agreable." To feel simultaneously wonder and agreeable terror—this is a state thoroughly congenial to the baroque mind. The Last Judgment is of course a subject found throughout all Christian art, and not exclusively associated with the baroque; but strangely enough its greatest representation in French poetry is the final book of d'Aubigné's *Les Tragiques*, "Jugement."

And then Saint-Amant has a vision. Like the witches' sabbath and the lover's ghost in "La Solitude," or the hair-raising nocturnal illusions of the

20. Ll. 311–20.   21. Ll. 325–30.

present poem, it is largely self-induced. Yet, despite the words "je m'imagine," he is probably closer to believing in its reality than in that of the night hallucinations. In any case, Christ's appearance in the center of the sun stands out in sharp contrast against the earlier demons of darkness:

> Je m'imagine au mesme instant
> Entendre le son eclattant
> De la trompette serafique,
> Et pense voir en appareil
> Espouvantable et magnifique
> JESUS au milieu du soleil.[22]

The name of JESUS, like the DUC and LOUYS, is printed in block letters. The double-sense imagery is particularly fine: the blast of trumpets blends with the blaze of sunlight; the word "eclattant" is actually one which can apply equally to sound or sight. "Espouvantable et magnifique" is a characteristic baroque juxtaposition: awe and spectacle are joined. The scene as a whole reminds us of Bernini's "Cathedra Petri," where, surrounded by a host of sculptured angels, the Holy Ghost appears in the center of a small sun-shaped window; or of Pozzo's ceiling of Sant'Ignazio where Christ holding His Cross floats in a burst of light before the saint's ecstatic eyes.

Stanzas XXXV–XL are devoted to the description of the dead emerging from their graves. Here the scene, while still theatrical, becomes realistic rather than visionary:

> L'un m'apparoist un bras devant;
> L'autre ne montre que la teste,
> Et n'estant qu'à moitié vivant,
> Force l'obstacle qui l'arreste.
> Cestuy-cy s'esveille en sursaut;
> Cestuy-la joint les mains en haut,
> Implorant la faveur divine;
> Et l'autre est à peine levé
> Que d'un cœur devot il s'incline
> Devers l'agneau qui l'a sauvé.[23]

The baroque, even in the midst of the merveilleux chrétien, remains intensely conscious of the physical. All this is no doubt implicit in the Christian dogma of the resurrection of the dead; yet I think it will be agreed that Saint-Amant's picture of the struggling man whose head sticks out of the ground has a singularly muscular quality. D'Aubigné, in his treatment of this theme, insists even more on naturalistic detail:

22. Ll. 345–50.   23. Ll. 351–60.

On void les os couverts de nerfs, les nerfs de peau,
La teste de cheveux; on void, à ce tombeau,
Percer en mille endroits les arenes bouillantes
De jambes & de bras & de testes grouillantes.[24]

Just as "Le Contemplateur" as a whole is made up of a succession of topics loosely linked through associations of ideas, so the account of the Last Judgment exhibits a variety of moods. After the visionary passage (Jesus in the sun) and the naturalistic passage (the bodies forcing their way out of their graves) we come to a mildly ribald stanza. In almost any age but the baroque, the following attempt at humor would be felt to be unsuited to a description of the Second Coming:

Près de là, le frère et la sœur,
Touchez de ce bruit dont tout tremble,
D'estre accusez d'inceste ont peur,
Pour se trouver couchez ensemble.
Icy, la femme et le mary,
Objet l'un de l'autre chery,
Voyans la clarté souhaittée,
Semblent s'estonner et gemir
D'avoir passé cette nuictée
Sans avoir rien fait que dormir.[25]

Modern taste may consider that, in such a context, the sly allusions to incest and to conjugal love are in dubious taste, or irritatingly coy; but baroque sensibility evidently enjoyed exploring the unexpected aspects of a situation. In stanza XXXVIII, Saint-Amant amuses himself by speculating on the astonishment of a man who died of gout and who is now able to run up to heaven; or again of the rich man who used to wear splendid clothes and is now disconcerted to find himself completely naked! Perhaps the classical principle of separating the genres continues, in the twentieth century, to influence us more than we realize; in any event, it is certain that men of the early seventeenth century were not troubled by curious mixtures of the humorous and serious. Immediately after the murder of Duncan in *Macbeth*, Shakespeare has the drunken porter joke about the effect of drunkenness on love-making, and Lady Macbeth puns about gilding the faces of the grooms (with blood) so that it may seem to be their guilt. We have seen how Bernini, in his loveliest church, Sant'Andrea in Quirinale, did not hesitate to introduce a playful series of cherubs doing gymnastics on the garland which surrounds the whole interior.

The poet does not dwell for very long on the damned; but a brief passage

24. *Jugement*, 609–12.   25. Ll. 361–70.

does hint, for a moment, at the favorite baroque themes of horror and metamorphosis. The torments of hell await the wicked, who have become
hideous and deformed:

> Mais les meschans desesperez,
> Pour qui desjà sont preparez
> De l'enfer les tourmens enormes,
> Ne se representent à moy
> Que si hideux et difformes
> Que mon ame en transit d'effroy.[26]

Beginning with stanza XLII, we have an apocalyptic vision of the end
of the world. This almost surrealistic picture combines a number of favorite baroque features: strangeness, metamorphosis, multiple-sense imagery,
and theatricality. It is reminiscent of d'Aubigné's treatment of the same
subject in "Jugement":

> Les estoilles tombent des cieux,
> Les flames devorent la terre,
> Le mont Gibel est en tous lieux,
> Et par tout gronde le tonnerre.
> La salemandre est sans vertu,
> L'asbeste passe pour festu,
> La mer brusle comme eau-de-vie,
> L'air n'est plus que soufre allumé,
> Et l'astre dont l'aube est suivie
> Est par soy-mesme consumé.
>
> Les metaux, ensemble fondus,
> Font des rivieres precieuses;
> Leur flots bouillants sont espandus
> Par les campagnes spacieuses.[27]

In one of the shorter odes of Théophile, there is a similar surrealistic accumulation of fantastic phenomena. Here it is not an eschatological vision; the
poet is simply allowing his imagination to play freely on baroque themes:

> Ce ruisseau remonte en sa source;
> Un boeuf gravit sur un clocher;
> Le sang coule de ce rocher;
> Un aspic s'accouple d'une ourse;
> Sur le haut d'une vieille tour
> Un serpent deschire un vautour;
> Le feu brusle dedans la glace;

26. Ll. 405-10.   27. Ll. 411-24.

> Le soleil est devenu noir;
> Je voy la Lune qui va cheoir;
> Cest arbre est sorty de sa place.[28]

Because of its versification, stanza form, and strange imagery, this passage might easily be taken to belong to "La Solitude" or "Le Contemplateur." There is the same tendency of the poet to indulge himself in illusions, the same technique of surprise and contrast, the same delight in transformations.

Saint-Amant's vision of the end of the world concludes with the words:

> Tout est destruit, et la Mort mesme
> Se voit contrainte de mourir.[29]

In the last and greatest metamorphosis of all natural things, the whole world is destroyed, and death itself dies. We should note the echo device ("Mort . . . mourir"), the personification of Death, and the fundamental paradox of the conception.

The last two stanzas of "Le Contemplateur" are addressed, respectively, to God and to the Bishop of Nantes. In praying to God for eternal life, the poet asks that on the Day of Judgment he may burn with no other flame than that of divine love:

> Et fay qu'en ce terrible jour
> Je ne brustle point d'autre flame
> Que de celle de ton amour.[30]

This is a typically baroque metaphoric antithesis. Saint-Amant is playing with two different meanings of the new word "flamme": the flame of hell, and the flame of religious fervor. And of course the expression of the love of God in terms of human passion is very much in accord with the sensibility of the age: compare Crashaw's "Carmen Deo Nostro," or Bernini's "St. Teresa."

We have now come full cycle: in lines 1–4, the poet had praised the bishop in extravagant terms, calling this prelate the cause of his salvation. "It is because of you," he declares, "that I hope to escape the flames of hell." With all due allowance for hyperbole, it would seem that such an invocation might have been more appropriately addressed to God than to Philippe Cospeau. At the end of the poem, after the prayer to God, comes a prayer to the bishop; the author clearly does not feel this to be an anticlimax:

> Vous, dis-je, à qui j'escris ces vers,
> Où dans la mort de l'univers
> Un haut renom s'immortalise,

28. Second stanza of ode beginning "Un corbeau devant moi croasse."
29. Ll. 439–40.   30. Ll. 448–50.

Veuillez estre leur protecteur,
Et permettez-moy qu'on y lise
Que je suis votre adorateur.[31]

This is the familiar Renaissance idea that poetry can confer immortality upon its subject. Saint-Amant, considering Cospeau to be the cause of his salvation, hopes that he may be the means of endowing his patron with everlasting renown. Thus, with typical baroque ingenuity, two different forms of immortality—religious and literary—are contrasted.

And so the twin themes of flattery and religious propaganda (united, actually, in the praise of the bishop), which first appeared in stanzas I and II, come back now to bring "Le Contemplateur" to a close. In somewhat the same way, Montaigne's essay begins with the theme of vanity, proceeds through a multitude of picturesque digressions, and reverts to vanity at the end. Despite all their movement and diversity, *De la vanité* and "Le Contemplateur" possess an organic unity; we realize this if we read each work through carefully from start to finish. In the first case, the theme of vanity is latent throughout; in the second, the poet, whatever his topic, conceives of himself as talking to a bishop. The conclusion of both works reveals the underlying unity which may at times have been hidden. Perhaps even more important as a unifying principle is the self-portraiture: through many varying moods and interests, the personalities of Montaigne and Saint-Amant emerge as living realities.

31. Ll. 455–60.

CHAPTER 5

A Baroque Dramatist Repents His Youth: Three Early Comedies of Corneille

IT IS with a certain diffidence that I embark on the subject of the baroque aspects of Corneille. I realize very well that in France especially such an idea appears almost heretical; at the Sorbonne, for example, M. Lebègue is one of the rare scholars to admit that part of the seventeenth century may be regarded as baroque.

Allow me, at the very outset, to define and delimit my subject. First of all, in this chapter I am concerned only with three of Corneille's youthful comedies. *L'Illusion comique,* which dates from 1636 (the year of *Le Cid,* I admit); *Clitandre;* and *Mélite* (both written in 1632). For a long time the early plays of Corneille were scorned and neglected; their progressive rehabilitation began in 1936, the year that M. Rivaille, at the Sorbonne, devoted his complementary thesis to this question, and 1937, when Louis Jouvet, at the Comédie française, created an ingenious and brilliant setting for *L'Illusion comique.*

For my part, I think I can see certain baroque aspects in *Le Cid* (for example, the celebrated conflict between love and duty—a dilemma which is never really resolved, as M. Nadal has pointed out; the bloody description that Chimène gives of her father's death, etc.), but I should prefer not to discuss this problem here. Besides, let the reader be reassured: my purpose is not to try to prove that all French classicism, Racine included, is baroque. On the contrary, I perceive three (possibly four) periods which follow one another: first the Renaissance; then (if certain recent scholars are to be believed) mannerism; next the baroque, which extends approximately from 1570 to 1650; and finally, I agree that the writers of the "great generation" are truly classical. To present the problem in another way: the baroque, for me, is not one of the basic categories of the human mind, a kind of phenomenon which recurs at very different epochs; thus in this I differ with Focillon's conception as he states it in *La Vie des formes.* No, I should like to treat the baroque as a chronological period; and without identifying myself with the positions taken by Weisbach and Mâle, who see in it primarily a manifestation of the Counter Reformation, I nevertheless think that the critic is less likely to go astray if he assigns relatively precise historical limits to the baroque style. For me, the baroque in the fine arts is the age of Bernini, Caravaggio, Rubens, and Jacques Callot; in literature, it is Montaigne, La

Ceppède, d'Aubigné, St. François de Sales, Saint-Amant, the early works of Corneille—and Rotrou. If you wish an architectural symbol, think of the Piazza Navona in Rome, with the marvelous façade of Sant'Agnese (by Borromini) and the extraordinary "Fountain of the Rivers" (by Bernini)— a spot which is, as M. Jean Rousset appropriately remarks in his recent book on baroque literature in France, one of the "hauts lieux" of the baroque. As literary representatives, consider the *Holy Sonnets* of Donne, Calderón's *La Vida es Sueño,* Agrippa d'Aubigné's *Les Tragiques,* or the three comedies which we are about to analyze here.

I shall begin by discussing *L'Illusion comique,* since this colorful and entertaining play will serve to illustrate my conception of a baroque comedy. It possesses, moreover, certain affinities with the tragedy which forms the subject of the final chapter of this book: Rotrou's *Saint Genest.* The other two Corneille comedies, though of lesser artistic merit, are particularly interesting because the author kept revising them—especially in 1644 and 1660. These successive emendations correspond, in my opinion, to an evolution of Corneille's taste, developing from the baroque to classicism. When the reader has studied *L'Illusion comique,* having gained an understanding of baroque comedy, he will be in a position to appreciate the changes which occur when Corneille begins to be ashamed of his baroque aspects. As early as 1936 people came to realize that it would be useful to make a comparative stylistic study of the different editions of Corneille; indeed, that year M. Louis Rivaille defended his thesis on *Pierre Corneille, correcteur de ses premières œuvres.* But this thesis confines itself to an examination of the 1644 edition of the *Œuvres,* comparing it with the first editions of *Mélite, Clitandre, La Veuve,* etc.; M. Rivaille is not concerned with the 1660 and 1682 editions. Thanks to his work, however, it was realized that it would be worth while to publish critical editions of the first comedies, using as the basic text the original rather than the definitive version. And so there have recently appeared, published by Mlle. Droz in Geneva, an edition of *Clitandre* by M. Wagner (1949; text of 1632 and variants) and an edition of *Mélite,* by MM. Mario Roques and Marion Lièvre (1950; text of 1633 and variants). My references to *Clitandre* and *Mélite* are, therefore, based on these two critical editions.

1. L'Illusion comique

It is possible that some of my readers may not have read or seen *L'Illusion comique* recently, or in any case that they find it difficult to recall the details of the plot. I shall begin, therefore, with a brief summary of the action of the play.

Pridamant, the father of Clindor, has no idea what has become of his son, who has been away for ten years. Despairing of ever seeing him again, and anxious as to the boy's fate, he goes to consult the great magician Alcandre. The latter, who apparently knows everything, reassures the father, and narrates, with a great abundance of picaresque details, the son's life up to a relatively recent period. Then, beginning with Act II, thanks to the magic procedures of Alcandre, Pridamant watches a kind of television show where he can see Clindor's daily life. And so we are the spectators of a play within the play. Clindor is in the service of a Gascon *capitan*, a grotesquely swaggering character named Matamore, who is forever boasting of his fantastic and hair-raising deeds. Pretending to help his master in the courtship of Isabelle, Clindor has taken advantage of the situation to woo this lady for himself. Isabelle also has a third lover, Adraste, but it is Clindor that she loves. A second lady, Lyse, has been deserted by Clindor; and so the two jilted lovers plot together to avenge themselves. Here the television program is interrupted for a few moments, and we return to Pridamant, who is beginning to be alarmed about his son's safety. When the curtain goes up on Act III, the television performance starts anew, and we continue to follow Clindor's adventures. Isabelle's father, Geronte, wants to force her, against her will, to marry Adraste and, annoyed by her resistance, he convinces himself that she is in love with Matamore. As a good common-sense bourgeois, Geronte refuses to be dazzled by Matamore, unmasks the pretensions of the braggart, and opposes his marriage to Isabelle. In another scene, Lyse demands an explanation from Clindor; the latter, hesitating, is unable to make up his mind:

> Vous partagez tous deux mes inclinations:
> J'adore sa fortune, et tes perfections.[1]

But despite this ungallant reply, Lyse continues to feel a secret tenderness for Clindor. Further on, Matamore, who has hidden in order to see whether Clindor is loyally serving him in the courtship of Isabelle, finds out that he has been betrayed. Bursting forth in rage from his hiding place, he threatens his squire with a thousand terrible deaths, but Clindor, who has come to realize the actual cowardice of his master, now adopts the swaggering tone himself. The capitan collapses like a pricked balloon and abandons Isabelle to Clindor. At this instant Adraste, with a band of armed companions, swoops down unexpectedly and lunges at Clindor. The latter succeeds in wounding Adraste, but is himself forced to yield before the number of his assailants. Now we have a new interruption of the televised drama: poor Pridamant is convinced that his son is dead, but the magician tells him to wait for the end of the story. The illusion of tragedy still persists at the begin-

1. Act III, scene 5.

ning of Act IV: Isabelle is in despair; her lover is in prison and condemned to death. However, thanks to the efforts of Lyse, who has been able to make the jailer fall in love with her, Clindor is delivered, and all three flee together. When we reach the third intermission of the television, Pridamant, overjoyed at his son's good fortune, exclaims: "A la fin je respire." But the performance is not over. There remains a final act. Alcandre explains that two years have passed; he waves his hand, and the magic play continues. We witness a violent quarrel between Clindor and Isabelle, who is accusing him of betraying her with Princess Rosine, and who threatens to commit suicide. The fickle lover repents, and promises to be faithful henceforth. But at that instant, Eraste, the prince's equerry, arrives and stabs Clindor to avenge his master's honor. Isabelle dies of grief. Once more there is a halt in the performance. Pridamant is now sure that his son is really dead, and gives vent to despair:

> Adieu, je vais mourir, puisque mon fils est mort.[2]

But the magician has a last scene to show us. Clindor, Isabelle, and the others are observed counting money on a table. It turns out that they have become actors, and that these are the day's receipts. The whole preceding scene was enacted on a stage, and is therefore only an illusion. Everyone is happy.

In the domain of fine arts, one of the most characteristic elements of the baroque is illusion. In order to realize this, it is sufficient to consider some of the principal monuments of Rome. In the Vatican Bernini has built the Scala Regia falsifying the perspective in such a way that the staircase appears twice as long as it really is; Borromini, by means of similar devices, has given the little colonnade of the Palazzo Spada, which is barely thirty feet long, a grandiose aspect; the charming church of Sant'Andrea al Quirinale, actually very small, is deceptively designed to seem very large; the Jesuit Father Pozzo has painted the ceiling of Sant'Ignazio in *trompe-l'œil* so as to make us believe in the existence of a vast upper storey surrounded by gigantic columns. And even when the baroque does not strive for pure effects of trompe-l'œil, it seeks to create, by means of the undulation of façades and the rhythmic grouping of columns, the illusion of movement, as in San Carlo alle Quattro Fontane or Sant'Agnese in the Piazza Navona. Think also of the famous series of pictures in the Medici Gallery in the Louvre: Rubens, painting the life of Henri IV and Marie de Médicis, manages to give us the illusion of a grandeur which does not correspond very closely to the reality of historic facts.

Now, in the comedy which we are examining, the poet tries above all to create illusions, to be amused by them, to rejoice at them. As a matter of fact,

2. Act V, scene 5.

the very title—*L'Illusion comique*—shows us how Corneille conceives of his art. And this magician, with his television shows, what does he do but procure for us constant illusions? The first thing Alcandre does, when Pridamant comes to consult him, is to wave his wand and to display on parade the actors' most beautiful costumes; "Jugez de votre fils par un tel equipage," he declares.[3] The father and the spectators are convinced that Clindor must be very rich—but it is all merely an illusion, since these are actors' costumes, as we discover in Act V. And before presenting the televised drama, the magician says,

> Toutefois, si votre âme étoit assez hardie,
> Sous une illusion vous pourriez voir sa vie.[4]

Clindor himself, in order to lead his life of adventures, has assumed a false name, which is of course a form of disguise or illusion:

> Il a caché son nom en battant la campagne,
> Et s'est fait de Clindor le sieur de la Montagne.[5]

When the magic play within the play begins, the first character we see is Matamore, proclaiming,

> Quand je veux, j'épouvante; et quand je veux, je charme [6]

or else,

> Contemple, mon ami, contemple ce visage:
> Tu vois un abrégé de toutes les vertus.[7]

We soon realize that the image which Matamore wishes to present to the world is pure illusion, for as early as the end of this first scene he trembles and flees upon the arrival of his not very formidable rival Adraste. Nevertheless, a little later, in his speeches to Isabelle, he attempts to recreate the illusion of bravery:

> Choisissez en quels lieux il vous plaît de régner:
> Ce bras aussitôt vous conquête un empire; [8]

But it becomes harder and harder for him to play this role in a convincing manner. Géronte is not fooled for a minute, and—culminating disgrace—his squire Clindor turns against him, reversing their parts and terrifying the master.

In Act III, scene 7, when Matamore is all alone, our disillusionment is complete. He who in the beginning used to say,

3. Act I, scene 2.   4. Ibid.   5. Act I, scene 3.
6. Act II, scene 2.   7. Ibid.   8. Act II, scene 4.

> Le seul bruit de mon nom renverse les murailles,
> Défait les escadrons et gagne les batailles.[9]

is now totally unmasked:

> Tout le corps me frissonne.
> Je les entends, fuyons.

and, further along:

> De deux mille ans et plus, je ne tremblai si fort.[10]

For baroque art, which delights in trompe-l'œil effects, also likes to destroy the illusions which it has created. When you have been thoroughly deceived by the perspective of Borromini's colonnade in the Palazzo Spada, you are intended to walk under this portico which seemed so vast: you then realize that it is actually tiny. It is all part of the game; the artist wanted it that way. You have perhaps been really moved by the ecstasy of St. Teresa, by Bernini; then look to the left and the right, and you will see that the sculpture has created opera boxes with spectators; what stirred you so much is thus only a dramatic performance. It is as if the artist were saying to you: "I fooled you, didn't I? How skillful I am!"

This is the way, I think, that we should conceive of the four interruptions in the television drama within the *Illusion comique*. Each time, we become completely absorbed by this play within the play. The magician Alcandre arranges these four intermissions in order to force us to return from "illusion" to "reality." With a certain psychological shock we are aroused from the adventures of Clindor, and hear his poor father say, "Je crains cette menace" or "Hélas! mon fils est mort!" or "Qu'Isabelle est changée et qu'elle est éclatante!" This is a technique employed by Alcandre to evoke admiration for his art. But that is not the only illusion; upon reflection we are forced to realize that the conversations between Pridamant and Alcandre which purport to be reality are obviously nothing but a theatrical illusion. This time it is no longer Alcandre but Corneille who is the great magician and creator of illusions.

But in this strange play, illusionistic art assumes still other forms. In spite of the title, Corneille twice succeeds in making us believe that his comedy is going to be a tragedy. This happens a first time when Clindor, who has wounded Adraste, is led to prison and condemned to death; however, thanks to the efforts of Lyse, he escapes and all is saved. Here it might be argued that we have an ordinary dramatic peripety—a thing which has always been common in the theatre. In spite of the father's fears, we are probably not altogether convinced. But the second time, when Eraste rushes in and kills

---

9. Act II, scene 2.   10. Act III, scene 7.

Clindor with a dagger, we are really unable to see how the young hero can be resuscitated. The tragic illusion is total; we actually believe that the play ends in this way. So it is with huge pleasure that Alcandre (and obviously Corneille also) shows us the comedians in the process of counting their box-office receipts. "Aha," says Corneille to us, "you allowed yourselves to be taken in by my art!" It should be observed that, in this fifth act, the illusion is threefold: a play within a play within a play. The tragedy enacted by Clindor and Isabelle is merely an illusion; it all takes place within the television show, which is in itself only another illusion; we ourselves, to the extent that we believe in the reality of Pridamant and Alcandre, are the victims of a third illusion. We finally come to wonder whether our own life is not an illusion. In any event, that is the conclusion to which another baroque dramatist seeks to lead us: in Calderón's play *La Vida es Sueño* (1640), Sigismondo can eventually no longer tell what is a truth and what a dream; in the end, we do not know either.

It is often surprising, in mannerist and baroque painting, to observe the intimate mixture of realistic and supernatural elements. In his masterpiece, the "Burial of Count Orgaz," El Greco has painted an extraordinary series of portraits of contemporaries who are present at the funeral. Both priest and congregation are represented with a powerful realism. However, in the midst of this faithfully historic scene, there is the miraculous element: St. Augustine and St. Stephen have come in person to hold the body during the entombment. Or—to pass from Christian to pagan marvels—consider the Rubens paintings in the Galerie des Médicis. We see there scenes from the life of Henri IV and Marie de Médicis; the portraits, the costumes, and some of the episodes are quite authentic and faithfully reproduced, but, in the midst of all this, there are Jupiter, Juno, Cupid, nymphs in the water, and little cherubs flying through the air.

If we study *L'Illusion comique,* we notice this same mixture of the magic and the naturalistic. The magic element is of course represented by Alcandre. At the very outset, Corneille seeks to create an atmosphere of mystery and the supernatural. The six first lines of the play are:

> Ce mage, qui d'un mot renverse la nature,
> N'a choisi pour palais que cette grotte obscure.
> La nuit qu'il entretient sur cet affreux séjour
> N'ouvrant son voile épais qu'aux rayons d'un faux jour,
> De leur éclat douteux n'admet en ces lieux sombres
> Que ce qu'en peut souffrir le commerce des ombres.[11]

Pridamant's friend explains that the magician

11. Act I, scene 1.

> . . . lit dans les pensées
> Qu'il connoît l'avenir et les choses passées; [12]

Alcandre himself, armed with his wand, conjures up a fashion show of the comedians' finest costumes; then, inviting Pridamant into his cave, he remarks,

> C'est qu'un charme ordinaire a trop peu de pouvoir
> Sur les spectres parlants qu'il faut vous faire voir.
> Entrons dedans ma grotte, afin que j'y prépare
> Quelques charmes nouveaux pour un effet si rare.[13]

Before beginning the performance, he warns Pridamant not to try to leave the grotto without him:

> Sinon, vous êtes mort.

And obviously this show, in an age when television had not yet been invented, is pure magic.

Yet in *L'Illusion comique,* alongside the marvelous elements, there are completely realistic elements, details which come from contemporary life. Alcandre may be an extraordinary magician, but all the same he was born in Rennes: we are explicitly told so. The life of Clindor, as Alcandre describes it before the beginning of his show, is full of realistic details: he has been a clerk in a lawyer's office, a solicitor at the Palais de Justice, has sold rosaries, and has exhibited a dancing monkey at the Foire Saint-Germain. Alcandre locates precisely the spot where Clindor is living at this moment: it is in Bordeaux, and not in some enchanted kingdom. Géronte, Isabelle's father, could easily be a character in a Molière comedy: down to earth and dictatorial, he grows most annoyed when his daughter rejects the husband he has chosen for her:

> Qu'à présent la jeunesse a d'étranges manies! [14]

he exclaims, and we might almost be listening to Gorgibus. Let us also recall what Clindor and Isabelle are doing when we see them for the last time; after so many extraordinary adventures, they are simply counting out their money on a table.

In my book on d'Aubigné, I tried to show that baroque art, whether in the fine arts or in poetry, loves change, transformation, and metamorphosis. One of Bernini's finest works is his "Apollo and Daphne," in the Borghese Gallery. Just at the moment when Apollo is about to seize the young girl, she transforms herself into an olive tree. Bernini has chosen the precise moment of the metamorphosis: Daphne is partly feminine flesh, partly bark and

12. Ibid.   13. Act I, scene 3.   14. Act III, scene 2.

leaves. D'Aubigné prefers to present things in movement and metamorphosis; and Montaigne himself declared, "Je ne peins pas l'estre, je peins le passage." The Corneille of the early comedies sees the world in this way also. We need not go back over scenes already discussed, but it is evident that the life of Clindor is nothing but a continuous series of changes; his destiny is transformed from scene to scene. Classical tragedy of the 1660 era, because of the rule of the unities, could not allow itself development: it shows us a crisis. Alcandre stages ten years of Clindor's life. And after all, is not a magician's role precisely to bring about marvelous transformations? That is just what Alcandre does with his magic wand.

This way of looking upon the world as a perpetual becoming influences the style of the play as well. The unhappy father, for instance, when told that the magician may be able to show him his son, replies,

Le sort m'est trop cruel pour devenir si doux.[15]

Most of Matamore's imaginary exploits are presented as transformations:

Je dépeuple l'Etat des plus heureux monarques;[16]

. . . . .

D'un souffle je réduis leurs projets en fumée;[17]

The baroque aspects of L'Illusion comique which we have just analyzed —illusionism, mingling of magic and realism, love of metamorphosis—can be looked at in another way: the baroque artist, above all, wishes to astonish. The Cavaliere Marino declared, in the preface to Adone, that every true poet succeeds in provoking surprise. Enough has been said of L'Illusion comique to demonstrate that the entire play is a continuous series of surprises: Clindor, who at first seems to be loyally serving Matamore, reveals himself to be disloyal, since he is courting Isabelle; then we observe that he is not faithful to her either, since he flirts with Lyse; when Matamore begins to threaten, Clindor suddenly adopts, in an unexpected way, the tone of his master, and actually terrifies him; the jailer leads Clindor off, saying "Vous mourrez de nuit," and instead of the scaffold, the hero finds Isabelle:

Trompeur trop obligeant, tu disois bien vraiment
Que je mourrois de nuit, mais de contentement.[18]

And above all, there is the final peripety: the hero and the heroine are not dead; they are actors.

A final baroque device, which I have had occasion to study at some length in d'Aubigné's Les Tragiques, is exaggeration and hyperbole. (It will be

15. Act I, scene 1.   16. Act II, scene 2.
17. Ibid.   18. Act IV, scene 9.

remembered that this constitutes one of the basic categories presented in the
chapter on Montaigne.) In *L'Illusion comique,* this aspect is represented
primarily by the braggadocio of Matamore, upon which I have already
touched; I shall not, therefore, discuss the ravings of this character any
further. Suffice it to say that, despite all ridicule, Corneille is secretly attracted to him. Thus, Matamore tells one of his adventures:

> Le Soleil fut un jour sans se pouvoir lever
> Et ce visible Dieu, que tant de monde adore,
> Pour marcher devant lui ne trouvoit point d'Aurore:

Clindor asks him:

> Où pouvoit être alors la reine des clartés?

And Matamore promptly replies:

> Au milieu de ma chambre, à m'offrir ses beautés.[19]

Lying, carried to such a degree, becomes art. Matamore in his way is a poet.
Exaggeration is an essential part of Corneille's poetry.

2. CLITANDRE

The scene is laid in Scotland, partly at the castle of the king, but mostly
in the neighboring forest. In spite of the title, the true hero of the play is
Rosidor, who loves Caliste and is loved by her. At the same time, Dorise is
also in love with Rosidor, and Clitandre with Caliste; both are spurned. The
situation is made still more complicated by the fact that a fifth character,
Pymante, has an unrequited passion for Dorise, and that the prince of
Scotland feels a sort of sentimental attachment for his friend Clitandre.

The action of the first act begins before sunrise; we progressively watch
the coming of dawn and full daylight—a spectacular transformation which
is pleasing to baroque taste. Caliste has been lured into the forest at this
early hour because Dorise has told her that Rosidor plans to tryst there with
another girl, Hipolyte. (This character, as a matter of fact, never appears on
the stage.) Rosidor appears, accompanied by his equerry, and Caliste hides
in a thicket. We learn that Rosidor has actually come into the forest to fight
a duel with his rival Clitandre, from whom he believes he has received a
challenge. In another part of the forest, Pymante, Géronte, and Lycaste (the
latter two being disloyal servitors of Clitandre) come out of a cave, disguised
as peasants. As a first surprise, we discover that it is they who forged the
letter of challenge, in order to draw Rosidor into an ambush where they hope
to kill him. In this way, Pymante will be rid of an inconvenient rival. A

19. Act II, scene 2.

little further on, there is a second surprise for the spectator: Dorise draws a sword from behind a bush, seizes her pretended friend Caliste, and prepares to kill her. (Thus the story of Rosidor's infidelity was only a lie to attract poor Caliste to a lonely spot.) But, just at this instant, a coup de théâtre occurs: Rosidor bursts upon the scene, covered with blood, and pursued by three masked murderers. As he enters, he kills Lycaste, but in pulling his sword out of the body, he accidentally breaks it on the branch of a tree. Then, in this extremity, he seizes Dorise's sword, and continues to fight with Pymante and Géronte, of whom he kills the latter and puts the former to flight. We have here several baroque effects: the surprise of the revelation of Dorise's treachery, the sudden dramatic arrival of Rosidor and the assassins, the disguises, the rivers of blood, two murders on the stage, a whole violent spectacle of unexpected horror. It is like a painting by Rubens—or, even more, a scene from an opera. Before fleeing, Dorise comments in précieux style on the fact that it is her beloved Rosidor who snatched the arms from her, and she laments because she is now obliged to run away from the person she loves most in the world.

After the effects of surprise and violence, we pass to effects of illusion— equally baroque in taste, as we know. Rosidor believes (and with him, the spectator) that Caliste is dead; then she revives and at first takes her lover for one of the murderers.

The second act contains varied and episodic scenes without much unity: Pymante wanders in the forest as an outlaw; the archers of the king discover the corpses of Géronte and Lycaste; then, under an elm tree, there is a strange tender scene between the prince and his favorite, Clitandre—a scene which is interrupted because the king, assuming that Clitandre is responsible for the murders, recalls him in order to throw him in prison. Further on, Dorise, also fleeing as an outlaw, and semiclad in Géronte's clothes, chances to meet Pymante. Each one mistakes the other's identity; he, not recognizing the woman he loves, takes her for Géronte, while she assumes that he is a peasant. (It should be recalled that he also is disguised.)

At the beginning of Act III the king, convinced by the forged letter of Clitandre's guilt, wants to hasten the latter's execution before the prince can return from the forest to stop it; in another scene, Clitandre laments his fate in a damp, evil-smelling dungeon. Next, we find ourselves back in the forest, where Pymante and Dorise have finally recognized each other; he drags her into a cave and (beginning of Act IV) attempts to rape her, but Dorise pulls a pin from her hair and puts out one of his eyes. This scene, which by its brutality recalls the passage in *King Lear* where Gloucester gouges his eyes out, is somewhat surprising in a play by a French author customarily classified as classical. When Pymante, recovering from the first shock of his wound, rushes after Dorise to kill her, a terrible storm suddenly breaks, with huge thunderbolts. At this moment the prince enters on foot, exclaiming:

> Que d'heur en ce péril! sans me faire aucun mal
> Le tonnerre sous moi a foudroyé mon cheval
> Et consommant sur lui toute sa violence
> M'a montré son respect parmi son insolence.

He arrives just in time to prevent Pymante from slaughtering Dorise; the huntsmen of the prince's suite gag Pymante and carry him off. Then the prince hurries back to the castle to forestall the execution of his dear Clitandre.

In the last act, matters get more or less settled. Clitandre, overwhelmed with gratitude toward the prince, who has saved his life, seems to wish to renounce Caliste and to devote himself entirely to friendship. In a very daring scene which I shall discuss a little later, Caliste comes to visit Rosidor in his sickroom, and sits on his bed. Finally, the king decides upon the marriage of the two unhappy lovers; and (a totally unforeseen development) the prince, obtaining Dorise's pardon, has her marry Clitandre—apparently without any great enthusiasm on the part of either bride or groom.

As you can see, *Clitandre* is an irregular play—that is the least that can be said of it.

Let us now examine the corrections made by Corneille on his original text. Caliste's monologue, which opens the play, has been changed in several ways. You will remember that the heroine is all alone in the forest at daybreak; she laments because she thinks that Rosidor has betrayed her. In the 1632 edition, addressing her absent lover, she said:

> Toi, que l'œil qui te blesse attend pour te guérir,
> Eveille-toi, brigand, hâte-toi d'acquérir
> Sur l'honneur d'Hipolyte une infâme victoire,
> Et de m'avoir trompée une honteuse gloire,
> Hâte-toi, déloyal, de me fausser la foi,[1]

In 1680 Corneille revised the passage and wrote:

> Toi qui fais ma douleur, et qui fis mon souci,
> Ne tarde plus, volage, à te montrer ici;
> Viens en hâte affermir ton indigne victoire,
> Viens t'assurer l'éclat de cette infâme gloire,
> Viens signaler ton nom par ton manque de foi;

As the reader can observe, the précieux image ("l'œil qui te blesse") has been suppressed, and the epithet "brigand" has given way to "volage." In

---

1. Ll. 23–7. (Line numbers refer to 1632 text.)

general the tone of the lines has become milder; they are less violent, less breathless, and not so concrete.

A little further on, in the 1632 edition, Caliste, fearing the sight which her own eyes may reveal to her, addressed them thus:

> Un infidèle encor régnant sur mon penser
> Votre fidélité ne peut que m'offenser,
> Apprenez, apprenez par le traître que j'aime
> Qu'il vous faut me trahir pour être aimé de même.
> Et toi, père du jour, dont le flambeau naissant
> Va chercher mon jour avec le croissant,
> S'il est vrai que Thétis te reçoit dans sa couche,
> Prends, Soleil, prends encor deux baisers sur sa bouche,
> Ton retour me va perdre, et retrancher ton bien,
> Prolonge en l'arrêtant mon bonheur et le tien; [2]

In 1660 these ten lines are reduced to two:

> Et toi, Soleil, qui vas en ramenant le jour,
> Dissiper une erreur si chère à mon amour,

The poet obviously felt that he should eliminate all these little rhetorical games, in particular the echoes and antitheses constituted by the words "infidèle"—"fidélité" and "traître"—"aimer." The comparison between the happiness of the sun in Thetis' couch and Caliste's happiness in the illusion of love (both to endure only so long as darkness hides the earth) is also removed. Of all the complicated images suggested by the sun ("flambeau," "croissant," "baisers," etc.) nothing remains but the bare word "Soleil."

It sometimes happens, as we shall see, that Corneille cuts lines for reasons of bienséance. In Act I, scene 2, Lysarque advises his master to take advantage of any opportunities for love-making which may arise while he is waiting for Caliste:

> Vous pouvez vous lasser de vivre d'espérance,
> Et tandis que l'attente amuse vos désirs
> Prendre ailleurs quelquefois de solides plaisirs. [3]

In 1660, apparently deciding that this conversation was improper, Corneille eliminated it from the text.

At the end of the first act, Rosidor, who has just killed Géronte and put Pymante to flight, sees the inanimate body of Caliste—she has fainted—and believes her to be dead. He gives vent to a verbose despair, and curses the gods who spared his own life. In the editions after 1632 the poet shortens this soliloquy very considerably. I shall not inflict upon the reader a recital of

2. Ll. 43–52.   3. Ll. 86–8.

the twenty-odd lines which have been cut, but the following, spoken while Rosidor bends over to gaze upon his mistress' face, are a representative sample. He is calling upon the gods:

> Sachez que Rosidor maudit votre secours,
> Vous ne méritez pas qu'il vous doive ses jours.
> Unique Déité qu'à présent je réclame,
> Belle âme, viens aider à sortir à mon âme,
> Reçois-la sur les bords de ce pale coral . . .[4]

In 1660, presumably, the curse uttered against the gods, the worship of Caliste as the only diety, and the image of the "pale coral" which is to receive the lover's expiring soul are considered in doubtful taste. It is perhaps a similar concern for the proprieties which brings about the suppression of a passage where, Caliste having recovered from her swoon, Rosidor says to her:

> Puisque un si doux appas se treuve en tes rudesses,
> Que feront tes faveurs, que feront tes caresses? [5]

By modern standards, this couplet is not very shocking, but to the classical mind even so veiled an allusion as this must have appeared indiscreet.

It frequently happens that a brutal and expressive term in the text of 1632 is later replaced by a milder and more elegant formula. And so

> Terre crève-toi donc afin de m'engloutir [6]

becomes

> Ouvre du moins ton sein, terre, pour m'engloutir

It may in general be said that the 1632 text is far richer in concrete and picturesque details than the latter versions. For example, in Act II, scene 6, Pymante and Dorise, both disguised (she in Géronte's clothing), encounter one another in the forest. Pymante, fearing unpleasant consequences because of the criminal action in which he has just been involved, wants to be taken for a peasant. In the earliest version, he says:

> Ne craignez point au reste un pauvre villageois
> Qui seul et désarmé cherche dedans ces bois
> Un boeuf piqué du taon, qui brisant nos closages
> Hier sur le chaud du jour s'enfuit des pâturages . . .[7]

Later this entire little picture disappears. Here is the 1660 version:

> Ne craignez point au reste un pauvre villageois
> Qui seul et désarmé court à travers ces bois.

4. Ll. 283–7.   5. Ll. 365–6.   6. L. 436.   7. Ll. 671–4.

The suppressed images are, it seems to me, precisely those which baroque poets enjoy: they are concrete, and they appeal to physical sensations ("un boeuf pique . . . brisant les closages . . . le chaud du jour"). This whole scene, as a matter of fact, has undergone important changes of the same kind. In 1632, Dorise says to Pymante:

> Tiens-moi dans ta cabane . . .

and he, seeking to avoid complications, replies:

> Tout lourdaud que je suis en ma rusticité
> Je vois bien quand on rit de ma simplicité,
> Je vais chercher mon bœuf . . .

As Dorise tries to detain him, he insists that he is in a great hurry because of

> Quelques rugissements entendus de là-bas

and dissuades her from following him:

> Vous me retarderiez, Monsieur, homme qui vive
> Ne peut à mon égal brosser dans ces buissons.[8]

To be sure, there is always something artificial about the seventeenth-century pastoral. It is difficult, in L'Astrée for example, to believe that we are really reading about shepherds and shepherdesses. And yet in the 1632 version of the scene, because of the abundance of picturesque rustic details, it is possible for us to imagine that this is taking place in the country; but in the 1660 edition, we have definitely come back into the salon. There is no longer any shack; Dorise expresses herself in more elegant fashion:

> . . . accorde une retraite
> Sous ton chaume rustique à ma fuite secrète.

He, instead of talking about his ox, bellowings, and bushes, simply says:

> L'affaire qui me presse est assez importante
> Pour ne pouvoir, Monsieur, répondre à votre attente;

The reader can observe how much more abstract all this has become.

I should not like, however, to give the impression that the 1660 and 1682 versions are totally devoid of concrete, picturesque, and sensuous images. In correcting his text Corneille did not feel an obligation to impoverish it to such an extent. In all the editions, for example, Clitandre in jail complains of the "air sale et puant," of the "foible jour," and of the "poids de ces fers"—a fine case of multiple-sense imagery. On the other hand, however, the poet cuts all that part of Clitandre's lamentations where the young man

8. Ll. 698-9.

abandons himself to *préciosité*. Thus the following passage disappears completely:

> Triste séjour! Qui dis-je? Osai-je appeler triste
> L'adorable prison ou me retient Caliste?
> En vain dorénavant mon esprit irrité
> Se plaindra d'un cachot qu'il a trop mérité,
> Puisque d'un tel blasphème il s'est rendu capable,
> D'innocent que j'entrai, j'y demeure coupable.[9]

Although in one way the baroque style is characterized by an abundance of concrete and picturesque details, it often presents another aspect, more précieux, too ingenious in its paradoxical elaboration. Corneille, under the influence of classical taste, has a tendency to reduce these two elements in his work. These two aspects of the baroque are of course different; but classicism is equally hostile to both. In the passage just quoted, it is hardly necessary to point out what is précieux: Clitandre finds his prison adorable because the love of Caliste has brought him there; to complain of this prison is, therefore, a blasphemy. (The reader will remember that I regard hyperbole and emphasis as an important baroque category.) I should like to dwell for a little longer on the last line of this ingenious development:

> D'innocent que j'entrai, j'y demeure coupable.

We find here several baroque devices used in conjunction. First of all, this is a pointe, produced at the end of a passage to create an effect of surprise. Then simultaneously, there is that antithetical mode of expression which is so congenial to the baroque mind. But above all, the idea is presented in the form of a metamorphosis: the lover *becomes* guilty. As a matter of fact, we have the impression of following the movement of Clitandre's thought as it comes into being: the idea develops progressively before our eyes, as so often happens in the *Essais* of Montaigne.

Let us now move on to the third scene of Act III, one of those which have undergone the most changes. Dorise and Pymante are still quarreling. However, from 1660 on they quarrel in a more classical manner. For instance, Pymante, who in the original version used to say:

> L'impétueux bouillon d'un courroux féminin
> Qui s'échappe sur l'heure, et jette son venin,
> Comme il est animé de la seule impuissance,
> A force de grossir il meurt en sa naissance,[10]

comes, in later editions, to say:

9. Ll. 901–6.   10. Ll. 1047–50.

> Le courroux d'une femme, impétueux d'abord,
> Promet tout ce qu'il ose à son premier transport;
> Mais comme il n'a pour lui que sa seule impuissance,
> A force de grossir il meurt en sa naissance,

And, when Corneille revises his text, he no longer makes Dorise scream:

> Sus, d'ongles et de dents . . .[11]

But aside from these considerations of literary style, it is evident that the whole manner of acting this scene was greatly modified in 1660 and 1682. In the earliest version, we witness a veritable wrestling match between the two lovers. Pymante seizes Dorise's hands and forcibly tries to kiss her; she resists, struggles, and lets out piercing screams. At last he drags her brutally into a cave which happens to be handy, while she howls, "A la force, au secours." None of all this violence remains when, some thirty years later, Corneille, influenced by the classical spirit, develops a case of bad conscience because of this scene. The new, chastened version eliminates all physical struggle between the lovers. Dorise merely leaves saying, "Traître, ne me suis point," and Pymante replies, "Mais vous n'irez pas loin que je ne vous rejoigne." Then the curtain falls. We are forced to conclude, however, that Corneille was not completely convinced by classical conceptions of propriety, for he retains, in all editions, the particularly brutal scene of the following act, which takes place in the cave. Pymante, declaring that "Il me faut un baiser malgré vos cruautés" [12]—in 1660, "Il me faut des faveurs"—attempts to rape Dorise, and she "lui crève un œil du poinçon qui lui étoit demeuré dans les cheveux." This stage direction—the partial blinding of Pymante—persists through all the editions. Corneille remains sufficiently under the influence of the baroque spirit to consider, throughout his life, that this episode is essential. Even in his "Examen" of the play, which dates from 1660, he refrains from any criticism of the incident. But the language of the scene is toned down as early as 1644; Pymante, when his eye is put out, cries in 1632, "Barbara je t'aurai," whereas later he merely says "Ton sang m'en répondra." One of Dorise's tirades is eliminated in 1660—perhaps because of its exaggerated préciosité, or perhaps simply because it is a little implausible, in view of the circumstances. She has just stabbed Pymante in the eye, and this is what she says:

> Ainsi dorénavant le Ciel plus favorable
> Me prête en ces malheurs une main secourable.
> Cependant pour loyer de sa lubricité,
> Son œil m'a répondu de ma pudicité,

11. L. 1057.   12. L. 1151.

Et dedans son cristal mon aiguille enfoncée,
Attirant ses deux mains m'a désembarrassée.[13]

Corneille has made important changes in the following scene, where the abandoned Pymante gives vent to his despair and his fury. Originally he represented the partially blinded lover as equally torn between rage and passion; the course of the 1632 soliloquy alternates several times from tenderness to anger and back again. Pymante is in that state of inner contradiction which especially interests baroque poets. In the corrected versions, on the other hand, anger triumphs. To realize this, we need only to compare two forms of one of the couplets:

1632: Et tous mes sens brouillés d'un désordre nouveau
      Au lieu de ma maîtresse adorent mon bourreau.

1660: Honteux restes d'amour qui brouillez mon cerveau
      Pourrois-je en ma maîtresse adorer mon bourreau?

Corneille tries here to eliminate the antithesis, and to make a single emotion dominate. But he wishes to attenuate the expression of that emotion, since at the end of the scene, after the storm and the thunderbolts, Pymante no longer contemplates "sur sa charogne achever sa colère" but (in 1660) confines himself to asking fate to avenge his injury.

It should be noticed that, in the course of his successive emendations of the play, Corneille has a tendency to cut certain scenes of secondary importance. Obviously, even the 1682 version retains the extreme profusion of different scenes, each one of which involves a change of place—"another part of the forest," as Shakespeare would say; but scenes like the fourth in the third act (a completely nonessential conversation between two confidants, Lysarque and Cléon), and Act IV, scene 5, where Cléon and a huntsman comment on the striking of the prince's horse by lightning—these scenes disappear. We are still very far from any observance of the unity of place, but the poet is probably beginning to feel embarrassed by the extreme variety of settings in his youthful plays.

After the examples which I have quoted, the reader has possibly gained the impression that, all things considered, Corneille was right to make the changes and cuts mentioned. Some people may side with the classicists in this argument, and condemn excesses of préciosité, violence, or even of too concrete imagery. It must be admitted, however, that the poet, in bowing to the demands of the new style, has completely mutilated the most charming scene in *Clitandre*. I refer to Act V, scene III. Because of the wounds received

13. Ll. 1173–8.

in the forest, Rosidor has been obliged to go to bed. Now Caliste comes to his room, and sitting on his bed, says:

> Que diras-tu mon cœur de voir que ta maîtresse
> Te vient effrontément trouver jusques au lit?

And Rosidor:

> Que dirai-je sinon que pour un tel délit
> On ne m'échappe à moins de trois baisers d'amende?

The scene develops, following this tone of tender flirtation, but progressively growing warmer and more passionate. Caliste resists her lover halfheartedly, and asks him to behave himself until the day of their wedding:

> Lorsque tu te verras ces privautés permises,
> Tu pourras t'assurer que nos contentements
> Ne redouteront plus aucuns empêchements.

And Rosidor:

> Vienne cet heureux jour, mais jusque-là, mauvaise
> N'avoir point de baisers à refraîchir ma braise!

Then, according to the stage direction, "Il la baise sans resistance." Naturally, we should not allow ourselves to be misled by modern colloquial usage as to the meaning of this phrase, but all the same we must admit that the situation scarcely conforms to the principles of classical bienséance. As a matter of fact, we observe that Rosidor himself is a little taken aback:

> Je ne m'étonne plus de te voir si privée
> Te mettre sur mon lit aussitôt qu'arrivée,

And Caliste, slightly alarmed by the way their tête-à-tête is tending, implores her lover:

> Retiens un peu la bride à tes bouillants désirs,

Rosidor's answer is simultaneously précieux and bold:

> Que le sort a pour moi de subtiles malices!
> Ce lit doit etre un jour le champ de mes délices,
> Et recule lui seul ce qu'il doit terminer,
> Lui seul il m'interdit ce qu'il me doit donner.[14]

Yet even in this 1632 version the proprieties are respected to a certain extent, since the lovers, considering that the state of Rosidor's health will permit

14. Cf. ll. 1606–84, passim.

him to leave his bed for an hour, finally decide to go to render personal thanks to the king. Rosidor begins to get dressed; and meanwhile, despite her lover's pleas, Caliste discreetly withdraws.

In 1660 the scene is reduced to a mere shadow of its former self. Both the actions and the language become more reserved. Corneille does not, however, do away with the bed. But Caliste does not sit on it, there are no embraces, and the erotic allusions are greatly attenuated. Caliste has a serene confidence that Rosidor will take no liberties with her:

> . . . je dédirois ce secret entretien
> Si ta pleine santé me donnoit lieu de dire
> Quelle borne à tes vœux je puis et dois prescrire.

And, a little further on, she says,

> N'espère qu'à demi, quand je parle à demi.

In fact the corrected scene is all in discreet half-tones. The lovers confine themselves to mutual assurances of affection, and Caliste expresses her hope for Rosidor's rapid recovery. In this particular case, the evolution from baroque to classicism constitutes an artistic decline. The earliest version seems to me definitely superior in dramatic movement, in elements of spectacle, and in poetic imagery. The later versions, a bit colorless and abstract, are lacking in life.

3. MÉLITE

The first performance of *Mélite* took place in 1633. Though the play was a great success, Corneille kept altering it throughout his life. M. Mario Roques' recent critical edition is based on the text of 1633 which is, as I shall attempt to show, the most baroque version. However, as French taste evolved, becoming more and more classical, Corneille published a succession of emended editions in an effort to make his comedy conform more closely to the new literary canons. These toned-down versions appeared in 1644, 1648, 1654, 1655, 1657, 1660, 1663, 1664, 1668, and 1682. The most considerable alterations occur in the edition of 1660—coinciding with the beginning of the greatest classical period in France.

As is often the case with Corneille's comedies, the plot of *Mélite* is somewhat complicated (although it is decidedly less so than *Clitandre*). Since many readers are unfamiliar with the play, a brief synopsis will probably prove helpful. Otherwise it will be difficult to appreciate the significance of the various emendations as they occur.

The action takes place in contemporary Paris, and the characters are the sort of people whom Corneille himself might have known. In the first scene, wealthy young Eraste, who is hopelessly in love with Mélite, is telling his troubles to his friend Tirsis, a cynical youth who scorns women, love, and marriage. In the midst of their discussion, Mélite herself arrives, and her lover reproaches her bitterly for her insensibility. But Tirsis, greatly struck by her beauty, begins to understand why a man may suffer through love. As soon as the two friends are alone again, Eraste turns triumphantly to Tirsis, saying, "Well, wasn't I right? Do you blame me now?" And he asks his friend, who apparently has some reputation as a poet, to compose a love sonnet for him, so that he can give it to Mélite. This Tirsis promises to do, swearing also that he will be loyal to Eraste and not try to win Mélite for himself. But in a brief soliloquy we learn that Tirsis really has fallen in love, and that he regards no promise as binding. Scene 4 introduces a new pair of lovers, Philandre and Cloris (the latter being Tirsis' sister). These two understand each other perfectly, and their conversation is one long happy flirtation. In fact, Tirsis interrupts them in the midst of an embrace; now that he understands love, he is in very good humor, and hints to the couple that he too has fallen in love.

A week or so elapses between Acts I and II; Corneille, at this date, had not yet heard of the unity of time. From the baroque point of view this is all to the good, because it permits an evolution of the relationships of the characters. The act begins with a long soliloquy of lamentation by Eraste, who has begun to be sorry that he insisted so strongly on making Tirsis admire Mélite; tortured by jealousy, he fears that he has been betrayed. Seeing Mélite, he expresses sarcastic surprise that Tirsis is not with her; in the ensuing quarrel she disavows having any responsibility toward her former lover. Eraste, left alone, plots vengeance. Rejecting the idea of a duel, he summons a neighbor, Cliton, and gives him a bribe of ten pistoles to carry out a nefarious scheme. In scene 5 Tirsis reads his sister the sonnet which he has composed on Mélite; with immediate intuition, she guesses the true state of affairs, and assures him that since the engagement between Eraste and Mélite has dragged on for two years, he really has nothing to fear from his rival. With scene 6 we learn further details of the plot which Eraste is concocting. He asks Cliton to take a forged letter to Philandre, and to tell him that Mélite can no longer restrain her passion for him. In the next scene this letter is delivered; while Philandre is reading it, Eraste sneaks up behind him and proceeds to urge him to desert Cloris in favor of Mélite. Tirsis now meets Eraste in the street in front of Mélite's house, and hands him the promised sonnet; but Eraste has lost interest, drops the poem on the ground, and goes away. Tirsis picks it up, and, annoyed at such capriciousness, vows henceforth to court Mélite for himself. The heroine, who has been watching the scene from her window, comes down to talk to him;

their conversation soon becomes most affectionate, and Tirsis slides the sonnet into her bosom.

We must also suppose an interval of a week or two between Acts II and III, because here again the situation has developed considerably. Whereas during the first entr'acte Tirsis' passion has grown, during this one Philandre has had the time to decide that he likes Mélite better than Cloris. We learn this during the opening soliloquy of the act; and when Tirsis, now confident of Mélite's love, comes to discuss his happiness with Philandre, he suffers a rude shock, for the latter produces two supposed love letters from Mélite. The first one, being somewhat ambiguous, can be explained away, but the second, which contains unflattering references to Tirsis, carries instant conviction. Philandre, challenged to a duel, insists with smug ingenuity that he no longer has the right to dispose of his own life, since it now belongs to Mélite. Tirsis, left alone, plans flight and suicide, but before accomplishing the final desperate act shows his sister the letters, which Philandre, in a moment of really extraordinary carelessness, has left in his possession. Cloris attempts to console her brother by assuring him that women in general are fickle and that Mélite in particular is not worth bothering about; she herself accepts Philandre's infidelity with surprising calm, feeling that if he really wants Mélite he can have her. By scene 6, Philandre has come to realize that he ought not to have left the letters in Tirsis' hands, and is now resolved to fight a duel, if necessary, to get them back. Encountering Cloris, he explains that he has to see her brother on important business; but she, suspecting at once what it is, allows him a glimpse of the letters, and when he attempts to seize them from her, slams the door in his face.

Act IV begins with a worldly-wise conversation between Mélite and her nurse, who is trying to persuade her that she should forget about Tirsis and marry Eraste: he is rich and of good family. The heroine remains unconvinced; at this point Cloris arrives to quarrel with her and to show her the letters. It is of course the first she has heard of them, and she denounces the forgery at once, but Cloris believes that she is lying. The dispute is interrupted by the report of Tirsis' death; Mélite reveals her true love by fainting; Cloris calls for help; the nurse and friends carry the inanimate Mélite home. In scene 5 Eraste exults at the success of his scheme, which has confounded his enemies, but shows some remorse at having made victims of Philandre and Cloris. And then his agent, the contemptible Cliton, comes trembling to announce that both Tirsis and Mélite are dead. Eraste goes mad with grief, and in long lyrical ravings imagines that he too has died and is in hell. He is by the river Styx, and Cliton is Charon; he leaps on Cliton's shoulders and is carried off the stage. Meanwhile Philandre is still looking for Tirsis, so that he can force him to give back the letters; in his wandering he runs into Eraste, who takes him to be Minos and remorsefully confesses his whole wicked plot and its tragic consequences. The horrified Philandre abandons Eraste to his deserved madness. However, in the last scene of the act, we learn that the report of Tirsis' death is untrue; his friend Lisis has circulated it for the purpose of testing Mélite.

Eraste's hallucinations continue during the early part of Act V; in fact they go so far that he mistakes the ugly old nurse for Mélite, but she, with rough common sense, brings him back to sanity by revealing that Mélite is not really dead. In scene 3 Philandre apologizes to Cloris for his fickleness, but is not forgiven; in scene 4, Tirsis and Mélite clear up their misunderstanding, and find that they love each other more than ever before. The lovers, seeing that Cloris envies their happiness, try to persuade her to make up with Philandre, but she proudly persists in her refusal. Eraste, now completely cured of his madness, asks to be forgiven his misdeeds. Mélite and Tirsis gladly grant him pardon since, as they say, the actual effect of his plot has been to strengthen their love. Finally, the nurse comes forward with a practical but rather surprising suggestion: Cloris should find her consolation by marrying Eraste, who is after all a most eligible young man. Eraste likes the idea, and Cloris intimates that she will ultimately consent. Thus all the problems are solved, except those of Philandre: fickleness is regarded as a more serious sin than deceit.

The ten revised editions of *Mélite* bring literally hundreds of changes to the original text, ranging in length from a single line to twenty lines or more. It is naturally not possible to study all of these alterations here, and indeed many of them have no great stylistic significance; for a complete listing the reader is referred to the variants given in the Roques-Lièvre edition. On the other hand, in numerous cases the emendations do reflect a change in Corneille's artistic sensibility; and this change, I feel, corresponds to the general evolution during the course of the century from the baroque to the classical. What follows is, therefore, a selection.

In Act I, scene 1, Eraste is describing to Tirsis the sufferings of love, and complaining of the way in which Mélite treats him. The 1633 text reads:

> Si sa rigueur m'aigrit, ce n'est qu'en son absence,
> Et j'ai beau mesnager dans un esloignement
> Un peu de liberté pour mon ressentiment,
> Un seul de ses regards l'estouffe, et le dissipe,
> Un seul de ses regards me seduit et me pipe,
> Et d'un tel ascendant maistrise ma raison,
> Que je chéris mon mal, et fuy ma guerison:

By 1660, this has become:

> Si j'ose en murmurer, ce n'est qu'en son absence,
> Et je ménage en vain dans un eloignement
> Un peu de liberté pour mon ressentiment,
> D'un seul de ses regards l'adorable contrainte
> Me rend tous mes liens, en resserre l'estrainte,
> Et par un si doux charme aveugle ma raison,
> Que je cherche mon mal, et fuy ma guérison.[1]

In general, it may be observed that the later version has been toned down, and is somewhat more abstract. "Si sa rigueur m'aigrit" is a stronger expression than "Si j'ose en murmurer." "J'ai beau mesnager" is a little more suggestive of personal struggle than "je ménage en vain." The echoing repetition of "un seul" has been eliminated; this echo technique, which is a great favorite of d'Aubigné's, produces an effect of heavy hammering—it is the baroque combination of mass and movement. Notice, as a part of this same technique, the heaping up of four verbs: "estouffe," "dissipe," "séduit," and "pipe"; in the later version these have been reduced to two: "rend" and "resserre." The idea of a violent struggle is more forcefully rendered by "Et d'un tel ascendant maistrise ma raison" than by "Et par un si doux charme aveugle ma raison." Finally, although in the last line the 1660 text establishes a more direct antithesis ("cherche"—"fuy") than the original version, the contrast is of a somewhat abstract and geometric character; the 1633 word "chéris" is warmer and more affective.

The Tirsis of this first scene is much more direct, cynical, and impolite in 1633 than later. In the original version Corneille has him make disparaging remarks about Mélite to Eraste's face:

> Je croy malaisément que tes affections
> Arrestent en un lieu si peu considerable
> D'une chaste moitié le choix invariable:

In other words, Mélite is an insignificant person, far beneath Eraste's level. Thirty years later, in 1663, the poet alters this speech, so that Tirsis is merely saying that a woman's beauty, being ephemeral, is an unsound basis for life-long marriage:

> Je croy malaisément que tes affections
> Sur l'éclat d'un beau teint qu'on voit si périssable
> Règlent d'une moitié le choix invariable.[2]

In all stages of the text, Tirsis advises his friend to marry for money rather than for love, and Eraste throughout reacts indignantly at the suggestion; but

---

1. Ll. 6–12. (Line numbers refer to the 1633 text.)   2. Ll. 44–6.

in 1633 his repudiation of mercenary considerations assumes a more précieux form than in 1660:

> 1633: Je ne sache point d'or capable de mes vœux
>   Que celuy dont Nature a paré ses cheveux.

> 1660: Il [his love] me rend insensible aux faux attraits de l'or,
>   Et trouve en sa personne un assez grand tresor.[3]

The visual image has been sacrificed, Tirsis regards this attitude as very immature; it is all very well for an adolescent to learn life through flirtation with pretty girls:

> 1633: C'est-là qu'un jeune oyseau doit s'apprendre à parler,

> 1660: C'est là qu'un apprentif doit d'instruire à parler,

The picturesque and colloquial "oyseau" has been replaced by the more formal and abstract "apprentif." Aside from these considerations, Tirsis is simply not attracted to marriage because he does not want to be bothered with children:

> 1633: Perdre pour des enfans le repos de son âme,
>   Quand leur nombre importun accable la maison!

In 1660 the second line is softened:

> Voir leur nombre importun remplir une maison! [4]

"Accable" is much more suggestive of violent motion than "remplir." The Tirsis of the first edition has moments of crude humor which disappear in the later revisions. As a realistic Frenchman, he is dedicated to the pleasures of the table, and he warns the ardent lover that he should make sure that his wife knows how to cook:

> La beauté, les attraits, le port, la bonne mine,
> Eschauffent bien les draps, mais non pas la cuisine,

In 1644, for reasons of bienséance, the allusion to sheets is removed, though the emphasis on gastronomy is preserved:

> La beauté, les attraits, l'esprit, la bonne mine,
> Eschauffent bien le cœur, mais non pas la cuisine,[5]

"Le port" has given way to "l'esprit," and "les draps" to "le cœur." Sensuous images are replaced by intellectual concepts. The same passage goes on to say:

3. Ll. 55–6.   4. Ll. 102–3.   5. Ll. 117–18.

> Et l'Hymen qui succede à ces folles amours
> Pour quelques bonnes nuits, a bien de mauvais jours;

By 1660 Corneille had decided that it would be better to change this too, and the second line of the couplet reads:

> Apres quelques douceurs a bien des mauvais jours; [6]

This emendation, like the preceding one, represents a step away from the physical toward the abstract; it also destroys an effective antithesis.

The scene where Tirsis meets Mélite, and begins to lose all his prejudices about women and love, has fewer significant changes. Yet there is an interesting variation, from 1633 to 1660, in Mélite's leave-taking:

> 1633: Mais outre qu'il m'est doux de m'entendre flatter
> Ma mère qui m'attend m'oblige à vous quitter,

> 1660: Mais je pourrois bien-tost à m'entendre flatter
> Concevoir quelque orgueil qu'il vaut mieux éviter. [7]

I do not think that it is stretching a point unduly to suggest that the Mélite of the first version is the more convincingly human. She admits frankly, rather than implying indirectly, that she enjoys Tirsis' attention; she is a real girl of everyday life with a mother who supervises her. By 1660 she has become a more remote and distinguished figure.

In revising his text, Corneille has not only rewritten certain passages; he has cut out others entirely. For example, he has somewhat shortened the scene in the first act between Philandre and Cloris, feeling perhaps that the flirtatious exchange between the two lovers is prolonged to the point of tediousness. In any event, a speech of protest by Philandre, ending with the lines,

> Ce refus obstiné d'une louange acquise
> M'accuseroit enfin de peu de jugement,
> D'avoir tant pris de peine, et souffert de tourment,
> Pour qui ne valoit pas l'offre de mon service, [8]

has been completely eliminated. Presumably it did not conform to 1660 conceptions of gallantry, and it is true that here Philandre, with his allusions to the troubles of courtship and to his own good taste in women, is being somewhat tactless and self-centered. By cutting this passage, Corneille has smoothed away some of the character's rough spots; yet we may question the author's wisdom in doing so, since (as it turns out) Philandre rather than Eraste is to be considered the villain of the piece. A certain amount of

6. Ll. 119–20.   7. Ll. 207–8.   8. Ll. 288–9.

psychological realism has been sacrificed for the sake of polish and bienséance. In places the speech of Cloris also has undergone a polishing process:

> 1633: Dois-je prendre cecy pour de l'argent comptant?
> Ouy Philandre, et mes yeux vont t'en montrer autant
> Nos brasiers tous pareils ont mesmes estincelles.[9]

> 1660: Le trait n'est pas mauvais, mais quisqu'il te plaist tant
> Regarde dans mes yeux, ils t'en montrent autant,
> 1668: Et nos feux tous pareils ont mesmes etincelles.

In the classical era the expression "argent comptant" probably seemed a little vulgar; the cash metaphor was felt to be inappropriate to the language of love. In 1668 the word "brasiers" appeared too ardent, and was attenuated to "feux." This scene ends with a kiss: the lines assigned to Philandre, Cloris, and Tirsis (who interrupts the embrace) are explicit on this point, and the poet never changed them; however, there is a stage direction which appears only in the 1633 edition: "Il les surprend sur ce baiser." As we shall see, Corneille shows a general tendency to remove more and more of his stage directions as he revises his play. It is well known that the plays of Molière and Racine contain very few stage directions: the whole emphasis, at the height of the classical period, is on text rather than staging. Naturally the spectator at an actual performance sees the action; but the reader is supposed to be influenced through his intellect rather than his senses. In some of the examples which I shall discuss later, not only the stage direction but the action itself is eliminated.

We have observed how Tirsis, in the early scenes of the play before he is transformed by true love, exhibits a Rabelaisian sense of humor. Such is his remark upon interrupting Philandre and Cloris:

> Je pense ne pouvoir vous estre qu'importun,
> Vous feries mieux un tiers, que d'en accepter un.

An older and more classical Corneille decided that this joke was out of place; the revised and more elegant version reads:

> 1644: De moins sorciers que moy pourroient bien deviner
> Qu'un troisième ne fait que vous importuner.[10]

Cloris, protesting, assures her brother that she and Philandre have not misconducted themselves, and that in any case a certain latitude is to be allowed an engaged couple. Tirsis replies that he knows they are impatient to be married:

9. Ll. 323–5.   10. Ll. 339–40.

> Ceste legere amorce irritant tes desirs
> Fait que l'illusion d'autres meilleurs plaisirs
> Vient la nuit chatoüiller ton esperance avide,
> Malsatisfaicte apres de tant mascher à vide.[11]

And here the poet, evidently at a loss to find a discreet way of expressing the idea, simply cuts the passage out (1644). The last sixteen lines of the scene, which closes the act, have been completely rewritten, partly because of some more of Tirsis' *gauloiseries,* and partly because Corneille wished to emphasize more clearly the fact that Cloris suspects her brother to be in love. In doing so, he prepares the audience more fully for Act II, scene 5, where Tirsis reads his sonnet aloud and Cloris extracts from him a complete confession of his love for Mélite. Generally speaking, the different scenes and acts of *Mélite* are not very tightly linked together; as the seventeenth century progressed, this was more and more felt to be a requirement of dramatic art, and Corneille attempted to remedy such weaknesses in his earlier plays. Actually, the sonnet scene is comprehensible even without foreshadowing; and the foreshadowing here at the end of Act I takes the form of a flirtatious argument between Philandre and Cloris (he tries to prevent her from leaving him, while she insists that she is curious about her brother), but the lovers' dialogue has, after all, already been sufficiently prolonged.

The first scene of the second act is a soliloquy in which Eraste curses himself for having insisted on introducing Tirsis to Mélite. A week or more has elapsed, and he has reason to suspect that his hitherto misogynous friend may have fallen in love with Mélite. The theme of jealous passion is expressed in every edition of the play; but the following passage from the 1633 version is suppressed in 1660:

> Mais helas! qui pourroit gauchir sa destinée.
> Son immuable loy dans le ciel burinée
> Nous fait si bien courir apres nostre malheur
> Que j'ay donné moy-mesme accez à ce voleur,
> Le perfide qu'il est me doit sa cognoissance,
> C'est moy qui l'ay conduit, et mis en sa puissance,
> C'est moy qui l'engageant à ce froid compliment
> Ay jetté de mes maux le premier fondement.[12]

In these lines Eraste appears almost as a romantic hero of the generation of 1830. There is first of all the idea of fatality (a law engraved in heaven makes us rush to our misfortune). Here we should note the use of the word "burinée," a strong physical image expressing deep engraving, often used

---

11. Ll. 347–50.   12. Ll. 385–92.

by d'Aubigné in a similar metaphorical sense. Then Eraste broods insistently and masochistically on his own perverse part in bringing about his misfortune. Naturally the torments of self-reproached guilt are to be encountered in classical tragedy—*Phèdre* for example—but here there is less sense of sin than of self-pity, and hence the feeling is closer to that of romanticism. I do not mean to suggest that the romantic and baroque styles are the same—in many respects they are very different—but it is surely the growing influence of classical taste which in 1660 made Corneille decide to present Eraste as less of an *homme maudit*. We shall see that he has the same concern in Eraste's scenes of madness (Acts IV and V).

The open expression of jealousy always defeats its own object; and after a stormy scene with Mélite, in which she evades his petulant interrogations and asserts her own independence, Eraste is left alone to make a more violent soliloquy than before. This is a speech which the poet has extensively revised. In 1633 it read:

> Tu me preferes donc un traistre qui te flatte?
> Inconstante beauté, lasche, perfide, ingratte
> De qui le choix brutal se porte au plus mal faict,
> Tu l'estimes à faux, tu verras à l'effect
> Par le peu de rapport que nous avons ensemble
> Qu'un honneste homme et luy n'ont rien qui se ressemble.
> Que dis-je, tu verras? il vaut autant que mort,
> Ma valeur, mon despit, ma flame en sont d'accord,
> Il suffit, les destins bandez à me desplaire
> Ne l'arracheroient pas à ma juste cholere.

The 1660 version has, in comparison, a dignified mildness:

> Tu m'oses préférer un traistre qui te flate,
> Mais dans ta lâcheté ne croy pas que j'éclate,
> Et que par la grandeur de mes ressentimens
> Je laisse aller au jour celle de mes tourmens
> Un adveu si public qu'en feroit ma cholère
> Enfleroit trop l'orgueil de ton âme légère,
> Et me convaincrait trop de ce désir abjet
> Qui m'a fait soupirer pour un indigne objet.[13]

The 1660 Eraste, though still suffering from jealousy, has more self-respect, and controls the brutality of his expression for the sake of dignity: in other words, he is more conscious of an audience which will judge him by classical standards of manners. The 1633 Eraste is more willful, more individualistic, closer to the Renaissance. The earlier text contains many more direct insults:

13. Ll. 469–77.

fickle, cowardly, perfidious, ungrateful; and Eraste frankly accuses Mélite of bad taste in preferring her less handsome suitor. In 1633 Eraste is full of threats of violence—his rival is as good as dead—whereas the Eraste who is being offered in competition with the young lovers of Molière and Racine politely disavows violence. The difference in tone may be measured by comparing the expressions "choix brutal" and "désir abject"; the fundamental meaning may be very much the same, but the first is actively violent, the second languidly perjorative. The following lines of the speech have been totally cut out; they refer to Tirsis:

> Tu demordras parjure, et ta desloyauté
> Maudira mille fois sa fatale beauté.
> Si tu peux te resoudre à mourir en brave homme,
> Dès demain un cartel, l'heure et le lieu te nomme.
> Insensé que je suis! helas, où me réduit
> Ce mouvement bouillant dont l'ardeur me seduit!
> Quel transport déreglé! quelle estrange eschappée!
> Avec un affronteur mesurer mon espée!
> C'est bien contre un brigand qu'il me faut hasarder,
> Contre un traistre qu'à peine on devroit regarder,
> Luy faisant trop d'honneur moy-mesme je m'abuse,
> C'est contre luy qu'il faut n'employer que la ruse:

In the place of this hyperbolic diatribe with all its exclamatory sentences, the author has substituted this single calmly dignified couplet:

> Je sçauray me vanger, mais avec l'apparence
> De n'avoir pour tous deux que de l'indifference,[14]

This is in fact the tone which Corneille, having toned down Eraste's threats of bloodthirsty reprisals, develops in the 1660 version of the closing lines of the scene: it provides a smoother transition to the plot of the forged letters. As we have already suggested, the 1633 text tends to consist of separate and contrasting episodes; the later version constitutes a more flowing unity. The earlier and the later endings of this scene 3 are worth contrasting:

> 1633: Vy doncques desloyal, vy, mais en asseurance
> Que tout va désormais tromper ton esperance,
> Que tes meilleurs amys s'armeront contre toy,
> Et te rendront encor plus malheureux que moy.
> J'en sçay l'invention qu'un voisin de Melite
> Escoutera trop aussi tost que prescrite.
> Pour n'estre qu'un maraut, il est assez subtil.

14. Ll. 479-90.

     1660: Tiens, desloyal amy, tiens ton ame asseurée
           Que ton heur surprenant aura peu de durée,
           Et que par une adresse égale à tes forfaits,
           Je mettrai le désordre où tu crois voir la paix.
           L'esprit fourbe et vénal d'un voisin de Mélite
           Donnera prompte issue à ce que je médite,
           A servir qui l'achepte il est toujours tout prest
           Et ne voit rien d'injuste où brille l'interest.
           Allons sans perdre temps luy payer ma vengeance,
           Et la pistole en main presser sa diligence.[15]

Spectators of the 1633 play witnessed an Eraste who, after a long speech of
murderous anger, decided to employ ruse rather than violence; in 1660 a
few brutal threats remain, but the insidious vengeance is more fully fore-
shadowed.

There follows immediately, in the 1633 text, a short scene where Eraste
plots with Cliton and offers him ten pistoles for some nefarious but as yet
unexplained service. In 1660 this scene is eliminated. When he first wrote the
play, Corneille wanted to show us, visually enacted on the stage, the mysterious beginnings of Eraste's plot; but later he chooses rather to alter
Eraste's speech of the preceding scene, and to give us these hints in words.
Regardless of the respective merits, dramatically speaking, of the two techniques, the visual method must be regarded as the more baroque, and the
verbal method the more classical. Actually, if we consider the 1633 play
in itself, scene 4 gives the audience no information not fully imparted in
scene 6, where the details of the forged-letters plot are explained; but the
little preliminary scene does create a certain amount of suspense. The 1660
version has sacrificed some vividness and excitement in favor of a more
flowing coherence of action.

Because of the elimination, in 1660, of scene 4, all subsequent scenes in this
act have to be renumbered; thus 1633's scene 5, in which Tirsis reads his
sonnet to his sister, becomes, from 1660 on, scene 4. Cloris, it will be
remembered, guesses at once that the sonnet expresses her brother's own
feelings, and proceeds to persuade him that Eraste is not a dangerous rival.
Mélite, she declares, is obviously not in love with Eraste; courtships which
are so prolonged never lead to anything:

     1633: On prend au premier bond les hommes de sa sorte,
           De crainte que la longue ils n'esteignent leur feu.

     1660: On prend soudain au mot les hommes de la sorte,
           Et sans rien hazarder à la moindre longueur.[16]

15. Ll. 493–9.   16. Ll. 592–3.

The imagery has been removed from the later version; the sprightly and concrete "premier bond" has been replaced by the abstract and colorless "mot"; the "feu" has disappeared entirely. At the end of their conversation, when the brother and sister part, Cloris says that she is going home to wait for Philandre; she is a little annoyed at her lover's delay in coming to see her:

> 1633: Un baiser refusé luy fera souvenir
> Qu'il faut une autre fois tarder moins à venir.

> 1663: Un moment de froideur le fera souvenir
> Qu'il faut une autre fois tarder moins à venir.[17]

Once more, concreteness has been sacrificed for the sake of bienséance. I think the reader will admit that the earlier version is the more lively.

After Eraste has given Cliton the forged letter to take to Philandre, he indulges in a disparaging speech on the venality of the lower classes:

> Ces âmes du commun font tout pour de l'argent
> Et sans prendre interest au dessein de personne
> Leur service, et leur foy sont à qui plus leur donne,
> Quand ils sont éblouys de ce traistre metal,
> Ils ne distinguent plus le bien d'avec le mal,
> Le seul espoir du gain regle leur conscience.[18]

In 1660 Corneille cuts out the four middle lines of this passage. He probably felt that, in rewriting the end of scene 3 (see above, p. 193), he had already dwelt sufficiently upon the mercenary theme. In any case, the excision removes another visual image—"éblouys de ce traistre métal."

In this part of the play, the later editions eliminate a great many of the stage directions. Scene 6, for example, originally contained the following:

Il [Eraste] baille une lettre à Cliton.

Cliton rentre.

Cliton ressort brusquement.

Philandre paroist, et Eraste se cache.

Scene 7 had:

Cependant que Philandre lit, Eraste s'approche par derrière, et feignant d'avoir leu par dessus son espaule, il luy saisit la main encore pleine de la lettre toute desployée.

In the last scene of the act, there were the following indications:

Elle [Mélite] paroist au travers d'une jalousie, et de ces vers, cependant qu'Eraste lit le Sonnet tout bas.

17. Ll. 605–6.   18. Ll. 622–7.

Il [Tirsis] monstre du doigt, la fin de son Sonnet a Eraste.

Feignant de luy rendre son Sonnet, il [Eraste] le fait choir et Tirsis le ramasse.

Melite se retire de la jalousie et descend.

Il [Tirsis] luy coule le Sonnet dans le sein comme elle se desrobe.

In 1644 all of these directions, except the last one, disappear from the text. As a matter of fact, all the actions described are more or less implicit in the spoken lines. From 1644 on, the actors studying their parts would in all probability decide to do the various things mentioned in the old directions. A spectator of the revised play would not be conscious of any change in these places. It is only the technique of presenting the play to the reading public which has changed: in other words, the alteration is literary rather than dramatic in nature. This is part of that evolution, which I have already mentioned, from a sensational to an intellectual conception of literature.

The last of these stage directions (Tirsis slides the sonnet into Mélite's bosom) merits special discussion. Here it is the stage action itself, rather than the method of indicating it to the reader, which troubles Corneille. In 1644 the playwright, judging Tirsis' gesture to be too daring, modifies it to "Tirsis, luy coulant le Sonnet dans le bras." The arm is a less controversial part of the body than the bosom. But he is still not happy about the scene; even this attenuated gesture is apparently regarded as somehow too physical. Four years later, in 1648, he removes the stage direction entirely, and this necessitates rewriting the final speech of Tirsis and of Mélite. Physical contact is here reduced to a minimum:

TIRSIS.

Ce sonnet que pour vous vient de tracer ma flame
Vous fera voir à nu jusqu'au fond de mon ame.

MÉLITE.

Garde bien ton Sonnet et pense qu'aujourd'huy
Mélite te veut croire autant et plus que luy.
Je le prens toutefois comme un précieux gage
Du pouvoir que mes yeux ont pris sur ton courage.[19]

Decorously he hands her the sonnet; decorously she at first declines, and then accepts it. Passion is expressed by words and glances only.

By the beginning of Act III, the letters which Philandre imagines he is receiving from Mélite have produced their insidious effect. A soliloquy informs us that he has resolved to change loves. He regrets that he has spent so much of the past in loving a woman other than Mélite, and expresses

19. Ll. 767-72 (1648 version).

the hope that Cloris, like himself, will be able to find improvement in change! And here four lines of the 1633 text are cut out in 1644:

> Dites luy de ma part, que depuis que le monde
> Du milieu du Chaos tira sa forme ronde,
> C'est la premiere fois que ces vieux ennemis
> Le change, et la raison sont devenus amis [20]

The passage has, of course, a distinctly baroque quality, with its theatrical evocation of the creation of the world, and its suggestions of mutability and metamorphosis. Corneille's reason for removing it is probably that he regarded it as too epic in tone for this particular situation: a faithless lover is trying to justify his own fickleness. It is true that he might have retained the lines, on the grounds that they are really mock-heroic; after all, thirty years later Boileau himself wrote the *Lutrin*. But the whole evolution of taste in the seventeenth century was moving against the mixing of tones within the same literary work; Corneille, feeling uneasy about these four lines, has struck them out. We shall see that Eraste's scenes of madness in Acts IV and V give the author similar moments of doubt.

In Act III, scene 2, Philandre is skeptical when Tirsis boasts of being beloved by Mélite:

> PHILANDRE.
>
> Encor c'est quelque chose, acheve et conte-moy
> Les douceurs que la belle à tout autre farouche
> T'a laissé desrobber sur ses yeux, sur sa bouche,
> Sur sa gorge, où, que sçay-je?
>
> TIRSIS.
>
>   Ah, ne présume pas
> Que ma temerité profane ses appas,
> Et quand bien j'aurois eu tant d'heur, ou d'insolence,
> Ce secret estouffé dans la nuit du silence
> N'eschapperoit jamais à ma discretion.[21]

This, of course, is from the 1633 edition; in 1660 the dialogue is considerably changed, and all indelicate allusions suppressed. Philandre now merely says,

>   . . . conte-moy
> Les petites douceurs, les aimables tendresses,
> Qu'elle se plaist à joindre à de telles promesses.

All very abstract and proper. Tirsis, altogether declining to discuss the degree of his intimacy with Mélite, says nothing, and thereupon Philandre

20. Ll. 795–8.   21. Ll. 854–61.

goes on to inquire whether he has received any letters. This leads inevitably to the production of the two letters which Mélite is supposed to have written to Philandre. Tirsis promptly challenges his rival to a duel. Philandre's form of refusal differs in 1633 and in 1660:

> 1633: Quant à moy, ton trespas me cousteroit trop cher,
> Il me faudroit après par une prompte fuite
> Esloigner trop long temps des beaux yeux de Melite.

> 1660: T. Quoy, tu crains le duel?—Ph. Non, mais j'en crains la suite
> Où la mort du vaincu met le vainqueur en fuite,
> Et du plus beau succez le dangereux éclat
> Nous fait perdre l'objet et le prix du combat.[22]

It should be noted that the original version expresses the idea in the first and second persons (*your* death would cost *me* too much; *I* should have to flee), whereas the revised text puts it in the third person (the loser's death puts the winner to flight). This difference in emphasis might almost be regarded as symbolically representative of the difference between the baroque and classical styles. The former, choosing the direct personal method of expression, is more vivid; the latter, removing itself from the concrete and particular, tends toward the universality of the aphorism. Another significant change in the same direction is that which befalls the beautiful eyes of Mélite: they become, very abstractly, the object and prize of the combat.

In both 1633 and 1660, Philandre's final argument for avoiding the duel is that his life now belongs to Mélite; but here again the two texts are not quite the same:

> 1633:   . . . je n'ose
> Ny mon sang, ny ma vie en peril exposer
> Ils ne sont plus à moy, je n'en puis disposer,
> Adieu, celle qui veut qu'à present je la serve
> Merite que pour elle ainsi je me conserve.

> 1660: Mon sang n'est plus à moy, je n'en puis disposer,
> Mais puisque ta douleur de mes raisons s'irrite,
> J'en prendrai dès ce soir le congé de Mélite.
> Adieu.[23]

This alteration changes somewhat both the dramatic situation and the character of Philandre. The original version precludes any possibility of a duel; the revised text still leaves a door open, since Mélite may allow the duel to take place. I think that Corneille was moved to make this emendation for

22. Ll. 906–8.   23. Ll. 913–16.

moral rather than aesthetic reasons. This is not the first time that we have seen moral considerations dictate changes ('Tirsis' manner of delivering the sonnet to Mélite, for example). Philandre is supposed to be the least sympathetic major character in the play, and in view of his opportunistic fickleness there is a good deal of doubt as to whether he may be regarded as an honnête homme; but the audience of 1660 would have been offended at the sight of a man who categorically refused to fight a duel.

Brokenhearted by Mélite's supposed letters, and angered by Philandre's refusal to fight, Tirsis voices his despair and fury in a soliloquy of ninety-two lines. Corneille seems to have felt that this speech was too long and too violent; by 1660 thirty-eight of the lines, including a good many of the more hyperbolic ones, have been removed. Since, as a consequence of the 1660 changes in the preceding scene, Philandre's cowardice is less evident, the following passage, now excessive in tone, is deleted:

> Fuy donc, homme sans cœur, va dire à ta volage
> Combien sur ton rival ta fuitte a d'avantage,
> Et que ton pied leger ne laisse à ma valeur
> Que les vains mouvemens d'une juste douleur,
> Ce lasche naturel qu'elle faict recognoistre
> Ne t'aymera pas moins estant poltron que traistre.
> Traistre, et poltron! voylà les belles qualitez
> Qui retiennent les sens de Melite enchantez [24]

Philandre's last words in the revised scene 2 were that he intended to ask Mélite's permission to fight the duel; the above passage would no longer be fully consistent. But here again I feel that in making the excision Corneille has in mind his contemporaries' ideals of human conduct. If he felt it necessary to tone down the weaknesses of one of his unsympathetic characters, it was even more essential that his hero, Tirsis, should appear in an attractive light. The playwright could not afford to let the hero make such brutally insulting remarks about the heroine, not even in a moment of jealous passion. The ideal of the gentleman in the salon is becoming paramount. As a result, the characters must be made blander and less individualistic. The Tirsis of 1633 makes vulgar jokes and yields to outbursts of passion; the Tirsis of 1660 is more polished and tamer. In making him conform to classical standards of manners, Corneille has had to sacrifice some picturesqueness and vitality. Even by 1644, the following mild allusions by Tirsis to his love-making are suppressed as indelicate:

> Je croyois à ses yeux, à sa mine embrasée,
> A ces petits larcins pris d'une force aisée,[25]

24. Ll. 943–50.   25. Ll. 959–60.

The climax of Tirsis' soliloquy, in the 1633 edition, is his resolve to flee to some lonely place, and there to commit suicide. Referring to his martyr-dom, the hero says:

> Aussi ma prompte mort le va bien tost finir,
> Desja mon cœur outré, ne cherchant qu'à bannir
> Cet amour qui l'a fait si lourdement mesprendre
> Pour luy donner passage, est tout prest de se fendre.
> Mon âme par despit, tasche d'abandonner
> Un corps que sa raison, sceut si mal gouverner
> Mes yeux jusqu'à present, couvers de mille nues,
> S'en vont distiller en larmes continues,
> Larmes qui donneront pour juste chastiment
> A leur aveugle erreur, un autre aveuglement
> Et mes pieds qui sçavoient sans eux, sans leur conduite
> Comme insensiblement me porter chez Melite
> Me porteront sans eux en quelque lieu desert
> En quelque lieu sauvage a peine descouvert,
> Ou ma main d'un poignard achevera le reste,
> Ou pour suyvre l'arrest de mon destin funeste
> Je respandrai mon sang, et j'auray pour le moins
> Ce foible et vain soulas en mourant sans tesmoins
> Que mon trespas secret fera que l'infidelle
> Ne pourra se vanter que je sois mort pour elle.[26]

Here Tirsis might almost be a nineteenth-century romantic hero. There are elements which suggest the mal du siècle and the works of Chateaubriand, Musset, or Hugo: the hero's belief in his "destin funeste," his contemplation of suicide in the wilderness, the broken heart, the tears, the dagger, the flowing blood—and above all, his sense of being tragically misunderstood. The feeling is not quite the same, however, for a true romantic would not reproach himself for being insufficiently governed by reason. And the lan-guage is often more précieux or baroque than romantic: one should note the image of the eyes which distill tears from the clouds, and also the feet which instinctively lead Tirsis to Mélite. The echo device is extremely fre-quent: "larmes continues . . . larmes qui donneront"; "aveugle erreur . . . un autre aveuglement"; "sans eux . . . sans leur conduite . . . sans eux"; "quelque lieu desert . . . quelque lieu sauvage"; "ou ma main . . . ou pour suyvre"; "mourant . . . mort." Such echoing repetitions are found through-out d'Aubigné's *Les Tragiques*.

By 1660 little remains of this tirade. Corneille replaces it with just four lines readapted from the end:

26. Ll. 989–1008.

> Mais cachons-en la honte et nous donnons du moins
> Ce faux soulagement en mourant sans témoins,
> Que mon trépas secret empesche l'infidelle
> D'avoir la vanité que je sois mort pour elle.

The thought of suicide is still present, though only by implication: the reader might very well interpret these lines to mean that Tirsis is going to die of a broken heart. And there are no gory details: the references to the dagger and bloodshed have been eliminated. Even the wilderness has disappeared—the "lieu desert" or "lieu sauvage." Instead, we have the much vaguer terms "sans témoins" and "secret." The dominant emotion is no longer self-pity but shame.

Cloris, coming upon her brother in his distracted state, exclaims (1633):

> Tu manques à la fois, de poulmon et d'haleine
> Ton pied mal affermy ne te soustient qu'à peine
> Quel accident nouveau te brouille ainsi les sens.[27]

The first of these lines, in 1663, is changed to

> Tu manques à la fois de couleur, et d'haleine!

(The word "poulmon" is now considered inappropriate for poetry.) The third line of the passage becomes, in 1660,

> Quel accident nouveau te trouble ainsi les sens.

(The verb "troubler" is more dignified than "brouiller.") In this scene between the brother and sister, the following stage direction is cut out (1644 and all subsequent editions):

> Elle lit les lettres que Tirsis luy avoit données.[28]

The actual stage business, however, is retained: it is evident from Cloris' next speech that she has read the letters. Some of her unflattering comments on Mélite are slightly toned down:

> 1633:   . . . ceste ecervelée
> Qui n'a d'ambition que d'estre cajolée
> Par les premiers venus qui flatans ses beautez

> 1660:   . . . ceste ecervelée
> Qui n'a d'ambition que d'estre cajolée
> Et rend à plaindre ceux qui flatant ses beautez [29]

The following passage (1633):

27. Ll. 1015–17.   28. Following l. 1030.   29. Ll. 1043–5.

> Ce n'est qu'une coquette, une teste à l'esvent
> Dont langue avec son cœur ne s'accorde jamais,
> A qui les trahisons deviennent ordinaires,

becomes in 1660:

> Ce n'est qu'une coquette avec tous ses attraits,
> Sa langue avec son cœur ne s'accorde jamais,
> Les infidelitez sont ses jeux ordinaires,[30]

Cloris, although she is annoyed with Mélite, takes her disappointment much less tragically than Tirsis. After all, she is armed with compromising letters, and she feels that if her crazy brother could only be induced to laugh at the situation, the two of them could have fun embarrassing Mélite and Philandre. Her sprightly enthusiasm for this little game is brought out much more strongly in the 1633 text than in the revised 1660 version:

> 1633:   Si je puis descovrir le lieu de sa retraite
> Et qu'il me veille croire estaignant tous ses feux
> Nous passerons le temps à ne rire que d'eux.
> Je la feray rougir, cette jeune esventée,
> Lors que son escriture à ses yeux presentée
> Mettant au jour un crime estimé si secret,
> Elle recognoistra qu'elle ayme un indiscret.
> Je luy veux dire alors pour aggraver l'offence,
> Que Philandre avec moy tousjours d'intelligence
> Me fait des contes d'elle, et de tous les discours
> Qui servent d'aliment à ses vaines amours,
> Si qu'à peine il reçoit de sa part une lettre,
> Qu'il ne vienne en mes mains aussi tost la remettre,

> 1660:   Si je puis le rejoindre, et qu'il me veuille croire,
> Nous leur ferons bien voir que leur change indiscret
> Ne vaut pas un soupir, ne vaut pas un regret.
> Je me veux toutefois en vanger par malice,
> Me divertir une heure à m'en faire justice,
> Ces lettres fourniront assez d'occasion
> D'un peu de deffiance et de division.
> Si je prens bien mon temps, j'auray plaine matiere
> A les jouer tous deux d'une belle maniere.[31]

In the first version, Cloris emerges as a much more positively mischievous personality than in the second. The 1633 text has more movement, more life, more visual details. The scheme of confronting Mélite with her letters is a

---

30. Ll. 1053–5.   31. Ll. 1096–1108.

little dramatic scene: Cloris and Tirsis are laughing, Mélite recognizes her handwriting and blushes at the public revelation of her indiscretions; then Cloris rubs salt in her rival's wounds by saying that Philandre always turns over the love letters to her. In the 1660 text the concreteness and drama are lost, and Cloris' plans for witty vengeance are outlined in a more remote and abstract manner.

In Act II, as we have already observed, there were originally two separate scenes between Eraste and Tirsis, showing the hatching of the forgery plot; and Corneille, judging that the first one was superfluous, later deleted it. There is a similar excision in Act III, which in 1633 contained two scenes (6 and 8) where Philandre alone on the stage is vainly looking for Tirsis in an effort to get back the letters. In both scenes his state of mind is substantially the same: he is so disturbed at Mélite's possible reaction if she finds out about the loss of the letters, that now he is ready to fight a duel if necessary. Scene 6, it must be admitted, contributes very little to the progress of the action, and so it is not surprising that the author, who undoubtedly felt that his play had too many detached episodes, should have cut it out in 1660. In the intervening scene (7 in 1633, 6 in 1660) Philandre discovers that Cloris has the letters, but is unable to make her surrender them. A brief comment is in order concerning the two suppressed stage directions of this scene: they occur only in the 1633 edition, disappearing as early as 1644. The first one reads

Il [Philandre] recognoist les lettres, et tasche de s'en saisir, mais Cloris les reserre.[32]

This indicates a definite physical struggle, since Philandre tries to snatch the letters, while Cloris clutches them firmly. With the removal of the above instructions, we have to fall back on the lines spoken by Philandre and Cloris, which do not tell us very much. He asks her to give him the letters, and she refuses, saying that she intends to show them to Mélite. In the 1644 edition, Corneille has cut out nearly all stage directions throughout the play, and these cuts, as we have seen, do not necessarily mean that the actions described are to be omitted. In this case, however, it seems likely that the author wanted to eliminate any suggestion of a wrestling match between the estranged lovers. I place a similar interpretation upon his removal of the other stage direction, at the close of their interview:

Elle luy ferme la porte au nez.[33]

In 1660 dramatic conflicts are to be expressed by intellectual and poetic means, not through physical violence visible on the stage.

32. Interrupting l. 1155.   33. Following l. 1162.

There are some changes at the beginning of Act IV, where Mélite's nurse is advising her how to catch a husband. The old woman frankly counsels coquetry:

> Ainsi lors que plusieurs te parlant à la fois,
> En respondant à l'un, serre à l'autre les doits,
> Et si l'un te desrobbe un baiser par surprise,
> Qu'à l'autre incontinent il soit en belle prise,[34]

These lines are eliminated in 1660. Did Corneille consider them too cynical, or did he regard the images as a little too concrete? One can only surmise, but whichever the reason, the fundamental motive is one of bienséance. It is interesting to notice what he does to the four lines immediately following:

> 1633: Que l'un et l'autre juge a ton visage esgal
> Que tu caches ta flame aux yeux de ton rival,
> Partage bien les tiens, et sur tout sçache feindre
> De sorte que pas un n'ayt sujet de se plaindre

> 1660: Que tout l'exterieur de son visage égal
> Ne rende aucun jaloux du bon-heur d'un rival,
> Que ses yeux partagez leur donnent de quoy craindre
> Sans donner à pas un aucun lieu de se plaindre.[35]

In the first passage, the verbs are in the second person; in the later one, they are in the third. This has the effect, as I have previously remarked, of creating a certain remoteness of tone: what was a direct personal conversation becomes a statement of general principles. In view of the frank, hearty personality of the nurse, the first way of speaking seems more appropriate than the second. She, by the way, is the sort of character we meet more frequently in Shakespeare than in French seventeenth-century theatre: we are reminded, for example, of the nurse in *Romeo and Juliet,* with her warm, earthy vulgarity. Mélite's nurse is given unusually full development for a secondary character, and while in the light of later, more classical standards Corneille might have had some misgivings about her, he actually makes few attempts to reduce the importance of the role. The old woman seems to have a secret fondness for Eraste, who is young, handsome, and very rich; in this scene she urges Mélite to marry him rather than Tirsis; later, it is she who by her common sense succeeds in curing Eraste's madness; and at the very end she solves matters by arranging the match between Eraste and Cloris. Also, the closing speech of the whole comedy is hers—though in later editions Corneille feels obliged to tone down its ribaldry.

The most abundant changes in Acts IV and V have to do with Eraste's

34. Ll. 1209-12.   35. Ll. 1213-16.

fit of madness. As might be expected, the later editions tend to make his
ravings milder. First of all, there is the mere question of quantity. At all
stages of the text, Eraste is mad during the following scenes: Act IV, scenes
6, 8, and 9; Act V, scene 2. But in 1633 he declaims two hundred alexandrines
while hallucinated; by 1660 fifty-five of these, or more than a quarter, have
been cut. Let me give a few samples of the type of passage which the older
Corneille condemned.

Hyperbole:

> [Que] j'ay toute une ville en larmes convertie,[36]

Hysterical remorse for his treatment of Tirsis:

> Mon courage au besoin se trouvant trop timide
> Pour attaquer Tirsis autrement qu'en perfide
> Je fis à mon deffaut combattre son ennuy,
> Son deuil, son desespoir, sa rage contre luy
>
> .   .   .   .   .
>
> Falloit-il, l'aveuglant d'une indiscrette erreur
> Contre une ame innocente allumer sa fureur?
> Falloit-il le forcer à dépeindre Melite
> Des infames couleurs d'une fille hipocrite? [37]

Desire to commit suicide on Mélite's body:

> Avançons donc, allons sur cet aymable corps
> Esprouver, s'il se peut, à la fois mille morts.[38]

Delusions of being in Hades:

> Le pere de l'oubly dessous ceste onde noire
> Pourroit-il conserver tant soit peu de memoire?
> Mais derechef que dis-je? imprudent, je confonds
> Le Lethé pesle-mesle, et ces gouffres profonds;
> Le styx de qui l'oubly ne prit jamais naissance
> De tout ce qui se passe a tant de cognoissance,
> Que les Dieux n'oseroient vers luy s'estre mespris,[39]

(In this connection, an eliminated stage direction should be mentioned.
Eraste, believing Cliton to be Charon, asks to be ferried across the Styx, and
"Il se jette sur les espaules de Cliton, qui l'emporte du Theatre.") Delirious
visions of horror (the Furies, fleeing in terror before him, have put out their
torches):

> Et tiré de leur chef les serpents d'alentour
> De crainte que leurs yeux fissent quelque faux jours

36. L. 1399.   37. Ll. 1423–6.   38. Ll. 1441–2.   39. Ll. 1467–73.

> Dont la foible lueur esclairant ma poursuite
> A travers ces horreurs me peust trahir leur fuite:
> Æaque espouvanté se croit trop en danger,
> Et fuit son criminel au lieu de le juger:
> Cloton mesme et ses sœurs à l'aspect de ma lame
> De peur de tarder trop n'osant couper ma trame [40]

In all fairness I must admit that, while a number of passages such as these have been removed, others like them still remain, even after 1660. Eraste still suffers torments of remorse, still has hallucinations, still imagines himself to be on the banks of the river Styx. Even in the later editions he continues to imagine that Cliton is Charon, though after 1644 he no longer physically has himself carried across the river. And in all editions, he for a time thinks that the nurse is Mélite. But one feels that this whole part of the play embarrasses Corneille, and that he would like to tone it down as much as possible. There remains the question of whether these scenes are to be taken seriously: would it not be possible to look upon them as mock-heroic, and to regard Eraste's hallucinations as a huge joke? This seems to me unlikely for several reasons. Whether or not we approve stylistically of the poetry in these passages, their effect is not primarily comical. Eraste's remorse is convincing, and his sufferings are genuine. We are more inclined to pity than to laugh at him. He does not strike us at all in the same way as, for example, Matamore in L'Illusion comique, whose hair-raising accounts of wild adventures are merely braggadocio. It is obvious, also, that the other characters do not think the madness of Eraste funny; his enemy Philandre takes it seriously, is glad to see him suffer, and considers the punishment deserved. Cliton is frankly terrified, and the nurse, who more than anyone else in the play represents common sense, realizes that these hallucinations are the result of grief, and immediately sets to work to cure Eraste. Furthermore, Eraste, whose treacherous plot has caused so much trouble for the other characters is not, in the end, treated as a villain; on the contrary, Mélite grants him full pardon, and he is finally to obtain the hand of Cloris. This is because he has redeemed himself through suffering. We are intended, therefore, to accept these sufferings as real. The mad scenes are tragic, not comic, in tone. This means that Mélite contains a mixture of genres and as such cannot be approved by true classicists.

One other important point should be made with regard to Eraste's hallucination. I am thinking particularly of the moment when, believing himself to be in the underworld, he meets the nurse and promptly takes her for Mélite. The baroque is an art of illusions, and in this specific situation in the play we have a compounding of illusions. First of all, the original cause of

40. Ll. 1629–36.

all this dramatic complication is an illusion: Philandre thought that the forged letters were really written by Mélite, and so did Tirsis. The news of Tirsis' death is an illusion: his friend Lisis made it up in order to test Mélite. Cliton, when he reports Mélite's death, is also under an illusion—as are the spectators, who are fooled for half an act. And then Eraste enters a complete world of illusion: he is in Hades, Cliton is Charon, Philandre is Minos, and —culminating illusion of all!—the nurse is Mélite.

Let us return now to Corneille's corrections of his first edition. There are a few more interesting examples, in the last act, of his change in artistic sensibility. Philandre, in begging Cloris for forgiveness, appeals principally to past sensuality. Cloris is unwilling to listen to him, and Corneille himself, in 1660, deletes one of these appeals:

> Par mes flames jadis si bien recompensées,
> Par ces mains si souvent dans les miennes pressées,
> Par ces chastes baisers qu'un amour vertueux
> Accordoit aux desirs d'un cœur respectueux,[41]

The standards of manners have become more severe in the generation since Corneille originally wrote his play, and self-indulgent images are now frowned upon. The evolution toward greater decorum and greater abstractness is even more apparent when Tirsis and Mélite meet in happy reconciliation (Act V, scene 4). The lover, as originally conceived by Corneille, is anxious to proceed to ardent love-making: now, he says, our delight is checked only

> Que par le souvenir de nos travaux passez
> Chassons le, ma chere ame, a force de caresses,
> Ne parlons plus d'ennuys, de tourmens, de tristesses,
> Et changeons en baisers ces traits d'œil langoureux,
> Qui ne font qu'irriter nos desirs amoureux.

This, in the more discreet 1660 version, becomes:

> Que par le souvenir de nos malheurs passez:
> Ouvrons nostre ame à ces douces tendresses
> Qu'inspirent aux amants les plaines allegresses,
> Et d'un commun accord cherissons nos ennuys
> Dont nous voyons sortir de si precieux fruits.[42]

The whole emphasis has been changed: originally Tirsis said, "Let us give ourselves over to sensual delight." In the revised version, his essential idea is: "We enjoy our present happiness all the more because of our past troubles." The same contrast is apparent, a few lines further on, between the

41. Ll. 1755–8.   42. Ll. 1797–1804.

earlier and the later texts; Tirsis mentions the lovers' first exchanged glances, and says:

> 1633: Je ne puis plus cherir vostre foible entretien
> Plus heureux je souspire apres un plus grand bien,
> Vous estiez bons jadis quand nos flames naissantes
> Prisoyent, faute de mieux, vos douceurs impuissantes,
> Mais au point où je suis ce ne sont que resveurs
> Qui vous peuvent tenir pour exquises faveurs,
> Il faut un aliment plus solide a nos flames
> Par où nous unissions nos bouches et nos ames.

And here it is not only the impatient lover who demands more solid food than words and glances but the baroque style itself which cannot be satisfied with intangible things. The older and more classical Corneille removes everything to a remote and elegant plane:

> 1660: Doux truchemens du cœur, qui desja tant de fois
> M'avez si bien appris ce que n'osoit la voix,
> Nous n'avons plus besoin de vostre confidence,
> L'amour en liberté peut dire ce qu'il pense,
> Et dédaigne un secours qu'en sa naissante ardeur
> Beaux yeux, à mon transport pardonnez ce blasphème,
> La bouche est impuissante où l'amour est extrême,
> Quand l'espoir est permis, elle a droit de parler,
> Mais vous allez plus loin qu'elle ne peut aller
> Ne vous lassez donc point d'en usurper l'usage,
> Et quoy qu'elle m'ait dit dites-moy davantage.[43]

This is one of the few cases where a revised passage is longer than the first edition. Préciosité, as a matter of fact, often takes more words than direct expression. This particular comparison should be instructive for those who are inclined to identify baroque and préciosité: often the vivid and direct expression of the baroque is directly opposed to préciosité. Here, the corrected and more précieux version is perhaps better poetry than the original; but the 1633 Tirsis, for all his clumsiness, is a more living and convincing person.

There is also a loss of naturalness when Corneille revises Act V, scene 5. As Corneille originally wrote the scene, the two lovers behave with uninhibited freedom in front of Cloris: it is almost as if they enjoyed having an audience. There is some pretense at trying to console her for having lost her lover, or indeed to encourage her to go back to him; but Mélite and Tirsis are primarily making an ostentatious display of their own happiness.

43. Ll. 1797–1804.

They are putting on a little play within the play, in the baroque manner;
or, to think of their actions in modern psychological terms, they feel a slight
sadistic pleasure in arousing the envy of their spectator. Tirsis offers to kiss
his sister to make her feel better, and she tartly replies:

> Les baisers d'une sœur satisfont mal un frere,
> Adresse mieux les tiens vers l'object que je voy.

> TIRSIS.

> De la part de ma sœur reçoy donc ce renvoy.

> MELITE.

> Recevoir le refus d'un autre! à Dieu ne plaise.

> TIRSIS.

> Refus d'un autre, ou non, il faut que je te baise,
> Et que dessus ta bouche un prompt redoublement
> Me vange des longueurs de ce retardement.

> CLORIS.

> A force de baiser vous m'en feriez envie,
> Trefve.

> TIRSIS.

> Si nostre exemple à baiser te convie
> Va trouver ton Philandre avec qui tu prendras
> De ces chastes plaisirs autant que tu voudras.[44]

But Cloris explains that she has no desire to go back to Philandre. This
entire conversation is suppressed in the 1660 edition. It is no mere question
of chastening the language, though the author may have felt that it was
desirable to do so. Corneille was as aware of the complicated psychological
overtones as the modern reader; but while the baroque age might find them
piquant, the classical critic would judge them to be in bad taste. And so
the playwright rigorously banishes from the scene whatever suggestions it
may originally have had of exhibitionistic, sadistic, or incestuous feeling.

Tirsis, who is eager for love, soon tires of arguing with his sister about
Philandre. He tells Mélite of his impatience to be alone with her:

> 1633: Tous nos pensers sont deubs à ces chastes delices
> Dont le ciel se prepare à borner nos supplices,
> Le terme en est si proche, il n'attend que la nuit,
> Voy qu'en nostre faveur desja le jour s'enfuit,
> Que desja le Soleil en cedant à la brune

44. Ll. 1848–58.

> Desrobbe tant qu'il peut sa lumiere importune,
> Et que pour luy donner mesmes contentements
> Thetis court audevant de ses embrassements.[45]

It is regrettable that the evolution of literary taste made Corneille feel ashamed of these charming lines. Sunset and Greek myth are blended to make one of the poet's most lyrical expressions of love. The 1660 version rewrites the first two couplets, and omits entirely the last two:

> 1660: Tous nos pensers sont dus, en l'état où nous sommes,
> A ce nœud qui me rend le plus heureux des hommes,
> Et ma fidelité qu'il va recompenser . . .

La Nourrice.

> Vous donnera bien-tost autre chose à penser,

Presumably an excessive eagerness for love-making had come to be regarded, in 1660, as contrary to la bienséance, and the word "supplice," to describe this impatience, as too strong. We can only conjecture why Corneille came to dislike the reference to sunset and to Thetis: he probably decided that this constituted a piece of superfluous decoration. The comparison of these two texts should be instructive for those who feel that the classical spirit came as an unmitigated blessing to literature.

In this very last scene of the play, Corneille has eliminated a bit of stage business which originally created a final moment of suspense. I refer to the arrival of Eraste, which in 1633 was indicated in the following manner:

> La Nourrice paroist à l'autre bout du Theatre avec Eraste, l'espee nuë à la main, et ayant parlé à luy quelque temps à l'oreille, elle le laisse à quartier et s'avance vers Tirsis.[46]

The nurse then informs Tirsis and the assembled company that Eraste has come to fight a duel for Mélite. Tirsis steps forward to accept the challenge, whereupon it all turns out to be a false alarm: Eraste, far from wishing to fight, begs for death and forgiveness. The 1644 edition cuts out the stage direction, and the 1660 edition eliminates those portions of dialogue which lead us to think that a duel is about to take place. Essentially these changes have the effect of simplifying the dramatic action by removing one peripety. Other than this, the alterations in Act V, scene 6 are relatively minor: Eraste's pleas for pardon are made slightly less intense in tone,[47] another allusion by Tirsis to the pleasures of the coming night is changed so as to be discreetly vague,[48] and the couplet with which the nurse closes the comedy undergoes a similar transformation:

45. Ll. 1895-1902.
47. See ll. 1909-18.
46. Following l. 1902.
48. See ll. 1985-6.

1633: Allez, je vay vous faire à ce soir telle niche
       Qu'au lieu de labourer, vous lairrez tout en friche.

1648: Et je feray bien voir à vos feux empressez
       Que vous n'en estes pas encor où vous pensez.[49]

In view of the very numerous revisions of *Mélite*, it is interesting to see what Corneille says about his play in the "Examen" (1660). As we might expect, he is somewhat apologetic. He explains that it was, after all, his first play, and that it observes none of the Rules, because at that time he did not know that there were any! Nevertheless, he asserts, his common sense did lead him to observe the unity of action: a single plot causes misunderstanding among four lovers.

Corneille points out what he feels to be the weaknesses of *Mélite*. First, Philandre is not a very convincing character; it is unlikely that a man would break with his fiancée because of love letters from a woman whom he knows so slightly as to be unfamiliar with her handwriting. Eraste is silly to imagine that his plot will bring about a break with Tirsis and Mélite. It is not plausible that Tirsis should believe the false letters instantly and make no attempt to get an explanation from Mélite in person. Corneille is not at all satisfied with Eraste's madness; he apologizes for these scenes, saying that he realized at the time that they were not good, but that he was catering to popular taste! He is, however, very proud of one incident which takes place as a result: Eraste, thinking that Philandre is Minos, confesses to him the whole plot of the forged letters. This, Corneille maintains, is the most skillful dénouement of his entire dramatic career. Finally, the whole fifth act is condemned as superfluous: the two principal lovers have already been reconciled, and Eraste's recovery from madness is merely an episode having nothing to do with the main plot. Philandre is left dangling at the end—he has no girl, and his anger leads to no dramatic consequence. In other words, the fifth act destroys that unity of action which the untutored author had somehow instinctively preserved in the first four.

Naturally, Corneille is also sensitive with regard to his comedy's violations of the unity of time. He points out, ruefully, that a week or two must elapse between Acts I and II, and just as long between Acts II and III. Furthermore, in cases where the same characters reappear twice in one act, he doubts whether they would actually have had the time to get from one quarter of the city to another. This suggests, in turn, that the unity of place has not been strictly observed. *Mélite*, alas, is full of irregularities: the playwright begs our indulgence for a youthful work. The weaknesses of this play, as a more mature Corneille sees them, may be summed up under two

49. Ll. 2019-20.

main headings: failure to observe the rules, and *invraisemblance*. The actions of many of the characters are implausible, and there is a lack of conformity to the three unities. Actually, it is clear from the "Examen" that in 1660 Corneille considered the Rules to be based on reason; they are not arbitrary, but determined by the concern for vraisemblance. The irregularities are, therefore, basically implausibilities. And here, in reality, the classical author is condemning his baroque youth. In the baroque era, literary irregularities were not necessarily to be avoided, nor was surprising conduct to be ruled out as unbelievable. Both art and life were rich with infinite variety. In the classical moment of French literature, a more severe taste came to demand a more logical consistency both in human psychology and in artistic structure.

In order to make *Mélite* a regular play, Corneille would have had to rewrite it completely. He would, indeed, have had to invent another plot, since in 1660 he regarded that of the false letters as incredible. He would also have had to transform the characters of Eraste, Philandre, and Tirsis, since their motivations had come to seem unconvincing. And yet there remained the disconcerting fact: the play had always been a success. So the author did the next best thing, in 1660 terms: he emended his text extensively. The stranger irregularities of his characters are smoothed away, particularly those which appeared violent and indecent. Above all, the language is chastened: improprieties are removed, brutalities toned down, concrete images replaced by elegant abstractions, disturbing agitation changed to civilized calm. Has Corneille, in making these transformations, improved *Mélite*? Perhaps he has succeeded in rendering his comedy more coherent and less bizarre; yet I hope that my readers will agree with me that the revised play has suffered a great loss of picturesqueness and vitality. It seems to me that Mario Roques and Marion Lièvre, in republishing the 1633 text, have done a service not only to scholarship but also to art.

CHAPTER 6. A Baroque Tragedy: *Saint Genest*

ROTROU's undoubted masterpiece is his tragedy *Saint Genest,* which dates from 1646, and is thus the latest baroque work studied here. The full title is somewhat more complicated and explains the subject: *Saint Genest, comédien païen, représentant le martyr d'Adrien.* There is probably no more interesting example in dramatic literature of a play within a play; and nowhere in baroque literature are the two great themes of illusion and metamorphosis more strikingly linked together.

The Emperor Diocletian is giving his daughter Valeria in marriage to Maximinus as a reward for military triumphs, and is naming him co-emperor. It is decided to celebrate these events by inviting a theatrical company to give a performance before the imperial court. The leading actor, Genest, is summoned, and the imperial personages discuss with him the choice of a play. It is apparent that Diocletian enjoys the theatre very much, and that he is grateful to Genest for having brought dramatic art to a high level during his reign. What Diocletian especially likes in drama is total illusion:

> Par ton art les héros, plutôt ressuscités
> Qu'imités en effet et que representés,
> Des cent et des mille ans après leur funérailles,
> Font encor des progrès, et gagnent des batailles,[1]

In other words, the summit of the actor's art is achieved when the spectator believes that he is witnessing a slice of life, with real people and real events. In recent times we have seen this theory in action when, in a Baltimore theatre, a member of the audience pulled out a pistol and shot Othello as he was strangling Desdemona. The same phenomenon has occurred when babies have been born to the heroines of soap opera programs; hundreds of listeners have sent infants' clothing to the radio studio. According to this conception drama is at its best when we can no longer distinguish between illusion and reality. (The trompe-l'œil of much baroque architecture rests upon a similar idea.) As we shall see, Rotrou's tragedy of *Saint Genest* is greatly preoccupied with this problem.

During the preliminary discussion, Valeria expresses another baroque attitude: she is tired of traditional subjects, no matter how beautiful; she

1. Act I, scene 5.

wants something new and surprising. In rejecting some of Genest's suggestions for the play to be given, she remarks:

> Mais leur sujets enfin sont des sujets connus;
> Et quoiqu'ils aient de beau, la plus rare merveille,
> Quand l'esprit la connaît, ne surprend plus l'oreille.[2]

In other words, art is not something statically and eternally beautiful; it
evolves, and is most alive when it surprises us. Valeria has heard that Genest's
most powerful role is that of a Christian martyr:

> Mais on vante surtout l'inimitable adresse
> Dont tu feins d'un chrétien le zèle et l'allégresse,
> Quand, le voyant marcher du baptême au trépas,
> Il semble que les feux soient des fleurs sous tes pas.[3]

It is worth considering why she wants to see this particular play. Her delight in novelty, strangeness, and surprise we have already noted; and once
again we see the general hunger for illusions. In this connection, the verb
"feindre," which forms a kind of leitmotif throughout this tragedy, is
significant. If you play this part, she is saying, we shall really believe that
you are a Christian martyr; caught up in the spirit of the thing, we too
shall think that fires are flowers. But it is also important that Valeria is
anxious to witness scenes of martyrdom; this taste she shares with those
patrons of the arts in the baroque period who ordered paintings of saints
being drawn and quartered or having their tongues cut out.[4] There is also
the appeal of forbidden fruit: Diocletian has forbidden Christianity on pain
of death, and it will be delightfully horrifying to see this criminal sight. If
we sum up the different reasons for Valeria's choice, we arrive at the conclusion that a single emotion underlies them all: the desire for strong
sensations.

Genest readily agrees to play this part, which clearly holds a great fascination for him. Perhaps his earlier suggestion of plays dealing with
Pompey or Augustus proceeded from a latent fear that the role of Adrien
the Christian martyr might completely take possession of him. In taking
leave of the imperial party, he again stresses the fact that, through his art,
illusion will appear truth:

> Et la mort d'Adrien, l'un de ses obstinés,
> Par vos derniers arrêts naguère condamnés,
> Vous sera figurée avec un art extrême,
> Et si peu différent de la vérité même,

2. Ibid.   3. Ibid.
4. Cf. Poussin's "St. Erasmus" or Rubens' "St. Livinus."

> Que vous nous avoûrez de cette liberté
> Où César à César sera représenté,
> Et que vous douterez si, dans Nicomédie,
> Vous verrez l'effet même ou bien la comédie.[5]

For the actors are undertaking, among other things, to play the part of Maximinus in front of the real Maximinus. They are supremely confident in their ability to present lifelike illusions!

So ends Act I of *Saint Genest;* at the beginning of the second act, the play within the play has not yet begun. We find Genest discussing the stage scenery with the "décorateur." He obviously wants to achieve an effect of splendor and ostentation:

> Il est beau; mais encore, avec peu de dépense,
> Vous pouviez ajouter à la magnificence,
> N'y laisser rien d'aveugle, y mettre plus de jour,
> Donner plus de hauteur aux travaux d'alentour,
> En marbrer les dehors, en jasper les colonnes,
> Enricher les tympans, leurs cimes, leurs couronnes,
> Mettre en vos coloris plus de diversité,
> En vos carnations plus de vivacité,
> Draper mieux ces habits, reculer ces paysages,
> Y lancer des jets d'eau, renfondrer leurs ombrages,
> Et surtout en la toile ou vous peignez vos cieux
> Faire un jour naturel au jugement des yeux,
> Au lieu que la couleur m'en semble un peu meurtrie.[6]

This picture has many affinities with the painting of Rubens or the baroque architecture of Rome. Let us examine some of the details. Genest starts by pointing out that a greater impression of magnificence could be achieved with very little added expense. The architects of many Roman churches sought to do just that; even when the site and the funds available were small, they used their ingenuity to create a sense of splendor and space. Thus Santa Maria della Pace has a false façade extending across the houses on either side, so that while actually a rather small church, it seems outwardly to be on a grand scale. Or, to consider an interior, the elliptical form of Sant'Andrea in Quirinale, running across the main axis of the observer, greatly increases the illusion of size.

Continuing with Genest's recommendations, the insistence upon introducing more light is also characteristic. In the above-mentioned church of Sant'Andrea, the impression of space is furthered by judiciously placed windows in side chapels. Bernini's group of St. Teresa in ecstasy is dramatically highlighted by hidden and unexpected windows. The idea of giving

5. Act I, scene 5.   6. Act II, scene 1.

a greater feeling of height ("Donner plus de hauteur") is carried out in churches like Sant'Ignazio, where Pozzo has made a flat ceiling appear to be a vast space enclosed by soaring columns. I scarcely need point out how baroque is the love for marble veneering, for gaudily decorated columns, for ornate tympana, for variegated color—the interior of the Gesù may serve as an example—or, if this is felt to be so extreme as to be really rococo, we may take the interior of Sant'Andrea della Valle (famous in another connection as the scene of the first act of *Tosca*). Genest also feels the dramatic effectiveness of drapery ("Draper mieux ces habits"), which Bernini utilized to the full in his "St. Teresa" or in his monuments to the popes in St. Peter's. When he speaks of the desirability of depth in the picture which is to be offered to the audience, he is touching upon a characteristic of baroque art which has been analyzed at great length by Wölfflin: the emphasis upon *recession* rather than planes. And then of course, for the delight of the baroque mind, there must be fountains ("jets d'eau"). The very soul of baroque Rome is its fountains.

The "décorateur's" arguments to justify what he has done reveal a similarly baroque point of view. First of all, he points out that time, rather than hard work on the part of the artists, has been lacking. This suggests, incidentally, that a minimum of time must have elapsed between Act I and Act II; even if they have been hurried, it has clearly taken some hours, or possibly days, for the players to get ready after the emperor commanded the performance. This does not necessarily require a violation of the unity of time, but it suggests more of an interruption than strict classicists would approve. But essentially, the stage designer is insisting that his scenery will look very different when seen from the audience's point of view. Genest is making criticisms because he is too close, right on the stage; if he were in the auditorium, the illusion would be more successful:

> Joint qu'on voit mieux de loin ces raccourcissements,
> Ces corps sortant du plan de ces refondrements;
> L'approche à ces dessins ôte leurs perspectives,
> En confond les faux jours, rend leurs couleurs moins vives,
> Et comme à la nature, est nuisible à notre art
> A qui l'éloignement semble apporter du fard:
> La grâce une autre fois y sera plus entière.[7]

There may be some disagreement as to whether Palladio's Teatro Olimpico in Vicenza (1580) is a mannerist or a baroque work; but I think that the reader will readily admit that it corresponds perfectly to the above description. Its architectural perspectives are completely convincing when seen from the

7. Ibid.

amphitheatre, and are fantastically distorted when one actually walks upon the stage. Of course it is universally true that the colors of stage scenery appear unnatural by daylight—there is nothing startlingly original in this; but I feel it to be interesting that the problem should be explicitly discussed in a play of 1646. One should note the phrase (referring to the too close view):

> Et comme à la nature, est nuisible à notre art.

The difference between art and nature is stressed; but even more, the stage designer wishes to point out that for both the point of view is important. Baroque ensembles like the Piazza Navona vary greatly with the point of view of the observer: Borromini's Sant'Agnese and Bernini's "Fountain of the Rivers" are best seen from a little distance away, and from an angle. "Eloignement" brings to these things a certain "fard." Baroque art, in other words, contemplates changes in position on the part of the spectator which will permit him to appreciate the "grâce . . . entière."

   This first scene of the second act ends with Genest rehearsing his part. The passage he is reciting is to be his opening speech. An obvious reason for this selection is that when, some ten minutes later, the play within the play begins, we receive an immediate shock of recognition, and realize the exact point at which we are passing from the "real" world of Diocletian's court to the "illusionistic" world of Adrien's martyrdom. I think that there is another reason for Rotrou's emphasizing these particular lines: he is setting the tone of torture, blood, and martyrdom which is to be such an important theme throughout the tragedy and which conforms so thoroughly to baroque taste:

> La torture, le fer et la flamme t'attend:
> Offre à leurs cruautés un cœur ferme et constant;
> Laisse à de lâches cœurs verser d'indignes larmes,
> Tendre aux tyrans les mains et mettre bas les armes;
> Offre ta gorge au fer, vois-en couler ton sang,
> Et meurs sans t'ébranler, debout et dans ton rang.[8]

As a matter of fact, the last four lines are rehearsed a second time before the performance starts. The "fer" and "flamme" call to mind another great baroque work; it will be remembered that two books of d'Aubigné's *Les Tragiques* are entitled, respectively, "Les Feux" and "Les Fers," and describe the torture and death of Protestant martyrs.

   In the next scene we see Marcelle, the actress who is to play the part of Adrien's wife Natalie, trying on her costume and reciting her lines. She

8. Ibid.

too stresses the theme of religious war and of victory through martyrdom. Just as d'Aubigné, in *Les Tragiques*, expresses the idea that the Protestant martyrs are preparing the way for the triumph of the true faith, similarly here the sufferings of Adrien are to bring about the defeat of paganism:

> Ce lion altéré du sacré sang des tiens,
> Qui de tant d'innocents crut la mort legitime,
> De ministre qu'il fut, s'offre enfin pour victime,
> Et, patient agneau, tend à ses ennemis
> Un col à ton saint joug heureusement soumis.[9]

Genest congratulates his leading lady on her histrionic skill, and assures her that the acting of this part will win her everlasting renown in the theatre. Then, warning that the audience will soon arrive, he orders the lights to be lit, and goes on rehearsing his own role:

> J'ai vu, Ciel, tu les sais par le nombre des âmes
> Que j'osai t'envoyer par des chemins de flammes,
> Dessus des grils ardents et dedans des taureaux
> Chanter les condamnés et trembler les bourreaux.[10]

The "grils ardents" are, of course, a reference to St. Laurence, who was burnt to death on a gridiron in 258—in other words, some thirty years before the action of this play and, therefore, quite possibly within the memory of Genest himself. The roasting of martyrs inside metallic bulls was apparently a frequent practice; d'Aubigné refers to it three times, in "Misères," in "La Chambre dorée," and in "Les Fers." [11] Although Rotrou has the singing of the victims terrify the executioners, this so-called bull of Phalaris was actually equipped with a steam device which produced music to cover up the martyrs' screams. Like the previous ones, the above lines are twice repeated in rehearsal.

Up to this point, we have thought of Genest exclusively as an actor; we have heard him discuss the problems of the theatre, and have watched him in rehearsal. Now there comes a halt in the preparations for the performance, and we see Genest not in his professional capacity but as a human being. Genest the man interrupts his reciting and pauses to consider his true situation; he appeals to the pagan gods to protect him from himself:

> Dieux prenez contre moi ma défense et la vôtre;
> D'effet comme de nom je me trouve être un autre;
> Je feins moins Adrien que je ne le deviens,
> Et prends avec son nom des sentiments chrétiens.[12]

9. Act II, scene 2.   10. Ibid.
11. Cf. *Les Tragiques:* I, 849; III, 533; V, 571.   12. Act II, scene 2.

In a moment of revelation and surprise, we discover the true subject of Rotrou's tragedy. Genest, while *pretending* to be Adrien, is *becoming* Adrien. Here are the two great baroque themes of illusion and metamorphosis. Where does reality lie, and where illusion? In Genest the man, or in Adrien the character from the play? But what was illusion is transforming itself before our eyes into reality. The two themes are inseparably fused. Struggling against himself, the actor tries to arouse his professional conscience, and to separate these two things. His job, after all, is not to become another person, but to create the illusion of another person.

> Il s'agit d'imiter et non de devenir.[13]

And here, in another dramatic surprise, the heavens open and flames descend. It is perhaps necessary to remind the reader that we have not yet reached the play within the play; in Rotrou's intention, what we are now witnessing is not illusion but reality. In Christian iconography, ever since St. Luke wrote the Book of the Acts, flames coming down from heaven have signified the descent of the Holy Ghost:

And when the day of the Pentecost was fully come, they were all with one accord in one place. And suddenly there came a sound from heaven as of a rushing mighty wind, and it filled all the house where they were sitting. And there appeared unto them cloven tongues as of fire, and it sat upon each of them. And they were all filled with the Holy Ghost . . .[14]

This, in a French seventeenth-century tragedy, is the merveilleux chrétien of which Boileau and all true classicists disapproved. Rotrou's employment of a device both supernatural and spectacular shows that his taste is essentially baroque rather than classical. It should be re-emphasized that this particular part of *Saint Genest* purports to represent actual historical events, since the curtain has not yet gone up on the "theatrical performance." In other words, this is a miracle taking place about the year 285 at the court of Diocletian. The mingling of the realistic and the miraculous is frequent in both mannerist and baroque art, whether in El Greco's "Burial of Count Orgaz," Caravaggio's "Calling of St. Matthew," or Rubens' "St. Ignatius Curing the Possessed." As the flames descend, a voice speaks to Genest:

> Poursuis, Genest, ton personnage;
> Tu n'imiteras point en vain;
> Ton salut ne dépend que d'un peu de courage.
> Et Dieu t'y prêtera la main.[15]

Note how many baroque elements are combined here: the appeal to several senses at once (flames suggest both color and heat, and a voice speaks at

---

13. Ibid.   14. Acts 2:1–4.   15. Act II, scene 2.

the same time); the theatrical in its most striking form (the merveilleux chrétien); the intervention of the miraculous in a realistically depicted scene; and finally the conception, expressed by the voice of God, that illusionistic art can lead to a supernatural metamorphosis.

As an immediate consequence of this miracle, the transformation of the character of Genest does in fact begin. He, who a few lines previously had prayed to the pagan gods to preserve him from conversion, now prays to the Holy Ghost for his salvation:

> Qu'entends-je, juste Ciel, et par quelle merveille,
> Pour me toucher le cœur, me frappes-tu l'oreille?
> Souffle doux et sacré qui me viens enflammer,
> Esprit saint et divin qui me viens animer,
> Et qui, me souhaitant, m'inspires le courage,
> Travaille à mon salut, achève ton ouvrage,
> Guide mes pas douteux dans le chemin des cieux,
> Et pour me les ouvrir dessille-moi les yeux.[16]

Yet Genest is not completely convinced; he fears that what he has just seen may be not truth but an illusion. His spirit is torn with doubts, and this inner conflict, as is so often the case in baroque poetry, is expressed in images of war. The pagan gods are struggling against Christ:

> Prenez, dieux, contre Christ, prenez votre parti,
> Dont ce rebelle cœur s'est presque départi;
> Et toi contre les dieux, ô Christ, prends ta défense,
> Puisqu'à tes lois ce cœur fait encor résistance,
> Et dans l'onde agitée où flottent mes esprits
> Terminez votre guerre, et m'en faites le prix,
> Rendez-moi le repos dont ce trouble me prive.[17]

It should be noted that in a mannerist poem, such as a sonnet by Sponde on death,[18] the inner tension would never be completely resolved, and the reader would be left with a feeling of anxiety; but the above lines suggest the resolution and catharsis that are to come.

Now almost everything is ready for the play within the play. The stage manager comes to light the candles and to tell Genest to hurry. The actor replies, somewhat ambiguously, that he is being disturbed in the rehearsal of a glorious role to be played before the court of heaven, and the "décorateur," in an aside, indulges himself in a play upon words:

> Il repassait son role et s'y veut surpasser [19]

16. Ibid.   17. Ibid.
18. Cf. Sponde, "Autres sonnets sur le mesme sujet," nos. II and XII.
19. Act II, scene 3.

There are a few points in which baroque taste seems rather remote from that of the twentieth century; and perhaps even more than the frequent fondness for effects which to us recall the Grand Guignol, this predilection for near puns in the midst of a tense dramatic situation seems alien to our sensibilities. Furthermore, I should like to point out that, in this exchange between Genest and the "décorateur," the two men are thinking in terms of different worlds: ultimate reality, on the one hand, and theatrical illusion on the other.

However, though Genest feels that he has been preparing a part to play before the court of heaven, it is now the very worldly court of the Emperor Diocletian that assembles for the performance. Valeria is pleased at the idea of seeing a tragedy (she explains that it is the kind of play she likes the best) and Maximinus is enthusiastic about witnessing the martyrdom of a Christian. Since he is not to see the actual event, a theatrical representation will be the next best thing, he declares. The dramatic irony of this statement will become fully apparent when, some time later, the pretended martyrdom turns into a real one. But then Diocletian tells the audience to be quiet, a lute sounds, and the tragedy of Adrien begins. We recognize the opening lines, which we have already heard in rehearsal, and moving into the inner play, we find ourselves one dimension deeper in the world of illusion.

The first *tirade,* as we have seen, sings the praises of martyrdom. Adrien is steeling his resolve to face torture, bloodshed, and death. He passes in review all the Christians whom he has seen led to the slaughter, and concludes that their superhuman courage must be of divine origin. He has witnessed the execution of young children:

> J'ai vu tendre aux enfants une gorge assurée
> A la sanglante mort qu'ils voyaient préparée,
> Et tomber sous le coup d'un trépas glorieux
> Ces fruits à peine éclos, déjà mûrs pour les cieux.[20]

It is not only the enjoyment of gory details that reveals the baroque sensibility; the fruit metaphor is characteristic also. This is the kind of imagery of which St. François de Sales is so fond: concrete, drawn from nature, lush. The adjectives "éclos" ("budding") and "mûrs" ("ripe") suggest the forces of metamorphosis, and are set against each other in antithesis. As I have often had occasion to remark, no single one of these traits is in itself evidence of the baroque style; but their conscious and simultaneous juxtaposition is conclusive.

20. Act II, scene 5.

Many baroque painters, such as Domenichino, have shown interest in the martyrdom of beautiful women,[21] and Adrien also lingers on this topic:

> J'ai vu mille beautés en la fleur de leur âge,
> A qui, jusq'aux tyrans, chacun rendait hommage,
> Voir avecque plaisir meurtris et déchirés
> Leur membres précieux de tant d'yeux adorés.[22]

It may perhaps be questioned whether the emotions aroused by such a sight are of a purely religious nature. It is, however, a characteristic of baroque that erotic and religious elements are blended in a curious manner,[23] and though Adrien's feelings may be complex, they lead him to believe that such feminine courage can come only from God. He is filled with the desire of emulation:

> C'est du ciel que me vient cette noble vigueur
> Qui me fait des tourments mépriser la rigueur,
> Qui me fait défier les puissances humaines,
> Et qui fait que mon sang se déplaît dans mes veines,
> Qu'il brûle d'arroser cet arbre précieux
> Où pend pour nous le fruit le plus chéri des cieux.
> J'ai peine à concevoir ce changement extrême . . .[24]

The passage deserves comment in several ways. First of all, it describes a transformation. Adrien, who at the beginning of his speech was still inwardly torn between fear and faith, still struggling to find the courage of martyrdom, is now converted to a firm resolve. It should be remembered also that, like everything else in this play within the play, the action is taking place upon two levels: that of Adrien and that of Genest. What on the Adrien level is a significant step toward the decision of martyrdom is on the Genest level also a stage in the process of conversion. By reciting these lines, the actor is gradually convincing himself. Note also the personification of "blood" —"mon sang se déplaît dans mes veines"—so similar in feeling to Thisbe's words at the end of Théophile's tragedy:

> Ha! voici le poignard qui du sang de son Maistre
> S'est souillé laschement: il en rougit, le traistre![25]

This is no cold and conventional personification but a living and original one. But the metaphor becomes still more elaborate: not only is Adrien's blood dissatisfied to remain in his veins; it burns to water the tree where

---

21. Cf. the "Martyrdom of St. Agnes."   22. Act II, scene 5.
23. Cf. Bernini's "St. Teresa" and Crashaw's "The Flaming Heart."
24. Act II, scene 5.   25. *Pyrame et Thisbe*, ll. 1227–8.

hangs the fruit of salvation! This again, like the image where infant martyrs were compared to budding yet ripe fruit, recalls the language of the *Introduction à la vie dévote*. It is also, of course, a curiously mixed metaphor: the blood burns, but is to water a tree. Adrien's change is, as he says, extreme, but nevertheless elements of inner conflict still remain; he is unhappy at the thought of abandoning his beloved wife Natalie:

> Si proche de la mort, j'ai l'amour en la bouche! [26]

In the next scene, Flavius the tribune comes to Adrien, sent by the emperor. Maximinus is alarmed by the rapid spread of Christianity, and still more by the rumor that his faithful Adrien, who has been absent from court for some time, has renounced the pagan gods for Christ. The tribune describes dramatically the atmosphere of supernatural awe in the palace when Titien brings the report:

> "Qu'est-ce, a dit l'empereur, interdit et troublé.
> Le ciel s'est-il ouvert? le monde a-t-il tremblé?
> Quelque foudre lancé menace-t-il ma tête?
> Rome d'un étranger est-elle la conquête?
> Ou quelque embrasement consume-t-il ces lieux?"
> "Adrien, a-t-il dit, pour Christ renonce aux dieux." [27]

To this embassy, Adrien firmly replies:

> Qu'il cesse de m'aimer, ou qu'il m'aime chrétien.[28]

There follows an argument wherein the pagan and Christian positions are juxtaposed in a series of striking antitheses. Tension and contrast are seldom absent in mannerist and baroque works: in the former, however, the two-fold view of the world is allowed to remain, producing a feeling of uneasiness; in the latter (as in the case here) one senses that the battle will lead to a victory. Flavius argues against the divinity of Christ:

> Sa mort sur un gibet marque son impuissance

and Adrien answers:

> Dites mieux, son amour et son obéissance.

The debate continues:

FLAVIE.

> Mais ce genre de mort ne pouvait etre pire.

ADRIEN.

> Mais, mourant de la mort il détruisit l'empire.

26. Act II, scene 5.   27. Act II, scene 6.   28. Ibid.

(Note the echoing repetition of "mort" and "mourant.")

FLAVIE.

L'auteur de l'univers entrer dans un cercueil!

ADRIEN.

Tout l'univers aussi s'en vit tendu de deuil,
Et le ciel effrayé nous cacha sa lumière.[29]

Adrien's statements are, to be sure, an exposition of Christian dogma; but
they are expressed in those terms of drama, movement, and antithesis which
are particularly congenial to the baroque mind. When all other arguments
fail, Flavius attempts to move Adrien by speaking of the love of Natalie;
but the martyr remains unshaken, and proclaims his resolve in a series of
hyperbolic statements which build up to a grand climax:

Allez, ni Maximin, courtois ou furieux,
Ni ce foudre qu'on peint en la main de vos dieux,
Ni la cour, ni le trône, avecque tous leurs charmes,
Ni Natalie enfin avec toutes ses larmes,
Ni l'univers rentrant dans son premier chaos,
Ne divertiraient pas un si ferme propos.[30]

There is in this passage that same combination of mass and movement
which we see in Roman baroque palaces and churches. Each line is massive
in its emphasis, and the whole speech rushes on with mounting tension
to the final words "ferme propos."

Words now give way to physical violence, the implied threats of imperial
punishment materialize before our eyes, and Adrien is bound in chains on
the stage. In my book on d'Aubigné, I have mentioned that the two fundamental aspects of the baroque are the paradoxical and the physical. We find
these two elements in the prisoner's words as he is led away. His chains are
to him "fardeaux précieux," and he is happy to go to the place where

Les soldats de Jésus triomphent de la mort.[31]

"Precious chains" is oxymoron, and the conception of soldiers of Jesus
(which, incidentally, is the basis of the Jesuit order) is paradoxical; the
whole final picture of Christian soldiers defeating death expresses spiritual
strife in the concrete imagery of war. On the one hand, we have préciosité;
on the other, violence.

Here the play within the play stops for a moment, and we return to
its audience: Diocletian, Maximinus, and Valeria. The comments of the
two emperors bring us back to "reality"—though of course this reality is

29. Ibid.   30. Ibid.   31. Ibid.

an illusion too, since the supposedly real imperial personages are themselves actors. Diocletian expresses the opinion that Genest has surpassed himself in this act, and Maximinus declares:

Il ne se peut rien feindre avecque plus de grâce.[32]

Valeria, rising from her seat, suggests that they take advantage of the intermission to go and congratulate Genest. The curtain falls on Act II of *Saint Genest,* and so the intermission of Rotrou's play coincides with that of Genest's play. The Parisian audience leaves its seats temporarily at exactly the same time as Diocletian's court, and so is led to identify itself with the Roman spectators. This ingenious device has the effect of bringing the play within the play closer to us.

In Act III, scene 1, the imperial personages have returned to their seats. Maximinus is excited because he is about to see himself represented on the stage:

L'art en est merveilleux, il faut que je l'avoue;
Mais l'acteur qui paraît est celui qui me joue,
Et qu'avecque Genest j'ai vu se concerter.
Voyons de quelle grâce il saura m'imiter.[33]

Once again Rotrou is playing with the problem of illusion and reality. On the inner stage, an actor is pretending to be an actor who is pretending to be Maximinus; on the outer stage, another actor is pretending to be Maximinus. Such is the magic of theatrical art that at various times we believe each of these illusions in turn to be realities.

Scene 2 belongs to the inner play. The enraged Maximinus, surrounded by high officials of his court and soldiers, confronts Adrien and, using every threat in his power, tries to make the martyr recant. Adrien, in chains, reaffirms his faith in the Christian God:

C'est lui qui du néant a tiré l'univers,
Lui qui dessus la terre a répandu les mers,
Qui de l'air étendit les humides contrées,
Qui sema de brillants les voûtes azurées,
Qui fit naître la guerre entre les éléments,
Et qui régla des cieux les divers mouvements;[34]

This passage has attracted the attention of Professor Raymond Lebègue in his article on "Rotrou dramaturge baroque."[35] He comments on the "baroque magnificence of the evocations of nature" in Genest's creed, and contrasts it with the intellectual, abstract creed of Polyeucte:

32. Ibid.   33. Act III, scene 1.   34. Act III, scene 2.
35. Raymond Lebègue, "Rotrou dramaturge baroque," in *Bibliothèque d'Humanisme et Renaissance,* 1942.

> Le Dieu de Polyeucte et celui de Néarque
> De la terre et du ciel est l'absolu monarque,
> Seul être indépendant, seul maître du destin,
> Seul principe éternel et souveraine fin.[36]

The comparison between the two passages is indeed an instructive one, and reveals some of the essential differences between the classical and baroque styles. I agree with M. Lebègue that, where Corneille is abstract, Rotrou is concrete and descriptive, but I think that one should also add that the lines from *Polyeucte* are essentially static; the only verb is "est," whereas the lines from *Saint Genest* are full of movement and the verbs are numerous and energetic: "tira," "répandu," "étendit," "sema," "fit naître la guerre," "régla . . . les mouvements." And perhaps it is not stretching the parallel with Wölfflin's categories too far to suggest that the Rotrou passage, with its evocation of vast space, corresponds to the concept of open form.

Maximinus reveals, in his violent diatribe against Christianity, that he is especially afraid of the spreading growth of the new religion. He considers himself to be the avenging arm of the gods, warning against Christians in all parts of the world; the fact that this "sacrilegious" faith should take root in his own court arouses his wrath and indignation:

> Ce que j'extirpe ici dans ma cour prend racine; [37]

D'Aubigné, in *Les Tragiques,* uses a similar image when he compares the ashes of martyrs to precious seeds of future growth of Christianity.[38] Another baroque stylist, St. François de Sales, likewise draws upon plant and animal life for much of his imagery; but the above-mentioned root and seed metaphors are particularly interesting because of their associations with germination, development, and metamorphosis.

Adrien defiantly praises the fortitude of Christian martyrs under torture. As usual in such passages, Rotrou is concrete and vivid:

> J'ai vu couler leur sang sous des ongles de fer,
> J'ai vu bouillir leur corps dans la poix et les flammes,
> J'ai vu leur chair tomber sous de flambantes lames,
> Et n'ai rien obtenu de ces cœurs glorieux
> Que de les avoir vus pousser des chants aux cieux,[39]

The iron claws the flesh, the bodies burn in pitch, the bright flames leap up, and the martyrs sing hymns: it is another example of multiple-sense imagery. Maximinus, in his threats of torture, goes into even more gruesome detail: he plans to cut Adrien's heart out and feed it to the crows. Then he orders Flavius to chain the martyr in a dungeon, and urges the soldiers to

36. Act III, scene 2, ll. 841–4.   37. Act III, scene 2.
38. "La Chambre dorée," 654–8.   39. Act III, scene 2.

use their utmost ingenuity in devising ways to make him suffer. Adrien's
lines as he is led off the stage are somewhat ambiguous:

> Comme je te soutiens, Seigneur, sois mon soutien:
> Qui commence à souffrir commence déjà d'être tien.[40]

The stage directions mark this couplet as an aside. There arises the question: Who is saying this, Adrien or Genest? The words are appropriate for
Adrien's situation, although it is a little strange that he speaks of *beginning*
to suffer, and *beginning* to belong to God. After all, he has already been
cast in chains in the previous act, and has already proclaimed his faith in
the Creed which we have just discussed. It is possible that "commence"
refers to Genest. My personal feeling is that the speech is intended for both
the actor and the man. In any case, we are not quite sure at this point whether
we are in the inner or the outer play, in the world of illusion or of reality.

Just as Flavius, the jailer, and the soldiers are escorting Adrien to prison,
his wife Natalie comes to meet him. The authorities, asking her to make
one final attempt to persuade her husband to renounce Christianity, leave
the couple alone together. Adrien's speech is a curious mixture of lofty
religious principle and down-to-earth, almost cynical, advice. Having staunchly
proclaimed the steadfastness of his faith, he advises Natalie to look around
for another husband:

> Ta jeunesse, tes biens, ta vertu, ta beauté
> Te feront mieux trouver que ce qui t'est ôté.[41]

"You are young, rich, and beautiful, and will certainly be able to do better
next time." This bourgeois and practical tone strikes us as incongruous in
a tragedy on martyrdom; probably we are influenced by classical taste. It
is certain that Racine would never have allowed so discordant a note. To
be sure, Corneille in *Polyeucte* has introduced a character—Felix—who tends
to think in worldly and mercenary terms; but here it is the martyr himself
who interrupts the atmosphere of heroism and tactlessly talks like a parent
in a Trollope novel. There is in the baroque a naturalistic side which at times
leads it to mix the realistic and the sublime.

And then, suddenly, there is a coup de théâtre, equally surprising to
Adrien and to the spectator. Natalie has been a Christian all along! Natalie's
mother brought her up from infancy as a Christian:

> Et presque en même instant le ciel versa sur moi
> La lumière du jour et celle de la foi.
> Il fit qu'avec le lait, pendante à la mamelle,
> Je suçai des chrétiens la créance et le zèle; [42]

40. Ibid.   41. Act III, scene 4.   42. Ibid.

The two cases of metaphoric antithesis should be noted. In this rhetorical device, which is also a favorite of d'Aubigné's, a literal image is set off against a figurative one. Natalie received simultaneously the light of day and the light of faith; at her mother's breast she sucked both milk and Christian faith. In each case the metaphor, being slightly unexpected, produces an effect of mild surprise; it receives, through contrast with the literal expression, an added emphasis. We may not be moved to admiration, but we are amused by the ingenuity; the device has some affinity with the pun. "Mamelle" is a word of frequent occurrence in *Les Tragiques;* the great classicists usually prefer "sein," and in any case eschew so physical a picture as "pendante à la mamelle," which is almost evocative of muscular strain and in any case does not conform to bienséance.

The idea of marriage to a pagan had apparently caused much distress and tension of spirit in Natalie and her mother. (We should remember that Adrien's conversion is of recent date, and coincides in fact with the beginning of the play.)

> Tu sais, s'il t'en souvient, de quelle résistance
> Ma mère en cet amour combattit ta constance
> Non qu'un si cher parti ne nous fût glorieux,
> Mais pour sa répugance au culte de tes dieux.

However, an order from the emperor had swept all opposition aside, and the mother, forced to consent to the marriage, in a parting speech had begged her daughter to remain faithful to Christianity

> Et détester autant les dieux de ton époux
> Que ses chastes baisers te doivent etre doux.[43]

Here are two constrasting duties: to love a man, and to hate his gods. Natalie explains that in the first days of her marriage this conflict troubled her greatly, but that eventually she succeeded in finding happiness in her love while remaining loyally Christian. This type of dichotomy is typically baroque; in a mannerist dichotomy the conflict would remain irreconcilable, and a sense of uneasiness would persist. And of course at this particular moment in the play, the tension has been ultimately resolved; the resolution will lead to martyrdom and tragedy, but it will produce a catharsis. There had been times in her marriage when Natalie, despite the modus vivendi which permitted her to love her husband while refusing to worship the pagan gods, experienced intense inner suffering; for Adrien had been active in the persecution of the Christians:

> Je m'en émus assez; mais eussé-je espéré
> De réprimer la soif d'un lion altéré,

43. Ibid.

> De contenir un fleuve inondant une terre,
> Et d'arrêter dans l'air la chute d'un tonnerre? [44]

(Note the hyperbole, and the spectacular quality of the imagery.) Now at last, thanks to Adrien's conversion, the dichotomy has transformed itself into a unity:

> Tous deux dignes de mort, et tous deux résolus,
> Puisque nous voici joints, ne nous séparons plus;
> Qu'aucun temps, qu'aucun lieu, jamais ne nous divisent:
> Un supplice, un cachot, un juge nous suffisent.[45]

However, Adrien does not want Natalie to share his martyrdom at this time. His motives appear to be mixed. If it were not for the fervor of his religious convictions, we would tend to believe that simple tenderness for his wife makes him wish to protect her from suffering and death. But we know that he considers martyrdom to be the greatest of glories. If he has paid any attention to Natalie's words, he must realize that she is of the same opinion; under the circumstances, it is hardly kindness to prevent her from sharing it with him. There is, of course, his own fear of weakening at the supreme moment. He tells his wife that he needs her encouragement and help; God is calling him now, and he must be sure not to miss this vocation:

> Mérite, en m'animant, ta part de la couronne
> Qu'en l'empire éternel le martyre nous donne: [46]

But if he needs Natalie's moral support to preserve him from failing, the "animation" would be infinitely stronger if she too were a martyr at his side. In mutual emulation, both would be sure to win the crown. I fear that part of the explanation is to be found in the line immediately following the couplet which I have just quoted:

> Au défaut du premier, obtiens le second rang.

Adrien does not want anyone else to share the leading role. He wants his wife to be a spectator. *Saint Genest* is a play about martyrdom; it is also a play about the theatre. The two elements are inextricably interwoven. D'Aubigné has remarked, in that canto of *Les Tragiques* which is essentially a Protestant martyrology, that martyrs are less happy if they die without an audience:

> Mais les martyrs ont eu moins de contentement
> De qui la laide nuict cache le beau tourment: [47]

44. Ibid.   45. Ibid.   46. Ibid.   47. "Les Feux," 987–8.

It is indeed a fundamental aspect of baroque art to be conscious of the audience; there is hardly a baroque piazza in Rome which is not primarily designed to impress spectators, and Bernini's "Vision of St. Teresa" is framed in a lighted stage, with an audience in boxes on each side.

Natalie submits to her husband's will in a speech which begins with an antithesis:

> Bien donc, choisis le ciel et me laisse la terre.[48]

She promises to follow and to encourage him at all times and in all places, hoping against hope that she too may finally attain martyrdom. For the moment, it is decided that she will continue to pretend in front of the authorities. When Flavius and his guards return, she tells them that all her pleas have been in vain, that Adrien has stubbornly continued to revile the pagan gods, and that he has even tried to convert her to Christianity! She plays this feigned role in front of the audience also; turning to Adrien, she pretends to try to dissuade him:

> . . . au nom de notre amour,
> Au nom saint et sacré de la céleste cour,
> Reçois de ton épouse un conseil salutaire:
> Déteste ton erreur, rends-toi le ciel prospère; [49]

It is worth pausing here to consider the various levels of illusion. If we were witnessing *Saint Genest* on the stage in Paris, this would be the situation. A young French actress is playing the part of Marcelle, a Roman actress of the third century. Marcelle, in the play within the play, has the role of Natalie. Natalie is really a Christian, but is here pretending to be pagan. The little scene where, in the presence of the authorities, she begs her husband to renounce Christianity and he turns a deaf ear to her pleas, is the art of disguise carried to the third degree. Here are the different levels, as we descend deeper into the world of illusion: (1.) we ourselves; (2.) Rotrou's play; (3.) Genest's play; (4.) the feigned scene between husband and wife.

When the tribune, jailer, and guards take Adrien away, Natalie is left alone. The process of deepening illusion is reversed, and we begin to make the ascent back to reality. In Natalie's soliloquy in praise of Christian martyrdom, we recognize her true sentiments and return to level 3, as indicated above. But we also recognize a familiar passage—lines which Marcelle the actress had been rehearsing in Act II, before the play within the play began ("Ce lion altéré du sacré sang des tiens," etc.). This brings us back to level 2, reawakening us to the fact that everything we have seen for the last

48. Act III, scene 4.   49. Act III, scene 5.

half-hour belongs to the play within the play. The impression that level 2 is reality is confirmed by the fact that now the curtain comes down on Genest's play. In a very brief scene, Genest (in his own character, not that of Adrien) complains to Diocletian that the crowd outside is making too much noise, and interfering with the performance. The emperor gives orders for quiet to be established, and at this point the curtain comes down on Act III of Rotrou's play. So it is that we are brought back to level 1— ourselves. Is our own life, in the words of Calderón and Shakespeare, a dream?

After the intermission, we return to Act IV, and successively re-enter the concentric circles of illusion. The noisy crowd has been silenced; the imperial party are eagerly awaiting the resumption of the performance; Diocletian tells his guests that, in this act, Genest reaches the summit of theatrical art. We pass to level 3, where Adrien continues to withstand the dire threats of Flavius. The dialogue, in violent contrast, opposes two points of view as to the nature of reality. To Adrien, pain and death belong to the world of superficial appearances; salvation through martyrdom is true reality. He defies the emperor to do his worst; God is with him:

> Si César m'est cruel, il me sera prospère;
> C'est lui que je soutiens, c'est en lui que j'espère;
> Par son soins, tous les jours, la rage des tyrans
> Croit faire des vaincus et fait des conquérants.[50]

God is reality, and Caesar is illusion. Defeat in Caesar's world means victory in God's world. Flavius accepts the philosophic basis of the argument, but reverses its terms; for him, physical things are real, spiritual ones an illusion:

> Souvent en ces ardeurs la mort qu'on se propose
> Ne semble qu'un ébat, qu'un souffle, qu'une rose;
> Mais quand ce spectre affreux sous un front inhumain,
> Les tenailles, les feux, les hâches à la main,
> Commence à nous paraître et faire ses approches,
> Pour ne s'effrayer pas il faut être des roches,[51]

In a sense this argument is connected with the great philosophical problem of accidents vs. substance, as related to the question of transubstantiation. Rotrou has so prepared this scene that our sympathies are entirely on the side of Adrien; in other words, like most baroque artists, he takes a sacramental view of the world. Our outward senses are struck by the details of torture and execution; our inner senses perceive the martyr and saint.

Although Flavius is a kind of imperial chief of police, he has moments of

50. Act IV, scene 2.   51. Ibid.

humanity and pity, and so he grants Adrien a final interview, without chains, to bid Natalie farewell. This gives Rotrou the opportunity of creating another scene of illusion (Act IV, scene 3) of which Natalie is the victim. Seeing her husband free, she is convinced that he has weakened and renounced Christianity:

> Comment! seul et sans fers?
> Est-ce là ce martyr, ce vainqueur des enfers,
> Dont l'illustre courage et la force infinie
> De ses persécuteurs bravait la tyrannie? [52]

For the major part of a scene, Adrien's attempts to interrupt her are unavailing, and she denounces his supposed cowardice and disloyalty in violent terms. But when he finally gets a chance to speak, telling her that in rushing toward martyrdom the one earthly relief he hopes for is the farewell kiss of his wife, she realizes her error and begs his forgiveness:

> Un Dieu te soutiendra, si tu soutiens ta foi.
> Cours, généreux athlète, en l'illustre carrière
> Où de la nuit du monde on passe à la lumière;
> Cours, puisqu'un Dieu t'appelle aux pieds de son autel,
> Dépouiller sans regret l'homme infirme et mortel;
> N'épargne point ton sang en cette sainte guerre; [53]

The imagery of this passage is characteristically baroque. The metaphor of the athlete, referring to Christ or to martyrs, is typical of the period; it is particularly frequent in the sonnets of La Ceppède on the Passion. Representative also of this style is the chiaroscuro contrast, the night of the world as opposed to the light of God: not otherwise does Caravaggio illuminate his pictures of divine intervention—the vocation of St. Matthew, or the conversion of St. Paul. The emphasis upon martyrdom as a sacrifice similar to Christ's, and similar to that of the Mass, is revealed by the reference to the altar; and while this conception may be regarded as a traditionally Catholic one, its specific and concrete expression in a work of art of the seventeenth century may be regarded as baroque. The verb "dépouiller," which suggests the casting off of outward appearance in favor of inner reality, brings to mind again the sacramental contrast between accidents and substance, to which we have just referred. Finally, the references to blood and holy war are in the spirit of the Council of Trent, the Society of Jesus, and the art of Rubens or Bernini.

Adrien's farewell to Natalie is a curious mixture of spiritual exaltation and worldly wisdom. In the same speech he expresses his eagerness for martyrdom:

52. Act IV, scene 3.   53. Ibid.

Adieu, je cours, je vole au bonheur qui m'arrive;
L'effet en est trop lent, l'heure en est trop tardive! [54]

and also his concern for the financial status of his widow. Roman law requires the confiscation of the property of a Christian. Indeed, he uses the very
worldly and modern term "le fisc"—he is sorry that the Bureau of Internal
Revenue is going to seize all his money, leaving Natalie without means of
support. But such a fusion of religious faith and practical materialism is
characteristic of an age which produced Rubens and Bernini. Adrien's
attitude is perhaps more typically baroque than the indignant protestations
of Natalie:

Quoi! le vol que tu prends vers les célestes plaines
Souffre encor tes regards sur les choses humaines? [55]

And now (scene 4) a Christian friend, Anthisme, comes to congratulate
Adrien on his conversion and imminent martyrdom. In praying that the
heavenly host of angels may open paradise for Adrien, he is clearly para-
phrasing the Sanctus of the Mass:

Et vous, hôtes du ciel, saintes légions d'anges,
Qui du nom trois fois saint célébrez les louanges,
Sans interruption de vos sacrés concerts,
A son aveuglement tenez les cieux ouverts.[56]

The Book of Common Prayer version of the Sanctus reads:

Therefore with Angels and Archangels, and with all the company of heaven,
we laud and magnify thy glorious Name; evermore praising thee, and saying:
Holy, Holy, Holy, Lord God of hosts, Heaven and Earth are full of thy
glory . . .[57]

The position of this passage in the Mass is significant: it immediately precedes the Consecration, or sacrifice of Christ. Similarly, Rotrou has placed
Anthisme's prayer as an introduction to the sacrifice which the martyr Adrien
is about to make. Adrien requests his friend to baptize him, but is assured
that the water of baptism is unnecessary; the blood of martyrdom will sacra-
mentally take its place.

We now reach the most significant point in the play. Adrien pauses to
meditate for a moment, and then addresses his fellow actor not as Anthisme
(his stage name) but as Lentulus (his real name). The spiritual transformation which has been taking place in the make-believe world of a
theatrical performance has also been occurring in the real world; it is time
to remove the mask:

54. Ibid.   55. Ibid.   56. Act IV, scene 4.
57. Book of Common Prayer, p. 77,

> Ah! Lentule! en l'ardeur dont mon ame est pressée,
> Il faut lever le masque et t'ouvrir ma pensée:
> Le Dieu que j'ai haï m'inspire son amour;
> Adrien a parlé, Genest parle à son tour.
> Ce n'est plus Adrien, c'est Genest qui respire
> La grâce du baptême et l'honneur du martyre; [58]

Genest himself has been converted, and from now on speaks in his own right. Henceforth the stage directions cease to refer to him as Adrien, and give him his real name. Genest looks up to heaven, and flames descend.

> Un ministre céleste, avec une eau sacrée,
> Pour laver mes forfaits fend la voûte azurée;
> Sa clarté m'environne, et l'air de toutes parts
> Résonne de concerts, et brille à mes regards,
> Descends, céleste acteur; tu m'attends, tu m'appelles.
> Attends, mon zèle ardent me fournira des ailes;
> Du Dieu qui t'a commis dépars-moi les bontés. [59]

Here Genest ascends a few steps and disappears behind a curtain.

Combining as it does almost every element of the baroque, this scene occupies a position in the history of that style as climactically important as the Piazza Navona. Let us recapitulate some of the significant items. Baroque art is essentially incarnational and, as we have observed, the preparation and development of this situation closely parallels the movement of the Mass, from Sanctus to Incarnation. Metamorphosis is one of the great themes of the baroque—and here we have been witnessing the progressive stages of a transformation: Genest the pagan has been made a Christian. There has also been another kind of metamorphosis: what was illusion has become reality. The basic dramatic situation of the play within the play has become the true human situation. Baroque artists pride themselves at their skill at producing illusions; here the illusionistic art par excellence—that of the actor—has been so great that it has achieved a kind of transubstantiation. The merveilleux chrétien manifests itself in the descent of fire from heaven. Genest describes his vision in terms of theatrical multiple-sense imagery: an angel bearing holy water breaks through the blue sky, dazzling light surrounds the actor, and the air resounds with heavenly music.

The other actors, though disconcerted by Genest's words, try to make sense, in theatrical terms, of what is happening. Marcelle, who has been playing the part of Natalie, has lost her cue:

> Ma réplique a manqué; ces vers sont ajoutés. [60]

58. Act IV, scene 4.   59. Ibid.   60. Ibid.

Lentulus (Anthisme) thinks that Genest has been improvising, and has disappeared behind the curtain to cover up a lapse of memory. The audience still does not realize that anything is wrong; indeed, they are greatly impressed by Genest's powers as an actor. Diocletian admires the skill with which Genest has been able to assume the expressions and feelings of another person, and Valeria comments:

> Pour tromper l'auditeur, abuser l'acteur même,
> De son métier, sans doute, est l'adresse suprême.[61]

In other words, the imperial spectators, who have just seen reality, are still convinced that it is an illusion. They are aware that the actors seem confused, but feel that that is a great tribute to Genest's skill: he has even succeeded in deceiving his colleagues! The actors stand around in embarrassment, awaiting Genest's return, and hope that Diocletian will not be annoyed at the interruption. They decide that Genest has been pardonably carried away by his role. There is dramatic irony in this, for he has indeed been carried away, but in a far more real sense than they imagine.

When Genest returns to the stage, he no longer makes any pretense of playing a part in a play. The theatrical performance has ceased to exist for him. Like the saints of Murillo or Baroccio, he looks up to heaven and prays:

> Suprême Majesté, qui jettes dans les âmes,
> Avec deux gouttes d'eau, de si sensibles flammes,
> Achève tes bontés, représente avec moi
> Les saints progrès des cœurs convertis à ta foi![62]

Even in his total sincerity, he continues to express himself with baroque antithesis and concreteness of imagary. The members of the audience are still sure that this is the height of dramatic art. Never have they seen such wonderful "feigning"!

MAXIMIN.

Il feint comme animé des grâces du baptême.

VALERIA.

Sa feinte passerait pour la vérité même.

PLANCIEN.

Certes, ou ce spectacle est une vérité
Ou jamais rien de faux ne fut mieux imité.[63]

Genest now turns to his companions, and calling Natalie and Flavius by their real names of Marcelle and Sergeste, apologizes for his pagan past,

61. Ibid.   62. Act IV, scene 6.   63. Ibid.

and implores them to worship the Christian God. Marcelle and Sergeste still do not grasp what is happening. Clinging to the conviction that he has forgotten his lines, they call for the prompter. But Genest, revealing his true self more and more, insists that the prompter is no longer needed. An angel is now the prompter; God Himself is concerned with the plot:

> Il n'en est plus besoin.
> Dedans cette action, où le Ciel s'intéresse,
> Un ange tient la pièce, un ange me redresse;
> Un ange, par son ordre, a comblé mes souhaits,
> Et de l'eau du baptême effacé mes forfaits.
> Ce monde périssable et sa gloire frivole
> Est une comédie où j'ignorais mon rôle.[64]

Throughout his life until this moment Genest has been feigning, but now he is speaking the truth. It is the material world which is the dream, the illusion, the theatrical performance; now at last Genest has found his true role. Regardless of what others may think, this is reality. Lentulus remarks that while this speech is not written down in the text of the play, Genest never seems to hesitate. Here the great actor, so soon to become a martyr in actual fact, grows impatient at his colleagues' persistent refusal to understand:

> Dieu m'apprend sur-le-champ ce que je vous récite,
> Et vous m'entendez mal, si dans cette action
> Mon rôle passe encor pour une fiction.[65]

It is now Diocletian's turn to lose patience. He reminds the actors that they are in the imperial presence, and tells them that this disorder has gone far enough. But Genest, with the new-found courage of a martyr, assumes full responsibility for the interruption of the play. He insists that he really means what he has been saying:

> Ce n'est plus Adrien, c'est Genest qui s'exprime;
> Ce jeu n'est plus un jeu, mais une vérité
> Où par mon action je suis représenté,
> Où moi-même, l'objet et l'acteur de moi-même,
> Purgé de mes forfaits par l'eau du saint baptême,
> Qu'une céleste main m'a daigné conférer,
> Je professe une loi que je dois déclarer.[66]

Speaking directly to the emperor, he proclaims again and again that he is really a Christian. His days of acting are over and, if necessary, he is ready for martyrdom:

64. Ibid.   65. Ibid.   66. Ibid.

Il est temps de passer du théâtre aux autels.
Si je l'ai mérité, qu'on me mène au martyre:
Mon rôle est achevé, je n'ai plus rien à dire.[67]

Diocletian is exasperated, but still inclined to think that this is a piece of superb acting:

Ta feinte passe enfin pour importunité.

Then, suddenly, he is convinced: this is the real thing, after all.

Quoi! tu renonces, traître, au culte de nos dieux? [68]

For him this is blasphemy and sacrilege. Enraged, he orders Plancien the prefect to have Genest tortured and put to death. Both spectators and actors plead for mercy, but the indignant emperor merely repeats his command and leads the audience from the hall. Genest offers thanks to God and joyfully looks forward to his martyrdom:

Je t'en rends grâce, ô Ciel! allons, me voila prêt:
Les anges, quelque jour, des fers que tu m'ordonnes
Dans ce palais d'azur me feront des couronnes.[69]

And now, in the final scene of Act IV, the prefect begins to interrogate the other actors. One senses that the whole dramatic profession has become suspect to him. Like the rest of the audience, he had greatly admired the acting of Genest. Now it turns out that it was not just magnificent acting —it was the sincere expression of real feelings. While he was marveling at Genest's power of creating an illusion, he was himself the victim of an illusion; for what seemed an illusion was truth. The other actors were good, too; can it be that they too really felt what they were pretending to feel? But they all—Marcelle, Sergeste, Lentulus, Octavius—assure him with many protestations that they are only actors, and that their job is to feign whatever feelings their roles require. Marcelle takes women's parts; Octavius plays kings and slaves; Lentulus, confidants and villains.

In their case, there is no confusion between illusion and reality. The contagion of Christianity has not spread to them. Convinced of their innocence, the prefect pronounces their acquittal. As he leaves, however, Plancien insists upon the gravity of Genest's crime. He is to die, and will bear the full responsibility for his own death, unless his fellow actors can dissuade him from his criminal folly.

The fifth act consists of six scenes. While the stage directions are somewhat incomplete, a careful examination makes it seem probable that the first three take place in Genest's prison, and the last three in Diocletian's palace.

---

67. Ibid.   68. Ibid.   69. Act IV, scene 7.

The first scene consists of *stances* recited by Genest, who is described as alone and in chains. These octosyllabic lines are the only ones in the entire tragedy which are not alexandrines. They constitute a lyric poem in which Genest meditates upon his impending martyrdom. It is characteristic of the sensibility of the age that he is experiencing a sensuous delight. It is thus, for example, that Bernini represents the death of the Blessed Ludovica Albertoni. As we look through the four stanzas, we notice a constant recurrence of this theme: "sensible et sainte volupté," "incroyable félicité," "douceur suprême," "bonheur volontaire," "doux de mourir," "céleste lumière." The poem is also constructed by an intertwining of the two familiar contrasting themes of illusion and reality: the delights of this world are deceptive, the joys of eternal life alone are true; our moments of apparent happiness on earth are only lulls in a storm; the gloom of the dungeon and the weight of the chains are less real than the blissful intimations of heavenly glory; what appears to be our bier is really our cradle.

At the conclusion of the stances, the jailer admits Marcelle to Genest's prison cell. She has been sent by the other actors of the company to beg Genest to renounce Christianity. The scene inevitably calls to mind Act III, scene 4 (in the play within the play). There Natalie had been sent on a similar mission to persuade Adrien. The two actors are the same, but the situation is different, and the difference makes us conscious of the two levels of illusion and reality. Natalie, left alone with Adrien, had immediately confessed that she too was a Christian. We wonder for an instant whether Marcelle will make the same revelation to Genest. We find, however, that this is far from the case: her principal concern is an economic one. How will the rest of the theatrical company be able to make a living if the star is dead?

> Car, séparés de toi, quelle est notre espérance? [70]

We have already seen this intrusion of economic problems into the world of religious ecstasy and martyrdom. It is, in effect, a realistic touch which makes us more ready to accept the elements of the merveilleux chrétien. People who worry about money must, we feel, be real people. And this thought leads us to contrast the Marcelle of this scene with the Natalie of the parallel scene. Obviously, we conclude, the ardently religious Natalie was a figment of the dramatist's imagination, while Marcelle is an actual everyday woman. But then there comes the disturbing antithesis: the Adrien of the make-believe scene has become real. Genest, who moves in a world where flesh-and-blood people discuss the difficulties of making a living, is an actual martyr and saint. His reality is emphasized by the contrast with

70. Act V, scene 2.

238

STUDIES IN THE BAROQUE

Marcelle. The economic plight of the theatrical troop no longer moves him; he invites Marcelle and the others to join him in martyrdom:

> Et vous reconnaîtrez s'il est un heur plus doux
> Que la mort, qu'en effet je vous souhaite à tous.
> Vous mourriez pour un Dieu dont la bonté suprême,
> Vous faisant en mourant détruire la mort même,
> Ferait l'éternité le prix de ce moment,
> Que j'appelle une grâce, et vous un châtiment.[71]

When Marcelle sees that she cannot persuade Genest to give up Christianity, she begs him to pretend to worship the pagan gods. Since she cannot change the reality of his religious faith, she at least hopes that he will be willing to use his actor's skill to create another illusion. This suggestion he indignantly rejects. When I was a pagan, he says,

> . . . j'ai fait d'un Dieu le jouet d'un théâtre,
> Aux oreilles d'un prince et d'un peuple idolâtre,[72]

but now that I have become a Christian, I will practice the arts of illusion no longer. The two former colleagues part exchanging antithetical exclamations:

MARCELLE.

O dur courage d'homme!

GENEST.

O faible cœur de femme!

MARCELLE.

Cruel! Sauve tes jours.

GENEST.

Lâche! sauve ton âme.[73]

The remaining scenes, as I have remarked, seem to take place in Diocletian's palace. It is evident that the emperor is alarmed at the failure of persecution as a policy. Bloodthirsty sacrifices to the pagan gods have been in vain:

> Mais j'ai beau leur offrir de sanglantes hosties,
> Et laver leurs autels du sang de ces impies,
> En vain j'en ai voulu purger ces régions,
> Je vois du sang d'un seul naître des légions.[74]

Note the sadistic emphasis on blood, and the echoing repetition of the word "sang" itself. We have again the favorite baroque metaphor of germination,

71. Ibid.   72. Ibid.   73. Ibid.   74. Act V, scene 4.

used by d'Aubigné, and by Rotrou elsewhere in this play: martyrdom is an irresistible natural force which promotes growth. Then Valeria, whose marriage day this is after all (we have quite forgotten her personal story!), makes a special plea on behalf of the theatrical company: the death of the leading actor will mean ruin for the troop. But though all the actors get down on their knees to implore Diocletian, the emperor is adamant. Christianity threatens the very existence of the state, and reasons of state must prevail.

In the last scene, Plancien arrives to announce the death of Genest:

> Par votre ordre, Seigneur, ce glorieux acteur,
> Des plus fameux héros fameux imitateur,
> Du théâtre romain la splendeur et la gloire,
> Mais si mauvais acteur dedans sa propre histoire,
> Plus entier que jamais en son impiété,
> Et par tous mes efforts en vain sollicité,
> A du courroux des dieux contre sa perfidie
> Par un acte sanglant fermé la tragédie . . .[75]

To the prefect, it is still all a dramatic performance—unfortunately Genest is a less successful actor in his life than in his plays! In any case, the martyrdom is merely the last act of a tragedy. From the Roman point of view, Genest's beliefs are an illusion. But Plancien clearly believes in the reality of the tortures inflicted; he enumerates them with a certain pleasure:

> Mais ni les chevalets, ni les lames flambantes,
> Ni les ongles de fer, ni les torches ardentes,
> N'ont contre ce rocher été qu'un doux zephyr,
> Et n'ont pu de son sein arracher un soupir.[76]

It remains for Maximinus to pronounce the last line of the tragedy, and in a sense to sum up its meaning. Genest, he declares, has through a conscious effort of the will decided to

> D'une feinte en mourant faire une vérité.[77]

The baroque will has operated a metamorphosis, and changed illusion into truth.

75. Act V, scene 6.   76. Ibid.   77. Ibid.

CONCLUSION

Now that we have come to the end of our investigation of six very different writers who flourished between 1570 and 1650, what can we conclude concerning the nature of the baroque style? The eight great categories which we postulated for the study of Montaigne seem, in fact, to be substantiated by a detailed examination of the text of the *Essais;* they appear, also, to have equivalents in the fine arts of the period. Indeed, in seeking parallels between painting, sculpture, and architecture on the one hand, and literature on the other, it is probably safer to adopt some such system as my eight categories: moral purpose, emphasis and exaggeration, horror, incarnation, theatricality and illusion, surprise and contrast, movement and metamorphosis, organic unity and the acceptance of life, rather than those of Wölfflin: linear vs. painterly, plane vs. recession, closed vs. open form, multiplicity vs. unity, clear vs. unclear. For Wölfflin's criteria are exclusively plastic and technical; and in the study of literature it is not possible to make such a sharp distinction between content and form. One of Wölfflin's key distinctions between the Renaissance and the baroque—multiplicity vs. unity —does have an affinity with my idea that baroque literature, despite all astonishment at the diversity of phenomena, is characterized by organic unity and the acceptance of life. Perhaps also it may be possible to discern, at the close of each of the sonnets of La Ceppède, an opening out toward infinite mysteries which bears some relationship to Wölfflin's open form; in general, however, the five basic headings of the *Principles of Art History* are more applicable to their own particular field than to that of literary history. In literary criticism we are constantly forced to deal with the basic intellectual presuppositions and spiritual attitudes of the writer. Thus I am led, in this book, to discuss, sometimes explicitly but always implicitly, the baroque spirit.

As we look at the five other writers studied here—St. François de Sales, La Ceppède, Saint-Amant, Corneille, and Rotrou—we find that my eight categories are, in varying degrees, applicable to them also. It must be stated immediately that no single one of these categories is sufficient to label a work as baroque: it would be easy, for example, to find several of them appropriate for works of the romantic period; and, in any case, such characteristics as exaggeration or concrete imagery are to be met with throughout the history of literature. Even between the years 1570 and 1650 we should proceed with caution. I should add also that the presence of all eight characteristics is not a *sine qua non;* this, I think, is evident from the works which we have been analyzing. For example, though seven of the categories are clearly present in the *Introduction à la vie dévote,* there is little trace of the third, horror. And in the poems of Saint-Amant, despite the lavish praise of the poet's patron, the Duc de Retz, and occasional protestations of patriotism or religious fervor, we cannot help feeling that moral purpose is a secondary consideration. Nor is this category very much in evidence in Corneille's early comedies. With regard to La Ceppède's *Théorèmes,* the baroque traits enumerated here are abundantly present, and yet we may be permitted to wonder whether organic unity and acceptance of life constitutes an adequate description. The sonnets themselves possess this unity, but the poet's attitude is not so much an acceptance of life as an acceptance of Christ as the Redeemer of the world. Perhaps a similar comment is in order with respect to *Saint Genest,* which is, after all, the story of a martyrdom; but there the author's manifest delight in the tricks of dramatic art incline us to believe that he too accepts the world despite its horror and cruelty; and, in any case, viewed as a whole this tragedy seems an almost perfect example of the baroque style in literature. Actually, the way in which the *Théorèmes* and *Saint Genest,* though they deal with horror and martyrdom, in the last analysis leave us with the feeling that life does possess positive meaning, is closely bound up with the Christian presuppositions of their authors; and of this connection between the baroque style and Christianity I shall have more to say in a moment. Returning to the question of the eight categories as touchstones: while no single one is sufficient, and none an indispensable prerequisite, the presence of the majority of them in self-conscious juxtaposition, in a literary work composed between 1570 and 1650, is sure evidence of the baroque style.

I have repeatedly remarked that, in literary criticism, the problems of style are inextricable from those of content. This truism is particularly valid with respect to the baroque. The reader has observed the importance of incarnation as one of the eight categories; and while this term is intended to describe the predilection of certain writers for sensuous imagery and the concrete expression of abstract concepts, my adoption of a word rich in Christian overtones is intentional. Underlying all baroque literature, even among those writers who are not specifically Christian in tone, is the idea of the Word made Flesh. In any event, a full understanding of the baroque style involves an awareness of the various writers' conscious or unconscious vision of the world. What, essentially, is the baroque spirit?

Here I should like to revert to a metaphor used in the Introduction: that of the navigator who, by plotting different lines on a chart, finds the position of his ship at their intersection. In order to discover the baroque spirit, let us review here a few of the significant attitudes reflected by our baroque writers. Though these men are very different, I think it will be agreed that they share in common a certain vision of the world.

Montaigne, though he suffered from a painful disease and lived in an age when barbarous civil war threatened his life every day, leaves us with an impression of serenity and optimism. He repeatedly declares that we should so far as possible spread joy and limit sadness. Rejecting the idea that man is either angel or beast, he accepts his own and all human nature—physical, intellectual, and spiritual functions alike—and simply ends by giving thanks to God for the gift of life. The contradictions and diversity of the world are a source of delight to him; he feels interest and sympathy for men of all nationalities; travel abroad is, for these very reasons, a constant joy. The world is especially interesting precisely because it is forever in a state of flux, change, and evolution. His own essays, though adorned with much fanciful and grotesque ornamentation, possess artistic unity: he has inserted little connecting links so that the attentive reader can perceive this unity. The essays teem with sensuous and physical life; throughout, we are aware of a man who seeks meaning in this life. The philosophical problem of the One and the Many, of the physical and the spiritual, of things visible and invisible, is forever kept in miraculous balance.

What of the world of St. François de Sales? Here is a saint who loved the physical world because God created it. Though for his own part leading an intense spiritual life, he accepts and welcomes with affection and charity the lawyer, the business man, the married woman, and hopes by his book to lead them to continual growth in the love and service of God. He presents to the ordinary human being, involved in mundane occupations, the ideal of resembling little children who walk along the hedgerows gathering strawberries, but who hold their father's hand for guidance and occasionally look up into his face to see whether he approves of what they are doing. Or, to recall another characteristic metaphor, ostriches cannot fly, hens fly badly, whereas larks and eagles soar in the sky: such are the different stages of spiritual life. We realize that, while in this respect the saint regards most of us as ostriches, he loves us nevertheless, and has an affection for ostriches also, because they are picturesque and amusing. To paraphrase the Ash Wednesday collect, St. François de Sales hates nothing that God has made; and in any case, he hopes to effect a transformation whereby all men shall come to love God. "Amoureuse de Dieu" is a phrase recurring constantly in the *Introduction à la vie dévote,* and Philothée is the name of his imaginary reader; yet, with characteristic desire to reconcile the claims of God and the world, the saint is always warning us against religious ecstasies.

The stylistic devices of the *Théorèmes* have been exhaustively analyzed in the chapter devoted to La Ceppède. The poet's basic presuppositions, so colorfully, trenchantly, and dramatically expressed in these sonnets, are so evident as to require no further comment here: essentially, they are the beliefs of any Christian concerning the significance of the events of the Passion and Resurrection.

Saint-Amant, because of his gastronomic and drunken excesses, and because of his sycophancy to his duke, must be regarded as a less temperate and a less independent figure than Montaigne, but we must remember that Montaigne did not scorn the pleasures of the table and that he was loyal to his king; in effect, we must recognize certain common elements in both men. As we think back over the three poems discussed in this book, perhaps what we remember most in Saint-Amant's delight in the diversity of phenomena: all the delicious dishes mentioned in "Le Melon," all the variegated pleasures enjoyed during the walks on Belle-Ile. We even find a love of wild nature uncommon before romanticism, and a sense that frightening experiences—thoughts of ghosts and suicide—can, within moderation, be pleasurable. The constant reiteration of "tantost . . . tantost" suggests a fondness for looking at the world from different aspects.

If Saint-Amant enjoys indulging himself in illusions, so also does the youthful Corneille. The title alone of *L'Illusion comique* would suffice to apprise us of this; but as we read the play, we find that we are forever in doubt as to what is actually happening. Is this, after all, to be a tragedy? No, apparently not; Corneille has succeeded in fooling us. These events which the magician shows us in the last act—are they real? No; it is all a play within a play within a play. What delight Corneille takes in his Alcandre, who is capable of conjuring up a magic television show! And how he enjoys his braggart Matamore, who raises lying to an art and thus creates still another world of make-believe! In *Clitandre* it is also the world of make-believe which we chiefly remember: that fantastic Scottish forest where, shifting from place to place, we witness extraordinary and melodramatic events. Probably, in addition, we are struck by two scenes which shock classical standards of taste: one where Pymante attempts to rape Dorise, and where she puts his eye out with a hatpin; and another where the two happy lovers, Rosidor and Caliste, effect their reconciliation upon the former's sickbed. Préciosité and brutal directness seem to alternate, as they do also in *Mélite*. There worldly drawing-room comedy is mingled with violent romantic love; the daemonic ravings of the desperate Eraste, who in his hallucination imagines himself to be in Hades, are brought back to sanity by the earthy and kindly nurse. The whole plot, we remember, is based on an illusion, that of the forged letters; in the end a solution is found, not altogether satisfactory to the demands of romantic idealism, but eminently sensible.

Saint Genest, I think the reader will agree, is an altogether extraordinary play: to an even greater degree than *L'Illusion comique* we are at a loss to distinguish, in certain scenes, between illusion and reality. And then we actually witness a conversion at the moment of its taking place; before our very eyes, the hero becomes a Christian. The full importance of this, for dramatic technique, may be appreciated if we compare Rotrou's tragedy with a classical one such as *Phèdre.* Racine's heroine does not *fall* in love with Hippolyte during the course of the play; her passion exists from the very outset, and the catastrophe is precipitated not by a change in her attitude but by two external events which act upon this basic *donnée:* the false news of Thésée's death, and his unexpected return. We are also struck, in *Saint Genest,* by the parallels between this literary work and certain important features of the Mass: just before the hero makes his sacrifice, a choir sings a Sanctus. The art of the actor has become a sort of sacrament.

What light do we find at the point where all these *feux croisés* meet? At the end of my study of Agrippa d'Aubigné's *Les Tragiques,* I arrived at the conclusion that there were two fundamental baroque elements: the physical and the paradoxical. Without wishing to repudiate these concepts, I now, after the examination of a greater variety of baroque works, find myself particularly impressed by the correspondence between baroque literature and a certain catholic Christian view of the world characteristic of the latter half of the sixteenth and the first half of the seventeenth centuries. It is not that I seek, as many scholars have done, to limit the baroque to the art of the Counter Reformation. In a certain way, the baroque appears to me to transcend specific religious dogmas and specific nationalities. In affirming implicitly throughout this book the existence of a baroque spirit, it is my conviction that Milton, Donne, and Rembrandt belong to this spirit as much as Rubens, Bernini, Montaigne, or St. François de Sales. However important an event the Reformation may have been in the history of ideas in the sixteenth century, a change in men's basic sensibilities could not be wrought overnight by the efforts of a Calvin or a Luther; and thus even unmistakably Protestant artists, such as some of those whom I have mentioned, or such as Agrippa d'Aubigné, to whom I devoted my earlier book, remained traditionally catholic in their imaginative view of the world. This underlying, often half-conscious, mode of envisioning reality is decisive even in those works of the period which are primarily secular: Rubens' Medici series, the *Essais* of Montaigne, the poems of Saint-Amant, the early comedies of Corneille, the engravings of Callot, the fountains of Rome. And in the religious domain, the basic religious text used by the Anglican church—the Book of Common Prayer, dating from 1549—must be regarded as fundamentally catholic in feeling.

Obviously the baroque spirit did not invent Christianity, though it may have given particularly spectacular affirmation to certain Christian beliefs. What, then, are the specific Christian dogmas to which the baroque gave so strong an emphasis that it affected even those artists and writers who were not specifically religious? For although not all Christian art is baroque, it is impossible to conceive of baroque art which, in its ultimate sources of inspiration (as regards both form and content), is not Christian. This, indeed, is the great gulf which separates romanticism from the baroque: romanticism, being the art of individualism, largely ignores the first Christian commandment—to love God—and tends to leave us only with the second —to love our fellow men.

An examination of the Nicene Creed would do much to inform us as to the essential elements of the baroque Zeitgeist. It is scarcely necessary to rehearse the tenets of this document here; but perhaps it should be pointed out that that very schism which, for the half-century preceding and following 1600, made Christians acutely aware of the basic dogmas of their faith, stressed the importance, for all aspects of life, of these concepts.

The Nicene Creed begins by asserting that God made all things visible and invisible. This statement can, I think, help us to understand the baroque delight in the physical world in all its diversity, together with the baroque interest in the contrast between illusion and reality. The baroque man, unlike the romanticist, does not think that the individual's emotion is the measure of things; nor does he think, like the existentialist, that man creates his own values: on the contrary, God is at the basis of all the phenomena which we can experience. This means that, in opposition to the ideas of puritans or Jansenists, the physical world is not evil: far from it, it is an object of delight. And, in opposition to the theories of Sartre or Camus, it is not absurd: life has, in absolute terms, a positive meaning.

In connection with this, we should point to another assertion of the Nicene Creed: that, at a certain point in recorded history, God was made man. This is, of course, a reinforcement of concepts just expressed, and bears an essential relationship with two of our baroque categories: that of incarnation, and that of metamorphosis. Writers and artists who are influenced by this dogma are inevitably led to feel that, in this world, ideas become meaningful to men only when they receive physical expression. The Holy Ghost, to paraphrase another passage, proceeds from the Father and the Son—or, to use the terminology of literary criticism, a work of art succeeds in communication only by means of its own medium. Furthermore, the operation of the Holy Ghost—or the effect of a work of art—is generally apprehended by us in terms of a transformation.

Basic also to our purpose are those passages of the creed which relate to Christ's Crucifixion and Resurrection. Insofar as these concepts formed the sensibility of men between 1570 and 1650, we must regard them as decisive in bringing about that feeling, observable in the majority of the works studied here, that horror and martyrdom are legitimate subjects of art, that human suffering has meaning, and that truth in the end will triumph. Man, though he once tried to do so, cannot kill God. Many recent art historians have devoted their attention to a style immediately preceding the baroque—mannerism—of which El Greco and Tintoretto are notable examples, and of which, if literary analysis were to be further pursued, Scève and Sponde would probably be found to be representative in French literature. Theologically speaking, I think it might be said that these men, despite their generally Christian orientation, reveal through their angoisse agonizing doubts as to the Resurrection. In baroque artists, whether they impress us as worldly like Montaigne, or deeply religious like St. François de Sales and La Ceppède, there is an optimism which, though aware of the tragedy of the world, and whether or not connected with an explicit Christian faith, corresponds to a belief in the Resurrection.

The generation of Racine was, of course, deeply Christian too; but here principles of bienséance and order and reason, together with the proscribing of the merveilleux chrétien in literature, tended to discipline the baroque taste of an earlier age and to produce that new style, more restrained, intellectual, and abstract, which we know as classicism.

Those who object to the view that the baroque is, in the last analysis, a Christian style, are probably also reluctant to consider Rubens or Montaigne as fundamentally Christian. It might be urged in reply that the many mansions of the New Testament are not necessarily limited to those of Calvin, Pascal, or Bossuet. The theologians' affirmation that Christ was both true God and true man has, we have seen, as one of its consequences the importance of the physical world; and this may be further extended to include the idea that all spheres of human activity are subjects of legitimate intellectual interest and artistic creativity. Once more it should be said that this does not open the way to unbridled passion, to crazy and disconnected efforts at making life picturesque; the baroque, like Christianity and unlike romanticism, realizes that discipline is necessary to make life meaningful. But whereas classicism has sometimes been defined as un baroque dompté, with the implication (felt as we have seen by Corneille) that the baroque needed toning down, we should like to argue that the essay De la vanité and the tragedy *Saint Genest* are themselves disciplined works of art, and that perhaps the discipline of later generations was excessive.

Naturally one does not exhaust the problem of the baroque by pointing out that it rests upon a Christian sensibility. To attempt another recapitulation: the baroque is a style often characterized by excess, and animated by a strong will toward that which it conceives as good; it is acutely aware of the physical aspects of the world, in all their beauty, horror, picturesqueness, diversity, and movement. While at times deriving an almost perverse pleasure at shock, surprise, and illusion, it ultimately hopes for the triumph of positive and meaningful values.

One way to feel the spirit of the baroque is to walk around the Piazza Navona in Rome, so as to see the varying aspects of the massive and undulant façade of Sant'Agnese reflected in Bernini's splashing fountain; and then to reflect that, many years before these things were built but still within the baroque age, Montaigne, the skeptical humanist and worldly Christian, loved this city because it reconciled man's diversity into a triumphant harmony; and, while aware of the vanity of vanities, was everlastingly proud that the ecclesiastical authorities of his day had made him a citizen of Rome.

BIBLIOGRAPHY

THIS BIBLIOGRAPHY, while not comprehensive, is nevertheless designed to help the reader interested in further study of the works analyzed here or of the literary baroque problem in general. To this end, I have adopted the following classifications: 1.) Editions of literary works discussed; 2.) Recent scholarly works on the baroque in literature, several of which, as indicated, contain further extensive bibliography; 3.) Books containing photographs of the paintings, sculpture, or architecture mentioned.

1. Editions of literary works discussed.

Corneille, P. *Clitandre*. Edited by R.-L. Wagner. Genève, Droz, 1949.
—— *Mélite*. Edited by Mario Roques and Marion Lièvre. Genève, Droz, 1950.
—— *Œuvres*. Edited by Marty-Laveaux. Collection des grands écrivains de la France, 1862–68.
La Ceppède, J. de. Choix des textes et préface par Jean Rousset. Paris, GLM, 1947.
—— Essai sur la vie et l'oeuvre de Jean de La Ceppède, poète chrétien et magistrat, 1548–1623. Edited by François Ruchon. Genève, Droz, 1953.
Montaigne, M. de. *Essais*. Edited by Pierre Villey. Paris, Alcan, 1922.
Rotrou, J. de. *Œuvres*. Edited by Viollet-le-Duc. Paris, 1820–22.
Saint-Amant, M.-A. de. *Œuvres complètes*. Edited by Ch.-L. Livet. Paris, Jannet, 1855.
Sales, St. François de. *Œuvres*. Editées par les religieuses de la visitation du premier monastère d'Annecy. Annecy, Niérat, 1893.

2. Recent scholarly works on the baroque in literature.

Blanchard, A. *Baroques et classiques: anthologie des lyriques français de 1550 à 1650*. Lyon, IAC, 1947.
Buffum, I. *Agrippa d'Aubigné's* Les Tragiques. *A Study of the Baroque Style in Poetry*. New Haven, Yale University Press, 1951. Contains a bibliography of items pertaining to the literary and aristic baroque.
"Le Baroque." *Revue des sciences humaines*. Numéro double. Juillet-Décembre 1949. Nos. 55–6.
Lebègue, R. La Poésie française de 1560 à 1630. Paris, Centre de documentation universitaire, 1951.
Le Préclassicisme français. Présenté par Jean Tortel. Les Cahiers du sud. Paris, 1952.
Mourgues, Odette de. Metaphysical, baroque and précieux poetry. Oxford, Clarendon Press, 1953.

Poésie du XVIIᶦᵉᵐᵉ siècle. Anthologie présentée par Thierry Maulnier. Paris, La Table ronde, 1945.

Poètes précieux et baroques du XVIIᵉ. Introduction by Thierry Maulnier. Choix de poèmes et notes de Dominique Aury. Angers, Editions Jacques Petit, 1941.

Rousset, J. *La Littérature de l'âge baroque en France: Circé et le paon.* Paris, Corti, 1953. Exhaustive bibliography of the literary baroque. A few photographs of the baroque in the fine arts.

Sayce, R. A. "Baroque Elements in Montaigne." *French Studies, 8,* January 1954.

Sponde, J. de. *Poésies.* Genève, Pierre Cailler, 1949. Containing also: "Essai sur la vie de Jean de Sponde," by François Ruchon, and "Etude sur les poésies de Jean de Sponde," by Alan Boase.

Wellek, R. "The Concept of Baroque in Literary Scholarship," *Journal of Aesthetics, 5,* 1946. Extensive bibliography.

3. Books containing photographs of the paintings, sculpture, or architecture mentioned.

Fokker, T. H. *Roman Baroque Art. The History of a Style.* London, Oxford University Press, 1938.

Magni, G. *Il Barocco a Roma.* Turin, C. Crudo, 1911–13.

Pevsner, N. "The Architecture of Mannerism." *The Mint,* edited by Geoffrey Grigson. London, Routledge, 1946.

Weisbach, W. *Der Barock als Kunst der Gegenreformation.* Berlin, Cassirer, 1921.

—— *Die Kunst des Barock.* Berlin, Im-Propläen-Verlag, 1924.

Wölfflin, H. *Principes fondamentaux de l'art.* Traduit par Claire et Marcel Raymon. Paris, Plon, 1952.

INDEX

"Fountain of the Rivers" (Rome), 45, 77, 107, 130, 136, 146, 164, 216
Fountains, 45–6; of Rome, 77 f., 145 f., 215, 245. *See also under names of fountains*
Frame, Donald, 16

Galerie de Médicis, 118
Gesù church (Rome), 86, 93, 215

Henri IV, 18, 77, 116, 119, 130, 136, 166, 169
Henri de Navarre, 116
Horror and violence. *See* Baroque style, elements
Hugo, Victor Marie, 199
Hyperbole, 18–19, 161. *See also* Baroque style, elements (exaggeration)

Imagery, excessive use of, 7–8. *See also* Baroque style, elements (incarnation); La Ceppède; Corneille; Montaigne; Rotrou; Saint-Amant; St. François de Sales
Impressionism, 36

Jouvet, Louis, 163

La Boétie, Etienne de, 20
La Ceppède, Jean de, vii, xiii, xiv, 231, 240 f., 243; *Théorèmes*, xiii, 115 ff.; *Vexilla regis*, 115; biographical summary, 116–17; admired by Malherbe, 117–18; text of the *Théorèmes*, 118–19; *Imitations des Psaumes*, 119; erotic religious sensibility, 120, 123; theatricality, 120; emphasis and exaggeration by exclamation and accumulation, 120; horror, 120, 124; contrast, 120, 124; movement, 120, 126, 133; moral purpose, 120; incarnation, 120, 129; image of darkness, 121; "surprise," 121; multiple-sense imagery, 121, 128; metamorphosis, 121, 126, 129, 131, 133; "heaping," 122; contrast and paradox, 122; echo technique, 122; antithesis, 123; impression of whiteness, 125; affinity with Wölfflin's "open form," 125; hyperbole, 126; material from varied biblical sources, 126–7; personification, 129; chiaroscuro, 131; examples from nature to illustrate a religious doctrine, 131; acceptance of life, 132
La Fontaine, Jean de, 97; *Fables*, viii
Lake of Annecy, 82
Lanson, Gustave, vii
La Tour, Georges de, 120 f., 124, 144
Lebègue, Raymond, vii, 163, 224 f.
Lecce, Italy, churches and palaces of, 45
Le Nain brothers, 8
Le Nôtre, André, 46
Lièvre, Marion, xiii, 164, 211
Literary style. *See* Montaigne
Louis XIII, 77, 116, 150
Louis XIV, 95

Louvre, 166
Luther, Martin, 48, 244

Maderna, Carlo, 77
Mâle, Emile, 134, 163
Malherbe, François de, 116, 117–18, 147; "Pour le Roi allant châtier la rebellion des Rochelois," 148 f., 156
Malines, Flanders, *chaires de vérité* of, 45
Mannerist style, viii, 86, 93, 163, 169
Marie de Médicis, 77, 116, 118, 136, 147, 149, 166, 169
Marino, Cavaliere, 42; *Adone,* 171
Massacre of St. Bartholomew, viii, 130
Maulnier, Thierry, *Poésie du XVIIᵉ siècle,* 115
Metamorphosis and mutability. *See* Baroque style, elements
Michelangelo Buonarroti, 57, 157
Milton, John, 135, 244; "L'Allegro," 156; *Paradise Lost,* 11; "Il Penseroso," 156 f.
Molière, *Le Misanthrope,* viii, 140; *Tartuffe,* 34
Montaigne, Michel de, viii–xii, xiv, xv, 116, 143 f., 147, 150, 152, 154, 171, 178, 240, 244, 247; importance of, more literary than ideological, ix; *un écrivain engagé,* ix; eight basic categories for consideration of his work, x–xi, 1 ff.; ideas more important than words, 1; his elements of good style, 1–2; his comments on his own style, 1–11; self-depreciation, 2; *De l'amité,* 3; disorder, 3; on rewriting, 4–7; unity in, 5; diversity in, 6; honesty of self-portraiture, 7; his view of repentance, 7 f.; "faults" of style, 7–8; improvisation, 8; recurrence in *Essais* of ideas of moral purpose and transformation of the author, 9; and "consubstantiality," 10–11; his moral purpose, 12 f., 24 f.; compared with Rabelais, 13; on education, 13, 47; on colonialism, 14; on redistribution of wealth, 14–15; essentially aristocratic, 15–16; his Pyrrhonism, 16; on atheism, 17; three forms of exaggeration (hyperbole, exclamatory sentences, and asyndeton), 18 ff.; horror, 23 ff.; his humanity, 25; condemns unrealistically high moral standards, 39; disparity between private and public morals, 39–40; use of antithesis, 40–2, of paradox, 42, of surprise, 42–3, of verbs, 43; his world of flux, 44–5; preoccupation with transformation, 45; on genius and insanity, 48; meeting with Tasso, 48; on Luther, 48; on scholarly activity, 48; impression of Roman ruins, 49; significant changes of *Essais* (*1572–92*), 52–3; acceptance of life, 53–4, 132; transformation of his thought, 54; fascination for individual mutability and infinite human variety, 54; belief that to know one man is to know all men, 56;